Four Steeples over the City Streets

Dear Maria,

Best wishes on your studies in history, race, and the human condition. I hold your entire family in great esteem and know you will do great things

Sincerely,
Kyle Bigley

Four Steeples over the City Streets

Religion and Society in New York's Early Republic Congregations

KYLE T. BULTHUIS

New York University Press

NEW YORK AND LONDON

NEW YORK UNIVERSITY PRESS
New York and London
www.nyupress.org

LIBRARY OF CONGRESS CATALOGING-IN-PUBLICATION DATA

Bulthuis, Kyle T.

  Four steeples over the city streets : religion and society in New York's early republic congregations / Kyle T. Bulthuis.

      pages cm. — (Early American places)

  Includes bibliographical references and index.

  ISBN 978-1-4798-1427-5 (cl : alk. paper)

  1. New York (N.Y.)—Church history—19th century. 2. New York (N.Y.)—Church history—18th century. I. Title.

BR560.N4B85 2014

277.47'1081—dc23

2014015104

Chapter 6 appeared in slightly different form as "Preacher Politics and People Power: Congregational Conflicts in New York City, 1810–1830," by Kyle T. Bulthuis, *Church History*, Volume 78, Issue 02 (2009), pp. 261–82. Copyright © 2009 American Society of Church History. Reprinted with the permission of Cambridge University Press.

New York University Press books are printed on acid-free paper, and their binding materials are chosen for strength and durability. We strive to use environmentally responsible suppliers and materials to the greatest extent possible in publishing our books.

Manufactured in the United States of America

10 9 8 7 6 5 4 3 2 1

Also available as an ebook

Contents

Acknowledgments

My wise advisor once remarked that academic research is a communal undertaking that masquerades as individual effort. This work is no exception, although any faults that remain are my own, including if I have overlooked any individuals here.

Graduate study is an apprenticeship, and often the graduate apprentice's work depends upon the skills of the master. There is perhaps no better master in the field of the early Republic than Alan Taylor. Alan wore many hats: a financier in keeping me funded through graduate school, a pathfinder through the thickets of early Republic historiography, a militia drillmaster in the mechanics of efficient prose, and Federalist father of the Davis chapter of townball players. I am grateful for his guidance. As for my other committee members, Steve Deyle ran wonderful graduate seminars, and introduced me to NYU Press and Debbie Gershenowitz. A patient reader of multiple drafts, Clarence Walker regularly displayed his unique blend of erudition, iconoclasm, and kindness. The transformation of this work from dissertation to book was extensive. Many archivists provided important aid in this project, especially Gwynydd Cannan at Trinity Church Archives and Kristin Miller of the American Bible Society. For help with images, thanks especially to Chris Anderson of Drew University, Joellen Elbashir of Howard University, and Maryellen Blumlein of the Sisters of Charity. I am indebted to the institutions that helped fund my research, particularly the Gilder-Lehrman Institute in this project's earliest phase, and the Office of the Vice-President for Research at Utah State University in the final stages. I am grateful for my editors, Debbie Gershenowitz, who shepherded this manuscript in its early form, and Clara Platter, who helpfully brought this book to completion. Thanks also to Constance Grady, my anonymous reviewers, and NYU Press. Alanna Beason's work on the maps was invaluable.

I am indebted to those history department administrators who helped in numerous ways, large and small, including Debbie Lyon, Gloria Kennison, Sharon Roehling, Sara Brown, Sharon Lee, Diane Buist, and Monica Ingold. Tammy Proctor has proven a wise leader and good friend as history department chair at Utah State University. Among the many friends and colleagues who have provided support in good times and bad, thanks are especially due to Eric Bryden, Robert Chester, Annika Frieberg, Steve Fountain, Shennan Hutton, Elizabeth LaCouture, Steve Leonard, Ken Miller, Brett Rushforth, Steven Seegel, and Robbie Weis. Special thanks for the insightful critiques I received on portions of this work from colleagues in the Rocky Mountain West and beyond, including Fred Anderson, Virginia Anderson, Jim Drake, Joyce Goodfriend, Eric Hinderaker, Chris Hodson, Susan Jones, Ann Little, Eric Love, Brian Luskey, Gloria Main, Mick Nicholls, Jenny Pulsipher, Nathan Rives, Brett Rushforth, Paul Sivitz, and Vikki Vickers. Susan Cogan's close reading of a late draft strengthened this work immensely. Kyle Roberts performed yeoman's work in his analysis of the near-finished product.

I still marvel at my parents' love and support, without which this book would not have been completed. For Tim and Andrew, I desire that they may find their own rewarding paths in life. Katherine and Hannah fill my days with joy. Susan, I am glad to have traveled this road with you, friend and love. I cannot conceive of a life without you.

Four Steeples over the City Streets

Introduction: The Pursuit of Religious, Racial, and Social Unity in an Early Republic Metropolis

Imagine, for a moment, the scenes that have defined major chapters in American religious history: a Puritan divine delivers rigorous, learned sermons inside whitewashed walls. Lonely backcountry Methodist circuit riders lead boisterous camp meetings and raise rough-hewn chapels. Black Baptists fervently pray as they boycott local businesses in a push for civil rights. A savvy evangelist preaches comfort in the spacious auditorium of a modern suburban megachurch.

None of these settings are necessarily urban. Yet each of these visions connects to metropolitan religious figures in one guise or another: village ministers read sermons from Puritan divines in Boston and London; circuit riders bought books from Methodist publishers in London and New York; civil rights activists drew influence from theology professors in Washington, D.C., and Philadelphia; and megachurch pastors in Scottsdale might model their congregational mission plans on those of pastors in Chicago or Seattle.[1]

Yet the assumption lingers that cities and religion do not mix. Far-sighted leaders of vital religious movements in America have viewed cities as places where religion dies. When Billy Graham held a revival in Manhattan in 1957, he prepared for spiritual war. Deeming his target "Sodom on the Subway," Graham rallied large crowds of faithful evangelicals to invade the secular city.[2] Graham's sentiments on the spiritual state of New York City were not new. The father of American Methodism, Francis Asbury, traveled nearly continuously throughout the United States and Canada from the 1770s to his death in 1815, observing and supervising Methodist churches. When he entered the Republic's cities, however, Asbury encountered worldliness and sin. Upon preaching to an unresponsive New York congregation, he bewailed: "[New] York, in all the congregations, is the valley of dry bones. Oh Lord, I will lament the deplorable state of religion in all our towns and cities!"[3] Asbury echoed the concerns of many observers who believed that religious faith best incubated in villages and the countryside.

This book begins to explain why Francis Asbury feared the growth of the city, and explores the effect the city had on religion. Historians of early Republic New York have examined how the city's growth affected where people lived, how they worked, what they ate, and even with whom they had sex.[4] Urban expansion also influenced religious experience. I wanted to determine how the city's churches responded to these changes: how their respective religious traditions shaped the way they reacted to the city, and how changes in the city affected the way they perceived and received religion in these years.

To answer these questions, I examined the creation and growth of four Protestant congregations in early Republic New York: Trinity Episcopal, John Street Methodist, African Methodist Episcopal Zion ("Mother Zion"), and the black congregation of St. Philip's Episcopal. These congregations varied in their wealth and racial makeup. But despite these differences in identity, all four shared a common theological tradition and institutional beginnings in the Anglican Church.

A study of religious experience in New York could pursue any number of religious traditions. The Dutch Reformed Church was central to Manhattan's development from the beginning, and its Calvinist theology and ethnic minority status intersected with American historical themes in unique ways. Moravians and Quakers shared dissenting theological trajectories and had important interactions with multiple races and ethnicities in the polyglot city, including its black population. Presbyterians in the early Republic perhaps best articulated the connections between evangelical religion and reform movements. These groups, and others, provide important illustrations of specific developments in religion, ethnicity, race, and reform in New York.[5] But all, including the Dutch, were outsiders and minorities in New York City in the late colonial and early Republic eras. None remained central throughout the entire sweep of time that the city grew from several thousand to a half million inhabitants.

In this study, I have focused on churches within the Anglican/Episcopalian tradition, including its Methodist offshoots. Anglican and

Methodist churches were not the first, and were rarely the most successful, religious groups in New York City, but their histories bring the reader close to the main stories of New York's development in the early Republic. The colonial-era British government promoted the Church of England as a model of cultural authority, so from its origins the Anglican Church in New York attempted to draw together different ethnic groups under its oversight. Methodists similarly welcomed different ethnicities, not to support the establishment but rather to create a new holy family in Christ. Both Anglicans and Methodists aspired to be geographically expansive and universally influential. Anglicans and Methodists were therefore well attuned to reflecting and recording the relationship between social and religious change, perhaps better than groups that were more marginal in the early Republic.

Further, both Anglicans and Methodists (at least, the vast majority of them) were Arminian in theology. In the early Republic, increasing numbers of Americans rejected the Calvinism that dominated the early colonial period. This stance placed Anglicans and Methodists in the theological mainstream of American religion for the time, in contrast with either the Calvinist traditionalism of the Dutch Reformed, Presbyterians, and Congregationalists (themselves soon to be modified from within) or the prophetic but decidedly minority status of Quakers and Moravians.[6]

The similarities between Methodism and Anglicanism help establish a common center of religious affiliation, but their differences ensure breadth to avoid a too-specialized, too-specific reading of any individual group. Methodists and Anglicans generally differed in their support for revivals; prorevival Methodists often gravitated toward evangelical groups, while antirevival Anglicans preferred communion with liturgical groups. They therefore straddled both sides of the most important theological divide in the American early Republic. Finally, the Anglicans and Methodists in these four congregations provide a study of varied social and ethnic populations. These churches contained rich and poor, native and immigrant, white and black, exalted and lowly. Thus the choice of Anglican and Methodist religious traditions allows this study to evaluate big themes in American religious and social history, even as the topic studied is small in scale.[7]

The study of congregations reveals dynamics that larger and more general studies might miss. Because congregations occupy specific geographic locations in the city, and are comprised of an easily identified set of individuals, their connections to the urban environment are clear and direct. As communal meeting places, congregations occupy public space; as places where individuals regularly experience the sacred, they touch upon private life. As such, a study of congregations allows the historian to bridge the dichotomy of public and private, of sacred and secular. They reconnect religion with social context, to provide a full analysis of individual experience and change.[8]

New Yorkers know these four congregations well. Trinity Episcopal Church was the oldest, formed in 1697, a mother of sorts to the later three groups. At its birth, British monarchs blessed Trinity with vast tracts of land that indicated its privilege and provided it wealth. Throughout the eighteenth century, and into the nineteenth, Trinity represented stability and social significance. It even dominated the physical landscape: not until the dawn of the twentieth century did any New York building rise above Trinity's steeple. Some of the city's most prominent families sat in its pews.

Methodism began as a movement within the Church of England. In 1768, John Street Methodist Chapel formed from members nominally affiliated with Trinity Church. Important English Methodist leaders visited John Street, which was the first permanent Methodist meetinghouse in America. In 1784, American Methodists broke from both Anglicanism and English Methodism, and by that decade's end, John Street was no longer a fledgling chapel, but a church in its own right. Although Methodism often attracted the working poor to its services, John Street housed some of the town's wealthiest Methodists.

The final two churches in this study established their identities on racial difference. Both Episcopal and Methodist churches welcomed blacks to worship, but widespread racism in America made biracial worship difficult. The African Methodist Episcopal Zion Church, or Mother Zion, started much like John Street as an informal chapel, where blacks held separate worship services. Over the following two decades, members grew estranged from the white church and established an independent denomination. Mother Zion remains a symbol of the birth of black Methodism, central to African American history. St. Philip's Episcopal Church also had beginnings in informal catechism study groups. In 1819, it erected its first building, but, unlike the African Methodists, its members remained under the white-run Episcopal hierarchy, and for decades remained without a voice or vote in the denomination. St. Philip's long path to recognition within the New York diocese is a dramatic story in its own right.[9] Mother Zion and St. Philip's were pathbreaking black congregations in New York; elite blacks attended these two churches alongside poorer coreligionists.

These four congregations shared common bonds through their institutional origins and in some of their theological assumptions, but each had a unique geographic location, social makeup, and forward trajectory. The development of these four churches provides a laboratory of sorts to closely observe and test the claims of urban religious transformation. Through them one can measure what role revivals played in an urban setting; when, why, and how black churches split from white bodies; or how urban and economic growth (and decay) affected religious identities.

In the early Republic, New York City underwent a massive transformation, growing from a provincial port town to a major commercial center. In 1790, New York's population stood at just over 30,000 inhabitants; the number doubled to 60,000 in 1800 and doubled again in 1820 to 123,000 inhabitants. This exponential growth accelerated in the following decades, exploding to a half million residents in 1850. New York overtook Philadelphia as the nation's most populous city at the beginning of the nineteenth century. By 1860, New York had become a world city in its influence.[10]

Amid all this growth, New York earned a secular reputation as a place where one could advance commercially.[11] New York was the financial and cultural center of the expanding nation, and important members of society, including John Jay, James Harper, Frederick Douglass, and Sojourner Truth, attended the city's churches.[12] The presence and interaction of these leading figures in a place where religious influence seemed to be dwindling made New York congregations central to developments that did not occur elsewhere until much later.

This study draws together several genres of historical inquiry. As a social history, it studies the interactions and relationships between different groups of New Yorkers in the early Republic. As a religious history, it recognizes that those groups claimed institutional affiliation with specific religious bodies. And as a record of lived experience, it works to combine the social reality and the religious choice of these New Yorkers, to see the city through the eyes of its inhabitants. While geographically precise, it is expansive to the degree that human perceptions are expansive, even messy.

Church history provides a base and a foil for the work. Traditionally, church histories narrated the institutional development of the church. Practicing adherents of the religion—often professional clergy—typically wrote them. Church histories usually privileged the actions of clergy over those of the laity, and theological issues over social and cultural contexts. While such studies can appear antiquarian or eso-teric to those outside the religious tradition, church histories provide an important starting point for this study. For one, church historians often focused on individual congregations. And their emphasis on theology provides a missing ingredient in determining the identity of religious actors. Finally, because church histories provided the earliest narrative of a religious group, they supply clues to the social identities of the his-torical actors, specifying people and places within a larger religious set-ting that later scholars have overlooked.[13]

Theologically and institutionally driven church histories have not been in vogue for nearly a century; the second major field used in this study, social history, largely supplanted church history in interpreting religion. Social histories place the religious actors of church history in their local environments, linking them to shared identities involving class, gender, race, and space. The classic models of social history often connected economic development and class identity to religion. A domi-nant strain of this historiography has suggested that evangelical reform-ers used a religious vocabulary of conversion to draw together troubled elites and a rising middle class, both of whom embraced religion as a form of social control over unruly laboring orders.[14] Historians of gen-der have built from, and challenged, this economic base by consider-ing the place of women in evangelical conversion attempts; such studies have pointed out that elite and bourgeois attempts to convert the lower orders often focused on working women, and the transformation of those women into genteel partners in domesticity.[15] Scholars of race and slavery have also connected religion and social experience. Historians have recognized the importance of religion to the slave experience, and of the black church to the formation and defense of the black community throughout the nineteenth and twentieth centuries.[16]

In recent years, other historians of religion have rejected church his-tory as too narrowly defined, but stepped away from the occasionally reductionist claims of social history, to promote the concept of lived reli-gion. Borrowing a page from anthropology, lived religion attempts thick description to uncover the web of symbols and meanings that historical participants experience as their culture.[17] This approach focuses on laity over clergy, and common perceptions over elite; it consequently blurs traditional religious categories such as sacred and secular that high theo-logical studies establish as rigid and distinct.[18] But this approach consid-ers religion as religion, and does not attempt to attribute other, social or historical, factors as primary in considering religious experience. Rather, religion is a highly individualized concept, molded and shaped for common consumption.

A number of historical works have navigated among these schools. In general, the fault lines have lain between scholars who place religion at the forefront, and those who put greater weight on social factors as causing or determining religious questions. Scholars of Methodism, for example, have either identified the movement as a popular religious expression birthed alongside the American Revolution, or have highlighted the social forces shaping Methodism, thus rendering its religious aspects secondary to tensions of class, race, or gender.[19] Historians of American Episcopalianism have similarly either considered the theological heritage and trajectories of the denomination, or probed the race and gender tensions arising within the church.[20] Historians of black religion have more closely blended the two categories, but bemoan the lack of truly biracial studies of religious experience.[21]

My focus on the congregation as a social unit cuts across these historiographical categories. Congregational studies must return, in part, to church history, because the individuals who attended the churches debated, defended, and fought over who led them, and their theologies. But congregations' small scale also allows historians to look closely at the class, gender, and racial identities individuals retained in their churches. A congregation bridges the dichotomy of public and private, or sacred and secular—as a communal meeting place (public) where individuals regularly experience the sacred (private). A congregation's specific geographic location allows the historian to connect religion with social context, to provide a full analysis of experience and change. As such, the congregation is an excellent avenue to combine social and cultural methodologies, and provides an ideal laboratory for this study.

Over the time of this study, the nature of the church, and its expected duty to society, changed dramatically. Before the American Revolution, church leaders held to an organic vision of church and community. As the Crown's spiritual representative, the Church of England linked state and society. Anglican missionaries with their Methodist partners undertook to evangelize all Americans. Under this system, leaders believed social tensions would dissolve in unity, for every person had a place in the church, no matter how lowly. Poor and rich, black and white, male and female could all take part in religious experience and reflect the greater good for both God and city. Although other congregations and other denominations held different institutional commitments, they generally shared this vision of organic community.

Urban development transformed the churches, and the organic vision crumbled. City growth heightened social differences. Rich and poor members lived in different neighborhoods and attended different congregations. The legal end of slavery in New York heightened racial prejudice, as working whites jostled to maintain their dominance over blacks. Whites and blacks segregated in worship as bourgeois blacks sought to create their own spaces of authority. And the number of those indifferent to religion grew too great to comprehend on a local, personal level. By 1850, ministers no longer expected the church to reflect society as a whole. Rather, each church reflected its local environment, its subsection of identity in city life. No longer was the church itself a new family, a separate structure that subsumed others within it. Rather, families became conduits of moral instruction and spiritual presence. Churches privatized their messages to reach individuals and families unconnected by a larger conception of society.

This book contains eight chapters. Each chapter covers a chronological time but also examines a theme, in overlapping segments. The first chapter traces the creations of Trinity Church and John Street Methodist. The colonial-era concept of religious establishment granted Trinity a prominent place in the city, which reinforced congregants' organic conception of society. Churchmen hoped that the Anglican Church would mediate between state and society, upper and lower orders, and different races, uniting them under its spiritual leadership. John Street Methodist Chapel initially shared these assumptions, for while Methodists believed they created a new close-knit family of believers, they accepted nominal oversight and leadership from the established Anglican Church. Both churches ministered to blacks, which made them unique among many of the city's religious groups. For their part, blacks attempted to use religious instruction to their own ends, as race relations in colonial New York were punctuated by periods of outright conflict.

The second chapter discusses the Revolutionary era's challenges to formal, legal establishment, and the persistence after the Revolution of a social vision of unity in both churches. Accusations of loyalism dogged both Anglicans and Methodists, and both groups' connections to blacks heightened such uncertainty, given British-black interaction in New York. During the American Revolution, the State of New York formally disestablished the Episcopal Church, and both churches faced signs of hostility. After the Revolution, however, many assumptions of organic society persisted. Episcopalian and Methodist leaders continued informal associations that promoted a vision of a united society under their leadership. Both groups included blacks within their communities, but kept them at a distance to conform more clearly to cultural assumptions that many white Americans shared.

The third chapter sketches a social portrait of each congregation during the 1790s. Trinity Episcopal Church retained its colonial-era aura of prestige. Prominent politicians, professionals, and merchants filled its front pews. Yet many from the middling and lower orders attended, and gentlemen who led the church viewed it as a model or reflection of the society at large, a piece of de facto establishment continued after the Revolution. In general, Methodism tended to attract artisans and laboring people. But John Street Methodist Chapel's location near merchant and retail centers caused social stratification within the church. As at Trinity, men of wealth and influence occupied positions of leadership at John Street, but the church contained members from all ranks and both genders, thereby illustrating the ideal of an organic society.

In the 1790s, black Methodists and Episcopalians took their first steps toward forming the distinct congregations of Mother Zion and St. Philip's. Many whites refused to worship with black members and attempted to push their black coreligionists to the margins. Consequently, free blacks in both white churches formed separate houses of worship. Black artisans tended to lead the Methodists, whereas black Episcopalians reflected a broader range of occupations. Both groups, however, remained firmly within their respective denominational traditions. While pushing to improve their own status, black churchmen remained theologically close to the white churches. And their early steps were tentative: black Methodists only met at times when white ministers did not offer services, and black Episcopalians delayed holding separate worship for another decade.

Chapter 4 explores the place of women in the churches in the growing city. Women constituted a numerical majority in each congregation. After 1800, wealthy women quietly entered the public sphere. They organized charitable institutions that focused on widows and children. These benevolent societies preserved traditional assumptions about poverty and the organic vision of society of the colonial era. Paradoxically, however, such organizations opened the way for more radical forms of action, as they provided public spaces, however circumscribed, for society's wealthiest women. Many more women in the churches preserved conventional gender roles by choosing private pious contemplation and steady attendance at worship services. The close connection of some of these women to their ministers heightened social tensions in the churches.

The fifth chapter explains the intersections of gender with race in church life. In the larger society, slavery, poverty, and menial status meant that black men risked being labeled feminine and without power. Thus in the black churches men, not women, took primary place, mimicking the white church's example in an exaggerated form. Black women, however, remained numerous in the churches, and supported their leaders through the emergence of auxiliary benevolent societies and in quiet, obedient forms of piety, similar to most white women. Just as white women gained a place in the public sphere through benevolence, so did black men in public processions and benevolent societies. These black men used a universal language of unity, which mirrored colonial-era church language, but like those earlier forms masked the strongly middle-class and masculine identities of the actors.

In chapter 6, to investigate the connections between religious and social experiences, I revisit the well-documented ecclesiastical battles within each congregation during the 1810s and early 1820s. The increased strains of city life frame these disputes, which church historians have long presented largely as internal theological issues. Episcopalians divided over the bishop's authority, and the right to form ecumenical evangelizing societies, but the struggles also represented a clash between competing Anglican forms of social organization within the congregation. Methodists divided over local and lay versus regional and clerical control over their congregations. Black Methodists tangentially entered white Methodists' debate by defining their identity as independent from white schismatics and churchmen alike, while keeping their local independence from other black churches. Black Episcopalians avoided serious battles in this decade, largely because their perilous financial position impelled them to cling to the High Church Party in the Episcopal Church leadership. In all these cases, ecclesiastical disputes had social dimensions. Local congregations' geographic locations helped determine their positions in these clashes.

Chapter 7 illustrates how the tensions of city growth shaped congregational life. After 1820, business and residential districts began to separate as poor and rich increasingly lived in distinct neighborhoods. All four congregations, located downtown, attracted wealthier worshipers than their coreligionists farther uptown. Even the black churches, near poor and crime-ridden areas, aspired to the bourgeois standards of the white leaders at the Trinity and John Street churches. As a result of this domestication, wealth brought greater privatization to church life. At St. Philip's, some service workers attained great prosperity, transforming the church into a body seeking collective refinement. At Mother Zion, gentility entailed male leadership and preaching bourgeois standards of education, respectability, and rationality. In the white churches, a suburban mentality encouraged some members to flee from the city. Trinity's chapels gained new prominence. Seeing its members less like one large family and more like a grouping of private families, John Street focused on a domesticity that limited the prior aims of Methodism. Education and cultural refinement joined spiritual fervor as paths to leadership.

The eighth chapter examines the full consequences of this domestication of church life in the 1830s and 1840s. Racial fissures grew absolute, and swept the last remains of hope for racial unity from the churches. Yet black churchmen continued to articulate loyalties to denominational traditions that recognized the local relationships fostered in each church. Many white Methodists and Episcopalians embraced nativist politics as a way to re-create the lost world promoted in the colonial era, a truncated version that continued racial separation while promising to soften class conflict among whites. But neither racial separation nor nativist dreams of unity could wind back the clock on the city's economic and demographic growth. Economic slowdowns and the flight of downtown residents caused the churches' once prominent position to decline.

A conclusion extends the narrative to the Civil War. In the 1840s and 1850s, a number of larger developments in American religious and intellectual history suggested that a new unity could be created in New York, whether it lay in evangelical revivalism, Broad Church Episcopalianism, or generalized Romanticism. But the reality of how church members lived highlighted major differences with the colonial era's promotion of organic unity. Social difference, and private religious experience, was the norm for the members of these churches.

In 1860, New York City was the United States' largest city, and a center of finance, fashion, and culture. Regular gridded streets and fine new houses uptown dwarfed the colonial era's small crooked alleys huddled at the south end of the island. The four congregations remained, or became, bastions of respectability. Church leaders could not offer a united vision similar to what their forebears had in the Revolutionary era. Rather, they reached out to individuals on a case-by-case basis, offering not social transformation but personal salvation and public respectability. While some historians note the importance of evangelicalism to nineteenth-century American cultural and political life, the experience of New York's churches suggests that social factors limited whatever influence that the churches and the churches' leaders could claim.

American religious scholars have posited that religion has functioned in a variety of important roles in different settings throughout American history. Paul Johnson, for example, asserted that evangelical religion helped newly bourgeois businessmen to control their laborers, and Nathan Hatch contended that the popularization of revival Christian movements liberated lowly upstarts and outsiders to attack the authority of learned clergymen and church hierarchies. For Johnson, religion was a tool of elite control; for Hatch, a force for popular liberation. In a similar vein, Graham Russell Hodges argued that religion invigorated the New York black community's resistance to white racism.[22]

As striking as the works of these scholars are, I found that the churches had a shorter reach in early Republic New York's urban setting. The expansion of the city, and the expansion and contraction of the city economy, battered and buffeted these downtown churches. Congregants paired their religious lives with identities borne of their living and working spaces. Religious groups rarely influenced events as dramatically as their leaders and prominent members initially hoped. Even when individual church members had important roles in their respective communities, their churches often hesitated in matters of social or political importance. Often, social, economic, and racial concerns eclipsed religious motivations. As time passed, religion became a more private, individual affair. While religion was certainly rich in meaning for the individual believer, the city's growth and commercialization meant in practical terms that, over time, the churches grew less relevant to the community as a whole.[23]

Even so, the parishioners at Trinity and St. Philip's and the congregants at John Street and Mother Zion chose to identify themselves religiously as well as socially or racially. Religion was significant because the participants deemed it such, not because it provided a functional or measurable tool for them. In an environment that was ultimately uncontrollable even for most elites, these city congregations offered havens where adherents might recapture some control, if only in claiming the option to worship and fellowship with the men and women around them.

1 / The Foundations of Religious Establishment: The Colonial Era

During the 1760s, the *New-York Mercury* was a modest four-page newspaper in a midsize colonial port town. Its rear section of advertisements typically dwarfed the few columns devoted to news, and most news relayed events occurring outside the city, in Philadelphia, London, and Paris. Nonetheless, on November 3, 1766, the *Mercury* gave much attention to a procession that had taken place in New York City's streets the previous Thursday, when Trinity Episcopal Church consecrated St. Paul's Chapel, its second daughter chapel in the city. New York's three Anglican worship houses equaled the Dutch Reformed in number for the first time and made the Anglican Church second to none in terms of prestige. The paper's printer, Episcopal layman Hugh Gaine, deemed the chapel's ornate Georgian architecture "one of the most elegant Edifices on the Continent."[1]

The proceedings began at 10:00 a.m. at Fort George, at the southern tip of Manhattan Island. A procession of religious and civic officials marched the half mile to St. Paul's in precise order. Children who received charity from the church walked in front. City and colonial officials followed, along with Trinity's clergy and prominent laity. At the chapel, Trinity's rector, the Reverend Doctor Samuel Auchmuty, led a worship service. In his sermon, Auchmuty preached on the text "the place whereon thy standest is holy ground." The service concluded with the "judicious execution" of several pieces of choral and instrumental music.[2]

When Samuel Auchmuty presided over St. Paul's consecration, he must have felt some satisfaction. During the 1750s and 1760s, Anglican

Figure 1.1. Samuel Auchmuty, Trinity's catechist of blacks and rector, champion of Anglican unity. (From Morgan Dix, *History of Trinity Church*, Vol. 1 [1898].)

opponents led a series of attacks on Anglicanism's prominence in New York. In his letters to his superiors in London, Auchmuty reported Presbyterian conspiracies against the Church of England around every corner. But at this ceremony only Anglican eminence showed. Gaine reported that thousands of individuals of "all Ranks and Denominations" observed the procession from the streets. Inside the chapel, several thousand more listened to the service with "fixed attention" and "devotion."[3] On this day

Trinity Episcopal Church and its two chapels, St. George's and St. Paul's, presented an Anglican establishment that, in the colony of New York, had never been stronger. Some Anglicans believed it augured a united, dominant Church of England throughout North America.

This chapter begins the study of four congregations by examining the origins of Trinity and John Street churches. The story opened with the consecration of St. Paul's because the Anglican concept of church establishment framed the Episcopalian and Methodist churches in colonial-era New York. Although religious pluralism weakened New York's establishment, Trinity Episcopal parish enjoyed a privileged place in Manhattan. The Methodists who began worship at John Street Chapel also associated with Episcopacy and borrowed from its cultural authority. Establishment provided a springboard for missions. Both groups aspired to a universal evangelism that would reach all members of society.

This chapter also examines the churches' attitudes toward black congregants, and black responses, in turn. Both Methodists and Anglicans ventured ministries toward blacks, whom other church groups had generally neglected during the colonial era. Before the Revolution, blacks' inclusion symbolized the universal, authoritative reach of these churches. For their part, black New Yorkers embraced Trinity's or John Street's missionizing efforts for their own ends; the Revolution would create an environment where black church members would attempt greater separation and independence from their white coreligionists. Black Anglicans and Methodists who first attended Trinity and John Street would provide the basis for St. Philip's Episcopal and Mother Zion African Methodist churches.

This background of religious establishment provided a cultural and social model that these churches' members would retain after the Revolution. Even though the political upheavals of the 1770s and 1780s formally ended official establishment, Anglicans and Methodists in New York promoted the idea of an organic, connected church body as normative. Growth of the city, not the Revolution, would alter the religious commitments of these congregants in the coming decades.

Anglican Religious Establishment, and Its Methodist Offshoots, in New York City

The concept of religious establishment seems strange now, but four hundred years ago it was the norm in European kingdoms and their American colonies. In the early modern period, most European elites believed that a stable and harmonious society required a linkage of church and state, with religious and secular authorities each supervising their subjects. In England, the Church of England was the church of the monarch, and the church of the realm. The monarch appointed its bishops, and these bishops in turn consecrated new monarchs. Public taxes went to church support, and in return, the church administered poor relief. Although England's colonies had no bishops, Anglican churchmen expected the model of establishment to expand across the Atlantic.[4]

The turbulent seventeenth century altered this ideal. A Civil War in England disestablished the church, but was followed by an intensely pro-church Restoration. At century's end, the Glorious Revolution resulted in a modified establishment that recognized the permanence, and significance, of dissenters. In the eighteenth century, pro- and anti-establishment camps periodically coalesced around politicized issues of church and state. In the English colonies, the reality of church establishment often varied considerably from the ideal model. Nine of thirteen colonies contained some form of religious establishment. From the Chesapeake region southward, the Anglican establishment mirrored the hierarchical conception of royal government, although wealthy tobacco planters in Virginia, not priests, dominated the parishes. In New England colonies, a thorn in the royal side, renegade Puritans established a Congregational Church, forcing loyal Anglicans to play the role of dissenters. In Pennsylvania, William Penn established a proprietary colony dominated (albeit unofficially) by the Society of Friends. In New York, Anglican interests were stronger than in New England, but weaker than in the South. As a result, pluralism limited formal religious establishments, requiring a shaky compromise with dissenters that lasted, in fits and starts, until the American Revolution.[5]

The English colony of New York had begun as the Dutch colony of New Netherland, and New York City had been New Amsterdam. Because the Dutch burghers who oversaw the colony sought profits more than religious orthodoxy, they allowed a degree of religious toleration remarkable for the seventeenth century.[6] When the English conquered the sparsely populated colony in 1664, the new elites did not wish to disturb old practices, and risk new rebellion, by imposing a heavy-handed religious conformity. In addition to de facto toleration of other Protestants, the new English leadership placated the Dutch landed elites by allowing Dutch Reformed churches to form corporations and own property, a grant denied to other denominations (the Anglican excepted). But accommodations soon extended beyond the former Dutch masters.[7]

Ethnic and religious pluralism hampered the royal governors at every turn, especially in New York City. By the late seventeenth century, the modest seaport of four thousand people displayed a remarkable variety of religions, and irreligion, to the consternation of Governor Thomas Dongan, who reported in 1687:

> New York has first a chaplain belonging to the Fort of the Church of England; secondly a Dutch Calvinist; thirdly a French Calvinist; fourthly a Dutch Lutheran—there be not many of the Church of England; few Roman Catholics; abundance of Quaker preachers men and women especially: singing Quakers, ranting Quakers, Sabbatarians, Anti-Sabbatarians, some Anabaptists, some Independents, some Jews: in short of all sort of opinion there are some, and the most part none at all.[8]

British governors struggled to nurture an Anglican conformity as existed in the mother country. The Anglican establishment that took hold in New York, however, was a veneer of respectability, barely masking both the continued pluralism and the tenuous hold of Anglican authority.

There were simply too few Anglicans in the colony to justify a full establishment. In the 1690s in New York, dissenters outnumbered Anglicans forty to one. In 1693, Governor Benjamin Fletcher strong-armed through the legislature a modified Anglican establishment in the four southernmost counties—New York, Westchester, Richmond, and Queens—where Anglicans were most numerous, although still a minority. This law, called the 1693 Ministry Act, called for the election of ten vestrymen and two wardens for each county. This vestry held the power to tax the citizenry for the local poor relief and the support of a minister. In New York, then, religious establishment encountered several limits from the start: it was not colony-wide, the local populace controlled it, and local interests could theoretically favor some other, non-Anglican church.[9]

In the three counties outside the city, the Anglican Church's control over the vestry was weak, nominal, and contested. The vestry tax often supported a non-Anglican minister. In New York City, Anglican interests fared better. In 1696, Anglicans captured a bare seven-to-five majority in the city vestry and elected William Vesey to serve as minister. Vesey had been raised in a non-Anglican family. Moderate in his theological views, Vesey willingly compromised on matters of faith. He proceeded to serve as Anglican rector in New York for more than forty years. His parish was Trinity Episcopal Church, incorporated in 1697, the year after his appointment, located at the foot of Wall Street on Broadway.

Vesey's easygoing tenure calmed suspicious dissenters and allowed Trinity parish the precedent of having its senior minister's salary supported by public tax. It also granted Trinity a measure of privilege and esteem otherwise lacking among skeptical antichurch colonists.[10]

At the beginning of the eighteenth century, two other sources of funding gave the Church of England in New York increased vitality, especially at Trinity parish. First, in 1705, New York's Governor Cornbury granted Trinity a land grant, or glebe, of the Queen's Farm on the west side of Manhattan Island, which secured a comfortable income to pay assistant ministers' salaries. Second, mission-minded Anglican priests founded the Society for the Propagation of the Gospel (or SPG) in 1701 in London. The SPG aimed to evangelize every subject in Her (soon thereafter, His) Majesty's realm. The SPG paid the salaries of missionary priests to staff the wide-flung parishes throughout the North American continent, and supported evangelization efforts among Native American tribes and African slaves. By the time of the Revolution, seventy-seven SPG-funded missionaries worked in North America, most serving north of the Chesapeake. They included a regular catechist at Trinity Church, who taught both poor white students and African slaves the fundamentals of Christianity, and non-English speakers the basics of the language.[11]

Such projects led to an increased optimism among Anglicans in the colonies over the eighteenth century, especially in the northern colonies where the church had lagged behind the southern colonies' full establishment. Trinity's steeple was the first in New York City with a bell to call congregants to worship. Trinity's rise initiated a flurry of church construction in New York, with parishes raised in Staten Island, Westchester, Eastchester, New Rochelle, and Queens. Between 1690 and 1750, the number of Anglican parishes in the British American colonies increased fourfold; the number north of the Chesapeake line of establishment increased one-hundredfold. By the time of the Revolution, Anglicans sustained more than 450 parishes, an increase of six times the number existing in 1690.[12]

Such growth was accompanied by theological compromise. Although most rectors at Trinity adopted a High Church position that stressed the significance of bishops, church hierarchy, and sacraments, in practice most Anglicans varied considerably in their beliefs and practices. Faced with Enlightenment challenges to tradition and revealed religion, many Anglican priests and congregants favored a latitudinarian stance in matters of orthodoxy, promoting a rational religion that allowed for broad differences on a variety of doctrines. One historian judged eighteenth-century Anglican sermons as "quiet and prosaic, and always genteel," appealing to the natural reason of each congregant in persuading him or her to act morally.[13] Such a position invited the support of many individuals who were not interested in orthodox doctrine.

This latitudinarianism in matters of faith complemented a pursuit of upward social mobility, as royal governors and government officials favored the church as an official faith. The combination proved irresistible to many ambitious colonists during the latter half of the eighteenth century. Repelled by the fatalism of Calvinist theology and chafing at the demands of strict morality, many merchant families in New England sought a more rationalist faith. Anglican parishes formed in New England's seaport cities, at the heart of a region traditionally hostile to the Church of England. Local-born Anglican converts ministered to them, encouraged by the famous defection of Yale's president and four tutors in 1722 from the Congregational to the Anglican Church. In New York, younger Dutch colonists rejected their ethnic heritage for the Anglicans' expansive vision and English-language services. Second-generation immigrants in German Lutheran and Reformed communities followed the Dutch, as did French Huguenots, whom the Church of England absorbed when Catholic monarchs in France destroyed their mother church.[14]

A new confidence at midcentury testified to the growth of Anglican influence in the colony. In a study of New York's colonial-era neighborhoods, historical geographer Nan Rothschild noted that the Anglican churches showed greater growth than those of the Dutch Reformed, and covered a greater population range in the expanding city. Old Trinity already occupied a prestigious spot at the foot of Wall Street on Broadway. Surrounded by three open blocks and commanding a view over the North River, Trinity stood apart from the rest of the city in its own bulk, and in the open space around it. St. George stood on the opposite pole from Trinity, at the higher population densities of the east side on Beekman and Cliff Streets. And St. Paul stood several blocks north of Trinity on Broadway, a stylish landmark of Anglicanism on "what was becoming the most fashionable street in Manhattan." The Anglican building spree thus reflected two aspects of expansion. Anglicans proliferated in all quarters of the city, surrendering none to their opponents. Second, in building near major thoroughfares, the church "dominat[ed] the prime areas of the city" and claimed a symbolic prestige and importance.[15]

By the 1760s, Trinity parish stood as the preeminent example of this expansive Anglican vision. At 148 by 72 feet, the church was the largest public building in the British colonies. It housed the first organ built

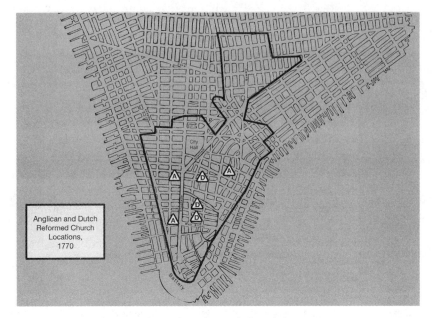

Figure 1.2. Anglican and Dutch Reformed church locations, circa 1770; the dark line reveals the extent of city settlement around that date. The Anglican churches claim more prominent locations, and are more geographically expansive, revealing greater confidence. (Map created by Alanna Beason, derived from map from United States Census Office, 1886.)

in the American colonies, where fashionable elites could attend elegant concerts.[16] The new church attracted the wealthiest New Yorkers, from Anglicized Dutch and Huguenot merchants to prominent British officials. Located at the foot of Wall Street on Broadway, the church stood at a major intersection of commerce.

Nurturing universal aspirations, the church also sheltered the city's poor and lowly. In the 1760s, Trinity became the city's leading landlord, as its vestry built affordable housing on its land west and north of the city. Many artisans soon resided there.[17] The Society for the Propagation of the Gospel, which had supplied missionary ministers to New York's churches since 1701, had also begun evangelization of both Native Americans and African slaves. The British defeat of the Roman Catholic French by 1763, and the subsequent French removal from the continent, seemed to open the continent to missionary expansion. Historian Henry May described such Anglican optimism:

With enough fervor and enough discretion, loyal churchmen could hope for almost anything: a North America all English, all Protestant, united in the same broad and tolerant Church, with even the harshness of slavery mitigated by Christian instruction to both races, with a place for the lowliest and a glorious career for the most talented and devoted, with new worlds to conquer in Africa and India, in an empire united by secular and religious ties.[18]

But the breadth of the church would prove especially difficult to manage.

Under the umbrella of Anglican evangelization efforts, Methodism stood out as particularly precocious, more energetic, and ultimately longer-lasting than the others. John Wesley founded Methodism as a missionary branch of the Anglican Church, originally analogous to the SPG. Wesley's Methodists experimented and adapted their methods to reach audiences where the established church had little exposure. In the eighteenth century, that meant success in the heart of a rapidly urbanizing and industrializing England. In these new industrial centers in the North, Midlands, and Southwest, the established church had failed to keep up. But Wesley famously remarked, "I look upon all the world as my parish." Eventually, Wesley's followers would take such missionary drive to the Americas, where the established church was present, but not prominent.[19]

An Oxford graduate, Tory in his politics, Wesley embraced Anglican rites and rituals. But along with his brother Charles, Wesley merged his High Church inclinations with Low Church innovations in worship. Scholars have focused on these innovations, for they came to dominate the story of Methodism in the early American Republic. Among them were small prayer groups and worship services held outside the standard (and state-mandated) times. Also important were hymns, especially the thousands of verses that flowed from Charles's pen, filled with piety and brimming with emotion. And Methodists styled their preaching to melt the heart, even as John Wesley described his own heart as "strangely warmed" in recounting his conversion experience.[20]

Such innovations did not make Methodists religious radicals, however. Methodists remained Anglicans until after the Revolution, when the vision of universal evangelization under the established church had tarnished. When John Wesley spoke of primitive Christianity, he did not necessarily mean it the same way early Republic evangelicals later did: as a Holy Spirit–filled ecstasy, ushering in the purity and truth of the early church, free from the corruption of succeeding centuries. Anglicans, like dissenting Protestants, embraced the term "primitive Christianity," but included with it the presence of bishops and sacramental rituals that had accompanied the Christian church in its first centuries.[21] Wesley, who straddled the line between High and Low, embraced this ambiguity. In New York, many of his leading congregants would keep it.

Wesley had little formal influence in the American colonies, at first, but his ideas about the importance of a heartfelt conversion paralleled colonial religious change generally. In the 1740s, evangelist George Whitefield promulgated a form of evangelical Anglicanism that many Americans then deemed Methodist. Whitefield was a master of self-promotion whose revivals drew thousands in the northern colonies, leading to what historians have popularly referred to as a Great Awakening. Although Whitefield was Calvinist, and Wesley Arminian, both emphasized conversion at the center of true religious faith. As Whitefield's and Wesley's converts from the British Isles filtered into the colonies in the eighteenth century, some added leaven to the Anglican churches that were growing in the seaport cities.[22]

These previously unidentified Methodists may have numbered in the hundreds by the 1760s. Over time, some rejected established Anglicanism and worshiped in home churches. The Methodist lay minister and former British military officer Thomas Webb discovered five New Yorkers who had begun worshiping at home in 1766. Webb introduced them to other coreligionists, and encouraged the fledgling group to acquire a house of worship. These early New York Methodists moved to a rigging loft on William Street in 1767. The next year they raised four hundred pounds from more than 250 contributors to move to a location on John Street. Lay preacher Philip Embury, one of the original five New York worshipers, preached the inaugural sermon at John Street in October 1768. Unlike the grand procession accompanying the consecration of St. Paul's, John Street Methodist's opening received no attention from the New York press. Almost immediately, however, John Street attracted large crowds: former closet Methodists, perhaps, or other evangelically inclined Protestants. Methodist itinerant minister Richard Boardman reported to John Wesley that 1,700 souls regularly attended Methodist services, only one-third of whom fit in the building.[23]

Trinity's Anglicans kept close ties with the city's Methodists. Methodists erected their first chapel on land bought from Mary Barclay, whose husband, Henry, had served as Trinity parish's second rector. She charged a nominal fee of five shillings in advance, and ground rent of just over fourteen pounds per year. Approximately 250 individuals pledged contributions to raise money for the erection of the chapel. Trinity's ministers Samuel Auchmuty, John Ogilvie, and Charles Inglis all donated. So did Trinity's vestry, including such prominent citizens as James Duane, Elias Desbrosses, Andrew Hamersley, Edward Laight, David Clarkson, Gabriel Ludlow, and Nicholas Stuyvesant. At least 10 percent of the individuals on the subscription list affiliated with Trinity.[24]

Colonial-era Methodists remained Anglicans, for John Wesley did not grant his followers the authority to conduct all the church's ordinances and rituals. Methodists attended Anglican worship services to receive the sacraments of baptism and the Lord's Supper, or Holy Communion. On one visit to the city, future Methodist bishop Francis Asbury partook of the Lord's Supper at St. Paul's Chapel with several Methodist church leaders, including Thomas Webb. Prominent Methodists Samuel Stilwell, Stephen Sands, William Valleau, and Andrew Mercein, all of whom were trustees, class leaders, or ministers at John Street, had their children baptized at Trinity parish in the late 1770s.[25]

Some of the Anglican cooperation with the Methodists contained an element of social control. Many of society's elites believed religious practice set a good example of moral character for the lower orders. Methodism deserved support because it encouraged unruly laborers and slaves to attend church. For this reason, Presbyterian Philip Livingston also contributed to John Street's building fund. But perhaps some at Trinity hoped that the Methodist chapel would draw the more enthusiastic members from their midst, thereby reinforcing the majesty and decorum of the church's most visible branch. Historian Richard Pointer notes that during the 1760s, Trinity, the "archetype of European traditionalism," had "developed an evangelical wing." As such, a Methodist preacher's fiery exhortations might upset the propriety of genteel latitudinarian morality, and be better placed outside the mother church.[26]

Trinity's attempt to create a broad church establishment confused many about the church's identity. Samuel Provoost stepped down as an assistant minister at Trinity in 1771. His biographer blamed Methodists for the resignation, for Provoost refused to deliver the enthusiastic, emotional sermons that many congregants desired. But another historian claims that a pro-establishment party forced Provoost's dismissal, for the theologically liberal Provoost sympathized with New York's dissenting religious groups, including the Methodists.[27] The opposing conclusions suggest that forms of worship divided the church.

Anglicans and Methodists remained officially linked during the colonial era, but the alliance fell short of true union. Trinity rector

Samuel Auchmuty viewed the Methodists with less concern than he did the Presbyterians, whom he believed conspired constantly against the established church. But he also considered Methodism an unwelcome nuisance. In one letter to London church officials, Auchmuty described the preacher-soldier Thomas Webb as "turn'd mad and do[ing] a good deal of mischief about the country." Auchmuty feared that Webb, who had already abandoned a military career, might attempt to gain clerical office from the Church of England, "which would be another affliction to the Clergy here."[28] Thus Auchmuty's greatest concern about the Methodists was not that they would attempt to destroy the church, but instead wanted to lead it! Even so, such concern did not compel him to bar Webb from taking communion at Trinity's chapel.

Although strains developed in the Anglican-Methodist alliance, both churches shared a common cultural and religious background that made movement between Episcopal and Methodist churches more likely than between other denominations. Well into the nineteenth century, after the churches had institutionally separated, Methodist ministers who wished to settle down and acquire a regular salary often joined the Episcopal Church. Upon surveying an area for evangelism, Francis Asbury confidently proclaimed that the local Methodists would achieve lasting success, "because the inhabitants are generally Episcopalians."[29] In addition to these affinities, both churches shared a willingness to evangelize black slaves.

Blacks under New York's Religious Establishment

The colony of New York contained more slaves, at a larger percentage of the population, than any other British colony north of the Chesapeake. In 1750, one in seven of the colony's population was enslaved blacks, with New York City's proportion closer to one in six. The Greater New York metropolitan region, including Long Island and east New Jersey, contained an especially dense slave population. Most slaves in the colony lived in rural regions adjoining New York City on Long Island, especially in King's County (later Brooklyn). By the early 1770s, an estimated 18,000 blacks lived in Greater New York City. In the city, slaveholding was widespread, with even poorer whites owning slaves.[30]

Historians have observed that racism toward blacks increased dramatically in the late-seventeenth-century British colonies. Antiblack racism became prominent, and more obvious, as the numbers of Africans imported through the Atlantic slave trade grew dramatically and after colonies stipulated clear slave codes in law. Under early Dutch rule, the city's blacks owned and accumulated property, drilled with the militia, and initiated lawsuits in courts of law. Blacks' status eroded in later New Netherland, as slavery grew more important, and under English rule slipped further. In the early eighteenth century, waves of new slaves from Africa bolstered general cultural assumptions about Africans' inability to assimilate, and their basic inequality with whites.[31]

On this issue, Anglican churchmen held a position contrary to that of most colonists. English imperialists looked to religious establishment to consolidate their control of English possessions. The aim of the Church of England in New York was not merely religious conversion, but also the cultural Anglicization of the population. The Society for the Propagation of the Gospel stood at the forefront of these efforts, seeking the education and conversion of not only Dutch subjects, but also African slaves. The SPG funded a missionary, Elias Neau, to catechize New York blacks at Trinity Church for the first two decades of the eighteenth century.[32]

Many Dutch and English alike remained suspicious of blacks' involvement in the church. A long-standing debate in Christendom involved whether Christians could enslave fellow baptized individuals. As such, many whites hoped to avoid the question by barring blacks from religious participation. Neau took another tack. A French Huguenot, Neau had been imprisoned in a French galley and sympathized with his charges as slaves. But Neau held a more personal and pietistic vision of faith than did the typical Anglican. He did not challenge the institution of slavery, but rather emphasized the heartfelt conversion of his charges. This gained him the grudging support of New York's more prominent Anglicans, who valued the cultural supremacy that the church promoted.[33]

Neau reported thirty regular communicants in his first years on the job, but such good fortune would not last. Neau's efforts nearly derailed in 1712, when almost three dozen enslaved blacks joined in a blood oath to throw off the shackles of slavery. Setting fire to buildings, they hacked apart fleeing whites with swords and hatchets before authorities subdued them. Six rebels killed themselves before capture. Officials tried twenty-five survivors, and executed seventeen. As one participant was a Neau convert, many white New Yorkers called for an end to the mission.[34]

The rebels of 1712 rejected most of the surrounding society's values, but did share a few connections with Neau's ministry. The conspirators' blood oaths and suicide before capture suggest African rituals, as pantribal confraternities participated in such undertakings. But blacks sought religious power where they could find it, including in the church of their masters. Neau's convert had reportedly been angry that his master had not granted him permission to be baptized, and other whites complained that blacks desired the magical (or possibly abolitionist) powers of baptism. Other rebels probably attended Neau's Anglican school to gain literacy, a form of power that could hold magical promise, but also pragmatic resistance. New York's blacks took Africa with them, but did not shut out the possibility of Christian influence.[35]

New York's governor, Robert Hunter, continued to support Neau's efforts, so the Anglican instruction of blacks continued through Neau's death in 1722. Neau complained in 1718 that it was nearly impossible for him to gain new pupils. Postrevolt laws severely limited blacks' religious activity. Black catechumens could meet only on Sunday afternoons, when slaves did not have to work, after regularly scheduled religious services, and when blacks could travel in daylight under the gaze of watchful authorities. These strictures limited opportunities for black religious instruction; white opposition nearly ended it completely. One observer contended in the 1720s, "Negroes instructed in Christianity are more conceited than their countrymen who are not."[36] After Neau, Anglican efforts to catechize slaves subsided until shortly before midcentury.

The next visible signs of black unrest, however, would lead to more, not fewer, attempts at evangelization. In 1741, another ostensible rebellion rocked New York City. Mysterious fires coupled with a wave of robberies fueled white fears of a full-scale slave revolt. The trail of evidence led to a few core conspirators, who under torture named others involved in a large-scale plot. City authorities executed thirty-one blacks—thirteen hanged, eighteen burned—and deported seventy more. Courts also condemned and executed four whites suspected of involvement.[37]

The truth behind the 1741 conspiracy remains shrouded in secrecy. The self-serving nature of the official trial report led an earlier generation of historians to doubt the truth of any rumors of concerted black revolt. They generally agreed with Winthrop Jordan's assessment that anxiety over a lack of social cohesion led whites to viciously turn on blacks. Ethnic and religious differences among New York's whites had fueled political factionalism for more than fifty years. The bitter conflicts did not obscure that blacks remained easy targets, lowest on the social ladder. Certainly the trials reveal that white prejudice toward blacks had strengthened by midcentury.[38]

The rise of anthropological approaches and recognition of African cultural survivals led more recent historians to find evidence of conspiracy in the events of 1741. But the motives for conspiracy remain wide-ranging in these interpretations. Some have stressed a proletarian union of blacks and laboring whites against elite merchant overlords; others have focused on the African influence on slaves, whose numbers swelled in the years before the trials. In all these interpretations, the attempted revolt would appear a natural response in the mid-eighteenth century; as Graham Russell Hodges has argued, the uprisings in 1712 and 1741 mark end points of a thirty-year revolt of Africans against white New Yorkers' increased attempts to strengthen the bonds of chattel slavery in the colony.[39]

The range of conspirators condemned in 1741 reveals a fragmented community, at best. Some blacks clearly had ties to African culture, but others embraced a more polyglot identity. New York's laboring culture could be interracial, as poorer whites and blacks joined in activities ranging from the leisurely to the criminal. And it was pluralistic, as some of the accused blacks were Hispanic sailors who occupied a higher social status in Latin America, but whose Catholic religion and darker skins nonetheless condemned them in the eyes of the judges, and in society as a whole.[40]

In an environment where both white and black communities remained fragmented, the Anglican Church and SPG advocated social cohesion. This stance gained the church new adherents. Throughout the eighteenth century, SPG officials contended that evangelization would make slaves less, not more, likely to revolt, and would increase their industry and honesty. Following tumultuous decades of master-slave relationships, after 1750 more masters were inclined to agree. SPG missionary Samuel Auchmuty noted a marked increase in the number of slaves attending catechism classes during the early 1760s. Every year he baptized dozens of children and a handful of adults. Each year, Auchmuty judged a few slaves advanced enough in their catechism studies to partake of the Lord's Supper at regular church services. Scores of African slaves received a rudimentary education under Auchmuty, who reported around thirty regular communicants during the 1760s and early 1770s. No other New York denomination made such an effort to convert blacks before the American Revolution.[41]

For their part, blacks were more likely to accept catechization after 1750. Slave imports into New York City dropped dramatically after the 1740 revolt, and while the black population grew, the number of new arrivals directly from Africa shrank. Auchmuty's catechumens were native New Yorkers, and perhaps saw in their activity a way to gain the patronage of the city's leading government officials and merchants, not to mention their own masters. But in these actions, their identity as outsiders to an inside faith remained. Analyses of New York City's African burial ground, which colonial blacks used throughout the eighteenth century, reveal continued survivals of tribal rituals.[42]

Black Movement toward Methodism

Aside from the SPG, most churches did not actively seek black members, yet over time blacks attended some churches. The outpouring of revivalist energy in George Whitefield's trips to America cracked the door for black conversion, as Whitefield attacked the proud and preached spiritual equality of all before Christ. Later revivalists grew more explicit in promoting social or political egalitarianism. The Great Awakening upended churches' old social relationships on many fronts. Lay ministers were especially successful among the poor. Blacks converted to Christianity in significant numbers for the first time. Some blacks and women took to the fields to preach. A few revival groups, like the Baptists in Virginia, willingly accepted black converts as equals, a drastic breach of social mores. The Methodists missed these early waves of revivals, but when they entered the colonies in the 1760s, they made up for lost time.[43]

Methodists fed from the energy of revivalism, and went further than Anglicans to welcome blacks to worship. According to oral tradition, at the first meetings of New York City's Methodists one of the five participants was a black slave named Betty. Methodist ministers preached the gospel to all individuals, white and black, and welcomed slaves as spiritual equals. Methodist church leaders repeatedly celebrated the presence of black worshipers at their services. New York City missionary Joseph Pilmoor wrote to John Wesley in 1770, "Even some of the poor, despised children of Ham are striving to wash their robes and make them white in the blood of the Lamb." Pilmoor closed with the verse "God is no respecter of persons." That same verse appeared in the journal of Francis Asbury when he recounted seeing blacks worship in New York. Asbury repeatedly voiced his enjoyment at seeing the "sable faces" of blacks in the services. In a few cases, black exhorters preached to crowds of white and black Methodists.[44]

Many blacks found low church Methodism more attractive than high church Anglicanism because early Methodists believed slavery to be a sin. Ministers denounced the institution of slavery from the pulpit, and many early Methodist converts freed their slaves after experiencing the grace of Christ.[45] In contrast, Anglican messages to black slaves stressed duty and obedience. Even so, both Anglicans and Methodists cared for Africans' spiritual needs, in marked contrast with most other New York religious groups.

Shortly after the midpoint of the eighteenth century, Anglicans and Methodists had an established place in colonial New York: established by law toward legal preference, but also established in fact as socially acceptable institutions in a burgeoning city. They were part of a church that had little formal power but did hold legal privileges, cultural prestige, and universal aspirations. And both groups ministered to blacks whose degraded status within the community marked them for prejudice and scorn. The American Revolution that would follow destroyed the legal privilege of these churches, but all their other characteristics—their cultural cachet, desire to reach all subjects (now citizens), and biracial missions—would remain.

2 / Religious Establishment Challenged, Destroyed, and Re-formed: The Revolutionary Era

Samuel Auchmuty did not live to see his vision of a unified Anglican Church establishment in New York fulfilled. His successor, Charles Inglis, had a front-row seat to its destruction. Inglis complained that the Church of England's loyalty to Crown in the 1770s only drew "peculiar envy" from "disaffected" patriots. He reported that in the run-up to Revolution, patriot laymen threatened, verbally abused, and jailed recalcitrant priests. Inglis had personally penned a response to Thomas Paine's *Common Sense*, but patriots had seized the essay directly from the press and destroyed it. Even though the British army occupied New York from 1776 until war's end, Inglis's anxiety remained. Fleeing American patriots plundered Inglis's house. And Inglis suspected that rebels under orders from George Washington set fires in the city. "It really seems the conflagration was directed against the interest of the Church," wrote Inglis, for the flames consumed Trinity's building. St. Paul's Chapel and King's College, directly in the fire's path, nearly met the same fate, but alert observers doused their roofs with water, sparing those two prominent Anglican symbols from destruction. For the rest of the war, as the king's troops marched through the streets of New York, His Majesty's largest church in the colonies would remain a burned-out husk. After the war, Inglis would leave New York alongside the British troops.[1]

This chapter traces the effects of the American Revolution on New York's Anglican and Methodist churches. Before the Revolution, proto-patriots attacked the Anglican clergy's vision as hostile to true liberty. During the Revolution, many patriots associated both groups, including their black coreligionists, with loyalism, and after the Revolution patriot lawmakers disestablished New York's Anglican Church. Such actions fatally destroyed the clergy's highest aspirations for political influence. Methodists similarly suffered in the shadow of the larger Anglican conflicts, harmed by their ambiguous relationship with the mother body. Yet most churchmen, especially Anglican lay elites who accepted independence, viewed these setbacks as temporary, and continued to embrace a cultural vision for the church that did not rely upon full political establishment. Both groups kept connections to blacks, a group tainted by all-out loyalism, but Americanized themselves by creating greater distance between white and black congregants. By 1790, many Episcopalians and Methodists expected that their institutions would shake off the setback of disestablishment and continue to provide a socially cohesive vision for the city.

Political Battles over Religious Establishment

During the eighteenth century, the political ramifications of religious establishment ebbed and flowed with the changing times. After heated debates in the 1710s, moderate Anglicanism dominated both sides of the Atlantic for an entire generation. But in the 1750s, old battles took on new forms. In the early 1750s, many New York elites championed the creation of a King's College to match their aspirations in a growing, prospering city. Anglican priests particularly welcomed the college as a necessary Anglican response to Congregationalist strongholds at Harvard and Yale. Many SPG missionaries had been American-born and American-trained, in hostile anti-Anglican environments: Trinity's rector Henry Barclay had attended Yale; Trinity's catechist Samuel Auchmuty had gone to Harvard. Such men hoped the college could train the Church of England's ministers in North America, ending the need for costly trips to England for education. Their influence, and the preponderance of Anglicanism in the governor's circle, led Anglicans to dominate the original board of trustees. When Trinity's vestry offered in 1752 to provide thirty-two acres for the college, provided it be Anglican-led, the matter appeared settled.[2]

Elites initially crossed denominational lines to support the effort, as a college would grant New York new cultural capital. But the attempt to link the school with religious establishment roused religious dissenters. Presbyterian William Livingston, a minority non-Anglican on the board of trustees, led the assault through a series of essays in the *Independent*

Reflector. Livingston strenuously opposed the church-state connection an Anglican college would imply. He particularly attacked the docility and deference that accompanied religious establishment.[3]

Livingston's opponents fired back, using the voice of the *New-York Mercury,* printed by the Anglican layman Hugh Gaine. Like Livingston, these High Churchmen dipped into the well of an earlier era, adopting the polemic of High Church debaters from the 1710s. Such men invoked a sacramental theology that stressed that God's invisible grace worked through visible signs, as it did in the Lord's Supper. No less did the visible and invisible intertwine in the working of civil and church laws, and in social and political institutions. In response to the *Independent Reflector's* invocation of a state of nature, which they deemed an ahistorical never-land, the *Mercury's* High Church champions suggested respect for God-given social and historical precedents. In the proper forms of deference, religion could steer a clear path between the twin dangers of emotional enthusiasm, on one hand, and infidelity, on the other.[4]

Livingston and allies responded in kind, extending the pamphlet war through 1756. The resulting political battles pitted the Anglican governor and council against a largely dissenting assembly. Like the original 1693 church establishment, the resulting compromise granted the college a limited form of Anglican influence. The board of directors would include both Anglicans and dissenters, and the college president would be Anglican. The college would provide a general instruction in Christian morality, without promoting the dogma of any individual sect. While this was technically an Anglican victory, it mostly suggested that support for full political-religious establishment was neither broad nor deep.[5]

The battles over King's College suggest that the High Church polemic attracted passionate support among the few clergy in the colony, but little beyond. Livingston's opponents were generally not laity, but clergy. Samuel Johnson was the eldest and most influential of these. Johnson's protégés wrote the *Mercury* essays, including New York priests Henry Barclay, Samuel Seabury Jr., Samuel Auchmuty, and Thomas Bradbury Chandler.[6]

For Anglican laity, however, such pure High Church principles were an embarrassment. The Tory principles that clerics championed in their responses to Livingston turned former Anglican allies, including a number of key Dutch Reformed clergy and laity, against the establishment. Opposition to such establishment made strange bedfellows, linking pietist revivalists with rationalist skeptics, radical with moderate Whigs, and opposition politicians with disaffected lower orders. Such unity would repeat in the Revolution. Anglican laymen who sought influence in their communities would rather channel such unity than beat against it.[7]

The King's College controversy would recur, in a larger register, in the bishop controversy. From the English colonies' inception, Anglican leadership had periodically tested the idea of establishing bishops in America. But none had seriously promoted the matter after 1720, as British politicians and colonial merchants alike turned their attention to the increase of commerce; none, that is, until the late 1760s. Historian Patricia Bonomi has suggested that the debate over establishing a bishop in the Americas consumed even more paper in the presses than the Stamp Act, and likely swung local elections in New York, where the debate ran hottest.[8]

The debate centered in New York because it was the center of Anglican missionary efforts. Anglican clergy had the ear of the colony's presses, as the city's two principal newspapers, the *Mercury* and *Gazette*, were both printed by Anglican laymen eager for church business. And clergymen started the debate when an English bishop, in a sermon delivered in support of the SPG, attacked colonial religion for its extremism and disorder, and suggested the planting of bishops as a remedy. As previously, William Livingston debated SPG affiliates or allies, most notably Anglican churchmen Charles Inglis and Thomas Bradbury Chandler.[9]

A minority of British Anglican churchmen considered it wise to plant bishops in the American colonies. Fewer American Anglicans supported the matter; most southern churchmen were dedicated to local lay control over parishes, and northern ones found the SPG's high Tory principles to be embarrassing, and certainly politically inexpedient after colonists unified to oppose the Stamp Act in 1765. Even ardent High Churchmen who supported a bishop suggested that such an office could be confined to spiritual authority, with no power to coerce colonial subjects. The debate over bishops had few real ecclesiastical results, then, even as it allowed antichurch opposition to coalesce.[10]

The Loyalist Taint on Anglicans and Methodists during the Revolution

The pre-Revolutionary debates over High Church establishment, in which patriots attacked church hierarchy and privilege, spilled over into the Revolution. The Revolutionary War undermined the Anglican vision of a unified colonial society. During the war, Episcopalians divided internally over politics and church governance, rejecting the supposed unity that Anglican clergy and SPG missionaries promoted. The Methodist institutional attachment to Anglicanism caused similar strains, and Methodists struggled to define themselves in relationship to their parent church. Both churches' connections to the British government created a special problem in New York City, where the military occupied the town for most of the war. Patriots (an increasing number of citizens identifying as such as the Continental Army's position improved) could paint Anglicans and Methodists as not only Tories, but also biracial disgraces, given their support for black evangelization.

New York's Anglican clergy stressed loyalty to the Crown; in fact, the northern colonies' Anglican churchmen were the strongest American voices for loyalism during the Revolution, and among the few to offer a coherent ideology. Priests such as New York's Samuel Seabury had publicly promoted an Anglican King's College and bishops in America; it was a short trip for him to denounce the emerging patriot cause. In 1774, Seabury wrote several tracts denouncing the delusional and fanatical tendencies of rebellion. He engaged in battle not with a Presbyterian, however, but an Episcopal layman, as then-teenaged Alexander Hamilton penned a series in reply.[11]

Priestly loyalism meant that, in the run-up to Revolution, Anglican churches suffered where patriots held sway. Trinity's rector Charles Inglis asserted that north of the Chesapeake, all Anglican clergy (save one lone exception) remained true to Britain. Inglis minimized his loyalism, noting only that his religious duty meant he could not advocate liberty from the pulpit, and had to adhere to the liturgies of the Book of Common Prayer, which included prayers for the king. Trinity, along with all other Anglican churches, also displayed the king's coat of arms. Consequently, Inglis complained that patriot committees of correspondence closed Anglican churches and harassed loyalist priests. As the British army occupied New York in 1776, Inglis insinuated that fleeing patriot forces burned down the church.[12]

Complicating matters, Anglican suffering under patriot rule disappeared under British oversight. During the British occupation of New York, Anglican churches fared better than other religious groups. Both of Trinity's chapels and John Street Methodist meetinghouse remained open during the conflict. Believing the Anglican charge that other denominations were havens for dissenting patriots, British officers forcibly closed most other churches. Some Presbyterian and Dutch Reformed congregations suffered the added indignity of serving as hospitals or barracks for British soldiers. But by remaining open, the Anglican Church garnered the same resentments applied to the occupying British army.

Condemning British soldiers as licentious and immoral, patriot moralists attributed the same vices to the Anglican churches that soldiers attended.[13]

Further, Trinity Church, rare among New York City's congregations, included a multiracial vision. Anglican priests baptized and married blacks, and served them communion. During the war Anglicans opened a school for black children. Methodist preachers, too, willingly ministered to blacks, and publicly rejoiced in their participation in revivals and prayer meetings. Such actions may have played a greater role in creating suspicion than the Anglican clergy's ideological loyalty to the Crown, for blacks occupied a conspicuous place at the bottom of the social hierarchy. When the Revolution offered opportunity for greater freedom, many blacks took advantage: historian Graham Russell Hodges has deemed black actions in Revolutionary New York an eight-year revolt against white New Yorkers.[14]

The most obvious threats to white colonists were blacks who joined British military actions. Eight hundred black soldiers trained on Staten Island, their Black Brigade serving as a segregated group within the British regular regiment known as the Queen's Rangers. Black soldiers' activities focused on the greater metropolitan area of Westchester County and east New Jersey. Colonel Tye, a runaway slave from a prominent Jersey Quaker, led an interracial group of irregular soldiers in terrorist attacks on patriot farms throughout New Jersey. Tye's men seized valuable provisions and freed slaves. While some elite loyalists such as Oliver DeLancey grumbled about blacks' military presence, British officers typically ignored such complaints.[15]

More visceral and immediate than military action was the large influx of blacks, mostly runaway slaves, who swelled the population of British-occupied New York City. An outside observer entering the city in the late 1770s might first notice the prominent scarlet-coated uniforms of the British army, for the city remained the army's headquarters throughout the war, an increasingly beleaguered center as the generals lost ground on the greater continent. But a close second to catch the eye would be the sheer numbers of blacks. Twelve thousand runaway slaves filled the city in 1779 (perhaps as much as half of the wartime population); at the time of British withdrawal in 1783, four thousand remained, despite thousands who fled with the army. The sea of black faces would appear striking in most American colonies north of the Chesapeake.[16]

Most of these blacks did not serve as soldiers. Paid less than white laborers, shunted to tent cities in Staten Island or the burned-out West

Ward, blacks nonetheless moved freely about the city and earned wages for their labor. They gained employment in rebuilding the charred West Ward in lower Manhattan, where more than one thousand buildings burned alongside Trinity. Others improved the military fortifications in the city and surrounding countryside. Teamsters carted arms from ports to magazines in the town. Black foragers ventured outside city limits to gather scarce foodstuffs to feed the teeming city. Black pilots navigated rivers for these foraging parties, and for British expeditions.[17]

Patriots had ample opportunity to complain about the mongrel nature of the British occupation. Patriot sympathizer Henry M. Muhlenberg suggested that the British regiment of blacks was "inclined towards barbarities . . . [and] lacking in human feeling." Blacks associated freely with British soldiers. Most scandalous to some were the "Ethiopian balls" in which white British officers mingled indiscriminately with African Americans.[18] Such criticisms of impropriety could be leveled directly at Anglicans, for their combined support of the British cause and black humanity.

Property and Patriotism: Trinity Rebuilds its Reputation

The traditional interpretation of the Revolution's effect on the Church of England is that the Anglican clergy's wartime loyalty to Britain nearly destroyed that denomination at war's end. In 1782, the SPG withdrew its aid to the American colonies, ending its longtime support for Trinity's catechists. Many SPG missionaries fled the country, among them Charles Inglis, who finally realized the High Church dream of a bishop in the Americas—in his case, in Nova Scotia. In 1784, the New York state legislature disestablished the Anglican Church, granted all denominations the right to incorporate, and legalized Catholic worship in the state. Further, state-appointed regents took control of King's College, removing it from Anglican hands and renaming it Columbia. At war's end, many Anglican loyalists fled the city, removing to havens in Britain or Canada. Lower attendance and smaller offering collections hurt the cash-strapped church. Resentment between patriot laity and loyalist clergy wracked the church in the 1780s. Relations also became strained between the colonial churches and the Anglican headquarters in England. Such conflicts and flagging numbers led some observers to conclude that the Church of England, in America, would not last beyond the Revolutionary generation.[19]

Figure 2.1. Charles Inglis, Trinity's ill-fated Revolutionary-era rector, later bishop of Nova Scotia. (From Morgan Dix, *History of Trinity Church*, vol. 1 [1898].)

As a branch of the Anglican Church, Methodists risked clear guilt by association. Like the High Church ideologues who promoted Tory principles, Methodist founder John Wesley was an arch-Tory in politics. During the Revolution, Wesley published loyalist tracts suggesting that all Christians should submit to their God-ordained governments. Certainly Methodism's status as a missionary wing of the church did not help matters, for the mission-focused SPG had been one of the most consistent voices for loyalism before and during the war. In fact, whereas most SPG missionaries had been American-born converts, most Methodist missionaries were British-born, culturally even more removed from the settings where they preached.[20]

Methodist preachers emphasized that building the kingdom of God was their primary aim, suggesting a commitment to political neutrality. But it might appear that Methodists tended, like their founder, to support the mother country. During British occupation, John Street Methodist Chapel remained open, when army officers forcibly closed all other churches (save the Anglican). Blacks and British soldiers (and black British soldiers) attended John Street, again reinforcing the strangeness and foreignness of the religion in many American eyes. After the war, most British Methodist missionaries left, if they had not been deported already. Such was the case for Thomas Webb, whose military background caused immediate suspicion. Patriot leaders captured Webb, held him as a prisoner of war, and deported him to England in 1778. Webb would never return to the church he helped found. Francis Asbury avoided the same fate by going into hiding. Asbury was virtually the only English minister, and licensed Methodist preacher, to remain at war's end. He would emerge as the symbolic and real leader of Methodism in America.[21]

As the Revolution ended, many patriot observers labeled New York's Methodist and Anglican Churches as loyalist and interracial. Both affiliated with a Church of England establishment that Whigs found hierarchical and tyrannical. But while both groups suffered damage to their reputations, neither faced extinction, or irrelevance. Both Methodists and Episcopalians resolved to continue their mission to society. While they deemphasized the colonial imperatives of hierarchy and patronage, they adapted older religious forms to new social realities. Independence muted their message, but did not destroy it.

While Anglican loyalists drew intense opposition, they had been small in number, and concentrated almost exclusively on high government officials and the clergy. Thus when church disestablishment forced most government officials and many priests to flee, few tangible signs of loyalism remained. Instead, an Anglican patriot laity forged a new elitism based upon the protection of property, and welcomed the return of any loyalist (especially those of means) willing to submit to the new government.

The transition from loyalist to Whig to an apolitical unity of wealth occurred quickly. In 1783, Trinity's loyalist vestry voted to replace the departed priest Charles Inglis with another loyalist, the moderate Tory Benjamin Moore. Fearing a political backlash against their parish, Trinity's Whigs protested. Using authority granted by the city council, in 1784 these Whigs took control of the vestry, deposed Moore, and replaced him with Samuel Provoost, whose patriot politics made him acceptable to more New Yorkers.[22]

The change in church governance accompanied a rearguard action to keep Trinity's property rights secure. Radical political groups in the city, the Sons of Liberty and Mechanics Committee, promoted the seizure of loyalist properties for the common good. When heirs of the original owner of Trinity's lands petitioned the New York state assembly to recover their lost property, assemblymen suggested that the lands, initially granted to Trinity by Queen Anne, properly belonged to the state. Trinity attendee Alexander Hamilton led the defense of Trinity's property, uncovering a deed that kept Trinity's lands from seizure. Hamilton's overtures to conservative Whigs also called for lenience toward former loyalists.[23]

These local actions paralleled Anglican actions on the national level. In 1785, the Anglican Church in America became the Protestant Episcopal Church, independent of its mother, the Church of England. Liturgical reform proceeded, with American Anglicans editing the Book of Common Prayer to fit its new republican setting. Authority in the new body resided with the laity, who attended and voted in diocesan conferences alongside priestly delegates. The issue of bishops rose again, briefly: when Samuel Seabury emerged as a candidate to be the first United States bishop, in Connecticut, Whig Episcopalians like John Jay and Rufus King (both at Trinity) fumed about Seabury's Tory views, and complained that the office of the bishop emphasized an unwelcome hierarchy in the church. But after Seabury's consecration in 1784, patriots gained access to the office: in 1787, Trinity's Samuel Provoost was elected as bishop of New York, and William White (chaplain of the wartime Continental Congress) was elected bishop in Pennsylvania. After the inclusion of lay checks on clergy, and of patriot clergy on loyalist ones, the old political resentments simply faded away.[24]

The wounds that the Revolution inflicted upon Trinity parish had healed by the 1790s, since the parish's patriots genially embraced their former political opponents. The 1784 shakeup that deposed the Tory vestry and rector Benjamin Moore was temporary and had few lasting effects on the church's governance. Evidence suggests that the men who joined the vestry in 1784 did so from expediency to preserve the church's property and image, and willingly stepped down when Trinity no longer faced danger. Vestry members who took office in 1784 served, on average, only four years—this was less than half of the eight years of service of the men they replaced. Further, those four years represented less than one-third of the twelve-and-a-half years of average service of the vestry-men who were elected after 1785. Men of unquestionable patriot pedigree such as Richard Morris, Francis Lewis, Lewis Morris, Isaac Sears, and Joshua Sands entered the vestry, served a few years, then stepped down. Their formerly loyalist neighbors and associates then returned to lead the church.[25] More important than political affiliation, Trinity offered continuity in the social composition of its leadership; in retaining its elite members, Trinity Church implied that hierarchy, privilege, and wealth would provide stability for the parish, in good times and bad.

The Whigs who shook up Trinity's leadership were reluctant revo-lutionaries, displaying a moderate and cautious stance in politics. The leader of the group that ousted the wartime vestry, James Duane, had been a careful conservative prior to the war. Duane acted as a liaison for, and sympathetic ally of, arch-loyalist Joseph Galloway. But unlike Gal-loway, Duane accepted the Declaration of Independence, figuring that "[i]t was more sensible to . . . become a careful neutral and look forward to the 'rich Encrease of our Estates,' which would assuredly follow in the wake of free trade with the world."[26] He was joined by men such as John Alsop, who had asserted a modest loyalism by resigning his position in the Provincial Congress after the passage of the Declaration of Indepen-dence. Alsop clearly adapted to his situation, marrying his daughter to Rufus King, a Massachusetts patriot and signer of the Constitution, who after marriage relocated to New York.[27]

Interested in the security of property rights, during the 1780s and 1790s Duane and his political allies welcomed loyalists back into the city, deeming their economic contributions to the city's prosperity more important than any past political irregularity.[28] This welcome extended to the ousted vestry of 1784. Miles Sherbrooke returned from abroad by 1787 to reestablish his merchant business on Little Dock Street. Simi-larly deposed, William Laight remained in the city, and worked as a merchant on Queen Street. He returned to the vestry in 1788, and served until 1802. His shop stood but a few houses down from the residence of William Bedlow, a Whig who had replaced him. Robert C. Livingston's Tory sympathies compelled him to remain in London for much of the war, although he occasionally visited British-occupied New York. He returned to the city at war's end, and in 1785, Livingston began a ten-year term of service as vestryman.[29]

Elites controlled Trinity Church and its property after the Revolution, as well as before. The new rector, Samuel Provoost, had been a patriot, alone among Episcopal clergymen in the northern colonies. As such, the patriot vestry knew he had the proper credentials to take Trinity's helm in 1784: political convictions that would silence radical opposition. But Provoost's credentials were more than intellectual, and appealed to the vestry for other reasons: he was related by marriage to the Livingstons, the wealthiest of the great landed families of the Hudson River Valley. This connection made him kin with John Jay, James Duane, and William Duer, the men who presided over the 1784 transfer of power to patriot interests in the church. The political shift from loyalist leaders in the 1770s to Whigs in the 1780s did not change the fact that a wealthy elite managed the church, and represented its public face.[30]

While the Episcopalians stressed their patriot bona fides and downplayed the church's earlier emphasis on hierarchy, the Methodists simply asserted that they were no longer Anglican. In 1784, at the "Christmas Conference," Methodist leaders voted for an official break with the Church of England. Methodists became a separate church, with their own self-sustaining ministry and administration of the sacraments. In 1789, the denomination sent greetings of congratulation to new President George Washington before any other denomination did so.[31] Methodism was no longer an English transplant, but an American original. Methodists' end goal remained the same, to preach the gospel message to all.

Trinity Church's vestry acted as if the holistic organic vision would revive despite disestablishment. Trinity cooperated with other religious bodies in the city but expected to lead them. As the city's most prominent church, Trinity's vestry felt a duty to aid their lesser brothers, just as they had supported the building of the Methodist church. But they modified the organic vision—no longer would all churches eventually join the Church of England, but rather the church might be a first among equals and lead by example. Anglican wealth helped its position.[32]

Trinity judiciously parceled out portions of its extensive lands to influence others. When British officers confiscated Garrit Lydekker's Dutch Reformed Church for a hospital, Trinity's vestry allowed Lydekker's group to use St. George's Chapel for worship. More striking were overtures of friendship to New York City's Presbyterians, who had been the Anglican Church establishment's most vocal critics. Trinity's vestry granted Brick Presbyterian Church the use of its chapels from 1783 to 1784, during a building restoration. Trinity further granted plots to Presbyterian congregations to build parsonages for the church's ministers. After the Revolution, Trinity vestry implicitly supported the state's legalization of the Roman Catholic Church, by leasing, then selling, Barclay Street land to trustees of St. Peter's Catholic Church.[33]

Painting the Churches White: Marginalizing Black Presence after the Revolution

The association of blacks with Anglicanism and Methodism hurt the churches' public images in post-Revolutionary America. Neither group, however, removed blacks from their communities. Trinity's ministers continued to marry and baptize black members, and restarted the African Free School in 1787 after a four-year hiatus. Methodists allowed blacks to speak at some meetings and organized class meetings where blacks could worship. Even so, both Methodists and Episcopalians more nearly entered the mainstream of American attitudes toward race by marginalizing their black members.[34]

In dealing with slavery and race, white Episcopalians expressed a condescending benevolence that promised gradual reform. This remained consistent with the humanitarianism the SPG had preached in catechizing blacks the previous century. In 1785, Trinity vestrymen James Duane, John Jay, Robert Troup, and Matthew Clarkson joined with Episcopalian Alexander Hamilton and other leading New Yorkers (including their political rival George Clinton) in founding the New York Manumission Society (NYMS), an institution dedicated to promoting gradual and voluntary manumission among the city's slaveholders. Trinity's Anglicans comprised a majority of its non-Quaker founders. Historians have noted the strong Quaker presence in the formation of the NYMS. However, the Anglican presence comprised a significant minority. Indeed, in its first years the society appears to be a nearly exclusive Anglican and Quaker undertaking, an alliance of the old order's elite politicians and churchmen with a prophetic, energetic, yet commercially connected majority.[35]

The New York Manumission Society attempted to undermine the worst effects of slavery in New York. It supported bans on out-of-state slave sales in an attempt to choke off the ready market for slaves and push owners toward manumission. NYMS lawyers legally represented free blacks accused as runaways, and filed suits for slaves who had been promised freedom that unscrupulous masters had later repudiated. The society also pushed the state to free slaves of loyalist masters, whom the state had seized and expected to sell.[36] As the institution's title suggested, members advocated for the direct end of slavery, albeit in a gradual and voluntary way. Shortly after the New York Manumission Society formed, the state legislature considered, but defeated, a law to implement gradual manumission. Over the next fifteen years, NYMS leadership would support efforts to push gradual manumission through the legislature, culminating in the successful law passed in 1799.[37]

Issues of black citizenship were embedded in questions of abolition. To make manumission more palatable to whites, NYMS members also attempted to exhort, and aid, the black community toward moral improvement. In 1787, the NYMS established a school for free blacks. Board members limited pupils to families who were "regular and orderly in their deportment." In limiting black "vice," white prejudice might decrease.[38] Thus, as patrons and teachers of blacks, society members placed themselves at the top of a social pyramid, in which grateful blacks at the bottom might reciprocate with hard work and clean living.

Joining the New York Manumission Society satisfied multiple parts of conservative Anglican elites' identities. The attack on slavery mirrored the Revolutionary rhetoric that asserted that all men are created equal, and that none should be held as slaves. Educating and exhorting blacks in efforts to humanize or civilize them placed members in line with the eighteenth-century Anglican mission to touch all members of the empire. Yet NYMS members did so in a way that respected the social order, including the right to property. The NYMS thus affirmed the Anglican conception of an organic society, in which everyone had a place, but tradition and hierarchy made it clear that even in liberty, not all places were equal.[39]

Less publicly minded Anglicans did resume the connections to blacks that had made the church suspect in the eyes of many colonists during British occupation. Trinity's ministers resumed the catechization of its black members on Sunday afternoons in the 1780s, an act they continued through the 1790s. A gap exists in the records between the colonial missions and the formation of the black-run parish of St. Philip's. Nonetheless, church historians surmise that the colonial-era efforts to catechize blacks led to the formation of the black-run parish of St. Philip's established in 1819.[40]

Early Methodist opposition to slavery did not completely disappear, but the church toned down its early insistence on the unity of all believers in Christ. By the 1780s, racial divisions began to show. Black Methodists approached white ministers with petitions to worship separately, but the white leadership repeatedly denied these efforts. At a 1780 conference, white Methodists resolved that church leaders should meet regularly with blacks, or appoint "proper white persons" in their stead, so that blacks not "stay late and meet alone."[41]

While denying blacks their own space and time for worship, white Methodists nonetheless marginalized blacks within the main body of Methodism. They did so primarily through the organization of the class meeting. Methodist classes were intense prayer meetings in which individual believers could work spiritual disciplines toward greater piety, removing individual tendencies toward sin from their lives. New York Methodist class records that survive from the 1780s reveal that while whites refused blacks the ability to lead themselves religiously, white Methodists nonetheless did not fully accept blacks into the main body of Methodists for worship.

Before the Revolution, no class records for John Street survive; missionary reports suggest that blacks and whites stayed in close contact. After the Revolution, black members were increasingly recorded and regulated in separate classes. In 1785, an unnumbered list of seventeen "Negroes" followed the class lists enumerating all white Methodists in New York, an afterthought to the main body of Methodists. In 1786, the Methodist society records formally placed blacks in their own class of twenty-five, with an addendum to the class lists adding nine more names. In 1787, Methodist leaders standardized their organization of black members, placing them in three clearly defined classes.[42] Without allowing blacks full self-governance, whites nonetheless shielded blacks from full Methodist fellowship, treating them as second-class citizens in separate classes. These actions made Methodists appear less unusual regarding racial issues, however.

Methodist cultural memories also stressed their patriotic impulses. While most blacks in New York had chosen loyalty to Britain during the war, the most famous Revolutionary-era black Methodist in New York was a patriot. Peter Williams was born a slave in New York City to African-born parents. He converted to Methodism at John Street Chapel in the 1760s, along with his wife, Mary (or Molly). Williams's master taught him the tobacconist trade. Although his master was a loyalist, Williams reportedly cherished the ideal of liberty that the patriot cause championed, as one oral history later recounted. While in New Jersey during the war, Williams helped a Methodist patriot minister hide from British authorities. The commanding officer pointed his sword at Williams, threatening to kill the slave if he did not reveal the preacher's position. Williams refused. The officer changed his tack, then offering Williams a purse of money, also rejected. The story, repeated in Methodist circles, had the dual aim of promoting a Methodist minister who was not a Tory or English subject, and championing a black Methodist who similarly refused to join the British.[43]

Figure 2.2. Old John Street Chapel. This image, often reproduced in different forms and styles in Methodist histories, displays the sexton Peter Williams, patriot, in the doorway. (Reproduced with permission from the Methodist Collections at Drew University.)

Williams's fleeing Tory owner sold his slave to John Street Chapel. Despite the general Methodist opposition to slavery, Methodist trustees bought Peter and put him to work as a sexton and gravedigger. The chapel apparently allowed Williams to purchase his freedom with his labor, combining a bartered watch and time served to gain his manumission papers in 1796. Thus in the 1780s, as Methodists attempted to integrate into American society, the New York chapel employed a black man in a position most New Yorkers would have recognized: as a slave. Williams's story entered the lore of New York history generally, and his image often appears in famous historic prints of John Street Chapel, suitably absent the context of widespread black loyalism during the war, or of his own status as a slave for more than a decade.[44]

Not only did New York Methodists downplay their unusual status on race, but they also minimized the presence of loyalism in the church. Another Methodist oral history surviving from the Revolutionary era (again, via Peter Williams) condemned the irreverence and immorality of British soldiers in New York. Williams recounted two instances of British soldiers' irreligion. In one tale, British soldiers dug a pit outside John Street Chapel for churchgoers to fall into when leaving religious services. In another striking passage, a British officer wore a devil's out-fit to frighten Methodist chapel attendees on Christmas Eve. Both cases ended with virtue rewarded and vice punished, but such stories served a larger role to emphasize Methodist patriotism. The tales obscured the facts that the Methodist church remained open in occupied New York when most other churches were forcibly shut, and that British soldiers attended Methodist meetings.[45]

While Peter Williams's stories were useful to white Methodists, they highlighted a problem for blacks who remained. Most black New York-ers had not shared Williams's support for the patriot cause. Instead, they cautiously, and sometimes incautiously, supported British efforts to gain freedom and to benefit themselves. When British troops left, thousands of blacks left with them. Until then, such actions of revolt had been a regular possibility for blacks in the colonial era. In 1712 and 1741, and from 1776 to 1783, unhappy slaves could forge alliances with poor whites, Anglicans or Methodists, or British or Spanish states to over-turn their bondage when their conditions grew too oppressive. But in the new Republic, blacks were under a clearly defined majoritarian regime, one that in fact (and eventually in most states, in law) recognized white superiority.[46]

New York blacks in the early Republic therefore traded revolution for hopes of reform. After 1788, blacks who remained in New York (and in all northern states) gambled that slavery was increasingly in decline, and that such decline would create the possibility of greater rights. They hoped that the language of liberty that patriots invoked in the Revolutionary struggle would truly include a universal promise that would accrue to them. Blacks first pushed for greater reform in the one arena open to them: the church, especially the Anglican and Methodist churches that previously accepted black participants. For churchgoing blacks, this also meant accepting white local church leadership, whether or not such lead-ers recognized black rights. Eventually, many blacks would form their own, separate, church, representing a possibility of a new revolutionary act. But in the Revolution's immediate aftermath, black religion would appear less confrontational or dangerous than before.[47]

Anglican and Methodist church leaders probably assumed that their congregations could continue as they had before the Revolution. Trinity

Church continued to house society's most important members, who would dispense the gospel and gradual humanitarian reform as they saw fit.[48] Cooperation in poor relief and among missionary efforts would be more informal and unofficial than before. The Methodists faced greater possibilities for change, as they now existed institutionally separate from their Anglican mother, but clung to their goals of reaching lost souls with the gospel, and encouraging saved souls to progress toward moral perfection.

New York City's Methodists and Anglicans could not foresee the greater changes that were in store with the dramatic growth of the city. These changes would strain the conceptions of Episcopalian social prominence and Methodist mission, and ultimately would cause deep fissures between white and black coreligionists. Such problems were not immediately apparent, for after the Revolution most churchmen were simply happy that they had averted complete disaster, that Trinity had not been divested of its property, and that the churches could continue with their missions.

3 / Creating Merchant Churches: The 1790s

During the 1790s, America's economic recession lifted, as the new federal government offered a secure platform from which commerce boomed. When war between Britain and France revived in 1793, the neutral United States benefited by assuming the carrying trade around the globe. With its fine harbor and expansive hinterland, New York capitalized on the opportunity. Between 1790 and 1800, the city's population doubled, growing from thirty thousand to sixty thousand inhabitants.[1]

By 1790, both Methodist and Episcopal churches could celebrate tangible signs of postwar recovery. In 1790, Rector Samuel Provoost consecrated a new Trinity Church, rising from the ashes of the old site to proclaim a new grandeur. Following Trinity's example, Episcopalians erected new churches throughout the state, and the denomination's numbers grew. The American Episcopal Church's prestige renewed with the election of Samuel Provoost as bishop of New York, emphasizing that hierarchy still had a place, even if it no longer emanated from the Crown of England.[2]

The Methodists also prospered. By 1784, the Methodist Episcopal Church was no longer an ambiguous branch of the Anglican Communion but a denomination in its own right. Shortly after the war, Methodist records first referred to John Street as a "church" instead of a "meeting house," suggesting a greater stability and permanency. In the expanding city, New York's Methodists added to their numbers. In 1789, they built a second chapel on Second Street (now Forsyth), near Division—also known as the Bowery church—to accommodate their growing membership. The Bowery church was the site of several revivals, in which new members joined in great numbers. By the end of the 1790s, New York's Methodists had built two more chapels.[3]

The city's growth posed new challenges to the churches. The Episcopal Church confronted an increasingly complex and divided community, one that defied the inclusive yet homogeneous vision that Anglicans had championed before the Revolution. The massive influx in immigrants strained conceptions of an organic society. The decline of deference by common people to their betters also challenged political elitism. After the Revolution, Anglicans ceased to automatically dominate political office. Church officials could not expect society's wealthiest and most prominent members, who sat in the front pews, to govern the city.

For the Methodists, the challenges of growth led to greater internal divisions within the church. Now several hundred members, and growing, Methodists were no longer the close-knit body of believers of the 1760s. The familial, communal nature of late-colonial Methodism necessarily strained as the church incorporated large numbers of rich and poor. During revivals, the poorer wards to the north generated more new members. Methodist leaders built a new chapel to accommodate them in 1789; these new converts thus had decreasing contact with the older, wealthier members downtown. In the 1790s, social stratification began to appear among the Methodists.

Episcopalians and Methodists also dealt with the challenges of being multiracial communities in a society that increasingly feared such as threats to the social order. Free blacks occupied an undefined space in a republican society, and often faced white hostility. Before the 1790s, both churches accepted blacks but relegated them to marginal positions. As the number of free blacks increased, the presence of blacks in both churches grew less welcome. In the first years of prosperity following independence, both groups encouraged racial separation in worship. Leaders in both groups, however, contended that blacks remained under their institutional oversight, a separate but unequal body of believers.

Black worshipers made steps to assert themselves in their respective congregations. Tensions over race at Trinity seemed less pressing in the decade, as many loyalist blacks had left the city. Black Anglicans who remained affirmed their denominational identity, accepting messages of obedience and promises of future liberation. They did so under the title of the African Society, which offered hints of a larger heritage and resistance, but as yet had little public presence, and firmly identified with white benefactors. Among Methodists, a group of skilled black males sought independent worship, taking steps to be not just Methodists, but African Methodists. Even so, these black Methodists remained connected to white church leaders. Further, black churchmen remained silent in the public sphere, whether due to the widespread presence of slavery in New York, or the lack of significant literate leadership to initiate debate. In 1790s New York, blacks were not able to disrupt the white churches' self-images as reflecting the religious norm.

In facing these social and racial challenges, both Trinity and John Street fashioned themselves as merchant congregations. They exemplified a preference for hierarchy, and organic connection, among their members. All had a place in the church—laborer or professional, black or white—but elites offered both bodies most of their stability and leadership. As such, the congregations exemplified connections to Federalism prominent in the era, albeit less in a political way than in a cultural and social preference. Therefore, in this decade the city's growth challenged, but did not disrupt, church leadership.

Federalists at Prayer: Trinity's Social Hierarchy

The wounds that the Revolution inflicted upon Trinity parish healed by the 1790s, as the parish's patriots genially embraced their former opponents. The radical bent of the city council demanded that in 1784, the parish's Whigs depose the Tory vestry and its hand-picked rector, Benjamin Moore. But the victors did not lord their triumph over the vanquished. This shakeup was temporary, and had few lasting effects on the church's governance. Shortly after this action, loyalists trickled back into positions of church leadership.[4] More important, the church retained its wealthy members, and its insistence that hierarchy, privilege, and wealth should persist.

Most of Trinity's Whigs became Federalists. During the later 1780s and 1790s, Federalists dominated political events. Having successfully framed and ratified the Constitution, Federalist officeholders occupied the majority position in state and federal legislatures. Federalism promoted hierarchy, the rule of society's betters, and a conception of an organic society. Culturally Anglophile, Federalists advocated improved relations with Britain, and welcomed back former loyalists; indeed, loyalists often joined conservative Whigs as party leaders.[5]

Although New York's Revolutionary state constitution abolished the Anglican religious establishment, Federalists strengthened the symbolic ties between church and state, between divine rule and temporal order.

Figure 3.1. Federalist-era Trinity Church at the end of Wall Street, with Federal Hall on the right displaying the connections between social, political, and religious prominence. (Collection of The New-York Historical Society.)

During the two years the federal government remained in New York City, Federalists emphasized the mutual ties of Episcopalianism and republican government. Trinity rector and bishop of New York Samuel Provoost served as chaplain to the United States Senate. Trinity's chapel, St. Paul's, became the destination of several governmental processions. Trinity's vestry affixed a presidential seal over the pew where George Washington sat at St. Paul's Chapel, and a seal of New York State on the pew reserved for the governor, at the opposite side from Washington.[6]

The Federalist emphasis on the benefits of hierarchy and order energized opponents suspicious of monarchy. Pennsylvania senator William Maclay sharply criticized any monarchical trappings. His censorious diary reveals a deep suspicion of pro-Anglican politicians who linked Episcopacy and government. He scorned the Episcopal "churchmen" who moved that Congress accompany the newly sworn-in President Washington to "attend divine service" at St. Paul's Chapel. Maclay failed

Figure 3.2. Samuel Provoost, patriot rector of Trinity
Church, first bishop of New York. (From Morgan Dix,
History of Trinity Church, vol. 2 [1901].)

to block the measure. Two weeks later, Washington addressed Congress,
and then led another procession to St. Paul's, where Provoost prayed.[7]

During the 1790s, Trinity's parishioners bolstered this Anglican vision,
which united the larger society behind a moderate and genial Christianity.
Samuel Provoost offered a rational and orthodox theology that persuaded
few but likewise offended few. He exemplified familial ties and kinship
alliances at the top. As Senate chaplain, and as minister of and relative to
leading government officials, he embodied a tangible connection between
church and government. Filled with pews arranged according to prominence and wealth, the church's building illustrated this organic vision of
all society united in a coherent whole, with the wealthiest at the front.

From Trinity's 1790 pew rent lists and New York City directories, I developed an occupational sketch of Trinity Church's members. Both sources display upward bias. City directories tended to record established individuals with their own businesses and residences.[8] Unskilled and poorer laborers would be more transient or more likely to board or share rooms, decreasing the possibility of their being listed in any given year. Likewise, pew lists record the congregation's wealthier members. Although every church provided a few pews without charge for those who could not afford a minimal rent, such individuals did not appear in the lists. Even given these caveats, Trinity parish's 1790s pew lists clearly portray a largely upper-class church. But because many occupations included both wealthier and poorer individuals, and because even poorer occupations appeared in the pews, an individual might scan the church building each Sunday morning and assume that Trinity represented New York as a whole.[9]

Politicians and professionals constituted a significant percentage of pewholders. Between 16 and 18 percent of Trinity's pewholders were in the professional and government category, a figure that more than doubled the 7 percent city average. At the beginning of the decade, John Jay served as the first Supreme Court justice of the United States, and by mid-decade he was elected governor of New York. At $17.50 annually, he paid the second-highest rent at Trinity Church, suggesting a prominent location. Jay's brother-in-law Robert R. Livingston, who served as chancellor of the state, also paid $17.50. Both men's pews probably overlooked the congregation from prominent spots in the gallery. Within this occupational category, the individual with the lowest pew rent, William Strong, appeared in the directory as an inspector; his rent of five dollars nevertheless placed him above the bottom decile of pewholders.[10]

Retailers and merchants comprised fully half of Trinity's pew renters. Between 46 and 54 percent were merchants, grocers, or other retailers, a number double the city average of 26 percent. Merchants such as Charles Ludlow and Edmund Seaman rented the most expensive pews prominently located in the front of the church. Not all merchants were as well-off as the Ludlows and Seamans, however, for many sat in pews priced in the middle ranges, around ten dollars annually. Grocers operated on narrow margins, and many grocery ventures were small-scale sales of produce grown just outside the city limits. A handful of small grocers and a merchant occupied the cheapest pews alongside poorer artisans, huddled in the backs of aisles or in corners of the gallery.[11]

The diverse and numerous artisan category included everyone from impecunious cordwainers and shoemakers to prosperous shipbuilders and silversmiths. They comprised from 19 to 22 percent of Trinity's pew-holders, half that of the 40 percent appearing in the directory, and about one-third the number of artisans historians believe resided in the city.[12] Trinity's artisans included many in lucrative and prestigious trades. Philip Hone and Robert Carter were both cabinetmakers, whose skills were "the most refined of the mechanic branches." If their rents are the only indication of wealth, however, the two had differing rates of success: Hone's pew rent of $14.75 placed him in the top quintile of rent prices, whereas Carter's $5.00 pew ranked just above the poorest rents. Hugh Gaine appears in the artisan category as a "printer-bookseller-stationer," and his pew rent of $15.00 reveals that he had made the transition from small-scale manufacturer to overseer of a larger shop and retailer. In general, however, artisans occupied the lower rent levels, including a tailor, cooper, and shoemaker each in the bottom decile.[13]

The lower occupational levels were especially underrepresented in Trinity's pews: from 9 to 13 percent of Trinity's pewholders filled the combined service-transport-marine category, also only half the city averages. Shipmaster Richard Black and branch pilot Matthew Daniel held positions of greater prestige than the typical mariner, and William Robinson, Edward Bardin, and John Battin as tavern keepers held greater sway than other service workers. All five, however, rented pews below the median rate of $10.00. Not surprisingly, the fewest pewholders in number were those identified as unskilled, the "laborer" category, making up no more than 4 percent of Trinity's pewholders. The number of unskilled workers attending must have been higher, for those too poor to pay for pews do not appear in the lists. Further, twenty-eight males on the pew lists do not appear in the directories at all, many of whom were probably unskilled workers.[14]

In the 1790s, Trinity church held a level of public prestige unmatched by other churches, for it participated in public displays associated with the new government in which other churches could not. Trinity's parishioners also tended to be in wealthier and more prestigious occupations than even upwardly weighted city averages. Individuals from all occupational categories rented pews at Trinity, however, and as John Jay took his seat above the sanctuary, or as Charles Ludlow walked to the front of the church, they surveyed poorer individuals who worshiped with them. More important, the poorer and middling individuals who attended Trinity saw the most prominent men at their head, or above them. On any given Sunday, Trinity remained white and affluent, but it still approximated the traditional image of an organic, inclusive church.

Anglican politicians also continued their attempt to properly educate blacks and move the state toward voluntary, gradual manumission. John Jay ascended to governor in 1795, and presided over a legislature that passed the gradual manumission law of 1799. Jay and his fellow Episcopalians in the New York Manumission Society had achieved one of the major goals that they had held at that institution's founding in 1785. The law offered nothing for existing slaves, promising freedom only to slaves born after July 4 of that year, and then only at age twenty-eight for men and twenty-five for women. Young slave men and women thus spent many of their most productive years paying for the ostensible costs of their childhood. Of the states north of the Chesapeake, only New Jersey was slower to pass a gradual manumission law.[15]

That a law was passed at all is testament, however, to the determination of NYMS members. In a burgeoning economy, successful shopkeepers became merchants, small merchants became large merchants, the numbers of professionals increased, and successful individuals at all levels bought slaves when they could afford them. In the 1790s, the percentage of men holding slaves rose from one-quarter to one-third of the population. It took a long, determined effort to convince a majority of New Yorkers that slavery should end.[16]

The New York Manumission Society's bylaws did not demand immediate manumission from its participants, and actually placed guidelines on its members more lenient than the 1799 law. Trinity's parishioners, who were also the most prominent politicians within the society, men such as John Jay, James Duane, Alexander Hamilton, and Rufus King, all held slaves. Historians have debated the significance of this connection. An older generation of scholars, now reinforced by new scholarship, has highlighted the real abolitionist intentions of the NYMS. David Gellman characteristically argued that "pragmatic incrementalism and moral idealism" marked the society's efforts, and that, no matter the compromises, society members always pushed the status quo toward, rather than away from, abolitionism. On the other side, scholars studying the black community have noted the heavy-handed paternalism of NYMS members, and critiqued the fact that those members widely held slaves even as a statewide manumission law passed. Shane White noted that the percentage of known slaveholders in the NYMS was significantly higher—perhaps double—than in the city as a whole, and further that slaveholding members owned nearly 50 percent more slaves than the average city slaveholder.[17]

Whereas Gellman finds idealism, and White hypocrisy, Trinity's Anglican abolitionists occupied a place where slavery was simply secondary to their larger concerns. Alexander Hamilton, for example, was consumed by ambition and a desire to remain within the social elite. Despite antislavery convictions on national or international issues, Hamilton kept his slaves because New York's elites kept slaves, as ultimate status symbols. John Jay, a more devout Episcopalian and more ardent abolitionist than Hamilton, nonetheless kept his slaves until he judged they had worked off their purchase cost. Further, Jay was not above selling recalcitrant slaves. And when earlier attempts at manumission failed to pass the legislature, Jay told friends that he was content to do his duty as best he could; the issue simply was not his greatest concern as a politician.[18]

Trinity's abolitionists opposed slavery as a part of a larger socioeconomic outlook. In supporting gradual manumission, they affirmed property rights and legal procedures, and further placed themselves at the head of organizations that stressed benevolence toward society's lower orders, including blacks. One cannot separate their opposition to slavery from what we might deem a cultural Federalism, which recognized hierarchy and property along with an organic interconnectedness of society's members.

Merchants and Methodists: John Street's Attempt at Social Unity

During the 1780s, Methodist leaders quickly distanced themselves from the stigma of loyalism that plagued the Episcopalians. Their English-born preachers had largely fled, and the church now revived under locally produced lay ministers.[19] New challenges lay ahead. Methodist leaders sought to bring others to Christ, and to make their own people holy in the process. Urban life challenged this ideal. As the first bishop of the Methodist Episcopal Church in America, Francis Asbury witnessed these problems firsthand and recorded them in his journal. He expressed ambivalence regarding urban growth, welcoming its opportunities, yet fearing its effects.

Although Methodist leaders avoided taking sides in political issues, many of their laity could not resist the temptation. During the Revolution, Asbury lamented that some Methodists "had dipped deep in politics."[20] After hostilities ended, electoral strife seduced many Methodists. In 1792, Asbury fretted, "This city has been agitated about the choice of Governor: it would be better for them all to be on the Lord's side."[21] In

1795, Asbury viewed Independence Day celebrations in New York with regret. Bells ringing, drums beating, and rifles firing: all proclaimed the nation's love of liberty, but Asbury lamented that, although the preachers shared a communal spirit, the city's Methodists "are far from being as spiritual as we ought to be."[22]

While politics led to obvious snares, more subtle and dangerous were the lures of moneymaking and wealth. After the Revolution, Asbury worried that, as peace brought prosperity, "our preachers will be far more likely to settle in the world; and our people, by getting into trade, and acquiring wealth, may drink into its spirit."[23] Suspicious of wealth, Asbury preferred that the poor fill his churches. During a 1787 visit to a Long Island church, just outside the city but miles away socially, he noted bluntly that "[t]he people on this island, who hear the gospel, are generally poor, and these are the kind I want, and expect to get."[24]

Late-eighteenth-century cities were notoriously unhealthy. New York's crowded, dirty conditions sorely aggravated Asbury's health. Seasonal epidemics made matters worse, with "fluxes, fevers, and influenzas" marking his congregational visits to all the eastern seaboard cities.[25] During those trips, Asbury regularly complained of sickness. In the late summer of 1791, he observed:

> The weather is extremely warm and dry: people are sickly and
> dying, especially children; I find my body very weak: preaching
> at night, added to the moschetoes [sic], causes me to sleep very
> little. . . . We rode to New-York; a very warm day. I found myself
> much injured, but was well nursed at the north side of the city. They
> have a touch of fever here in George-Street. Sabbath, Oct. 1 We had
> much rain. Live or die, I preached at the old and new church. . . . I
> had some disagreeable things and was but ill-fitted in body to bear
> them.[26]

Asbury rode thousands of miles on horseback, but despite these physical exertions, his worst health complaints came in tight urban quarters.

For circuit-riding Methodist ministers, the crowded city also meant much work in a short time, with an intensity unmatched in rural locations. On July 5, 1795, for example, Asbury preached in Brooklyn in the morning. He then crossed the river to administer the Lord's Supper at the Bowery church and met with the black classes. In the evening, Asbury preached at John Street and afterward met with two men's classes. The next day, Asbury met with nine more classes, "so that I have now spoken to most of the members here, one by one."[27]

For Asbury and other Methodist ministers, ungodliness flourished in the city. New York was an especially worldly place of bustle and business. Great wealth and noisy poverty crowded out thoughts of God. Urban anonymity allowed sins to pass unnoticed, far more than in the socially confining small towns and villages of rural America. On one trip into New York, Asbury feared during the ferry crossing that the boarding party had uttered so many curses that God would sink the boat! He then asked another passenger for a piece of chalk, that he might keep track of the number of curses for the duration of the trip. At John Street, after preaching on self-denial, Asbury noted, with great exasperation, "a more gay and indevout congregation I have seldom seen; they were talking, laughing, bowing, and trifling both with God and their minister, as well as their own unawakened souls." After preaching to another unresponsive congregation in 1804, Asbury concluded, "[New] York, in all the congregations, is the valley of dry bones. Oh Lord, I will lament the deplorable state of religion in all our towns and cities!"[28]

Despite these lamentations, Asbury valued the stability that prominent members gave to the city's Methodist congregations. Although Asbury railed against the wealthy in the abstract, his personal friendship with long-standing members anchored him during trying visits to the city. Asbury regularly lodged with such "Old Friends," strong in the faith, who provided him a deep sense of calm. In 1796, he noted simply "I lodged with Elijah Crawford: this house is for God."[29]

To foster holiness, Methodists scorned ostentatious living and public displays of wealth and social status. This stance attracted many poor people into their churches. Methodists welcomed women, blacks, and the poor, groups that republican politics explicitly excluded from the public sphere. As historian Dee Andrews noted in her pathbreaking study of American Methodism, the Methodist societies were socially and racially heterogeneous. They included the poorest and the richest: unskilled laborers and hardscrabble journeymen on one hand, and great planters and emerging capitalists on the other.[30] But in the bustle of city life, merchants and entrepreneurial "new artisans" remained when laborers came and went, and they funded the struggling churches in ways that the poor could not.

Divisions over occupation or wealth within Methodism therefore imbedded in the movement from its start; they did not merely represent a later declension, but rather the realities of a movement that appealed to groups across the social spectrum.[31] A study of churches on the congregational level reveals this clearly. When John Street Chapel was the only

Methodist building in New York City, believers could hail the spiritual unity of its members. As John Street Church in the 1790s, the building represented a congregation, one of two (and by 1800, four) Methodist bodies. Occupational and wealth divisions very quickly strained the unity of early Methodism and highlighted the difficulties of preserving a heterogeneous movement.[32] But at the congregational level, the wealthiest members, merchant-professionals, attended John Street alongside workingmen. Such elites befriended ministers and could view the church as a unity of believers. While Methodists in New York did not typically share outright their Episcopalian brothers' tendency toward political Federalism, John Street's Methodists specifically embraced an organic unity in Christ that functioned very similarly on a social and cultural level.

New York City's 1796 Methodist classes reveal a church largely drawn from laboring occupations. One-third of all white males in the lists did not appear in the city directories, which suggests that their position was too poor or transient to enter the record. In the occupation categories of government, professional, retail, service, and marine workers, the Methodist society members were, compared to city averages, underrepresented in all categories. Within the service sector, cartmen accounted for two-thirds to three-quarters of the category. Cartmen might be considered closer to artisans in spirit than to other service workers, given their group solidarity, and their ability to regulate entry to their occupation through licensure. The largest job category in the Methodist classes, well above city averages, belonged to artisans.[33]

Artisans in the early Republic were hardworking, but not necessarily working-class. Artisans typically placed themselves in a middling category between the parasites at the top of society—ranging from bankers to lawyers to landlords—and the under classes at the bottom, with few skills or prospects. Some Methodist artisans had transcended the daily grind of production to manage and oversee shops. The New York Methodist society's large artisan population thus reveals not a church of the poor, but rather one dominated by a large middling section, many of whom were anxious of their eroding status and increasingly militant in defending it.

During the 1790s, class meetings lay at the center of Methodist spiritual life. Through 1820, New York's Methodist ministers recorded membership by class lists, not congregation. They listed each class one after the other, numbered consecutively, with no mention of what church each group may have attended. Assuming that geographic proximity to a church made attendance more likely, I identified individual white male Methodists as either John Street or Bowery attendees depending upon their places of residence as listed in city directories. If a class had a preponderance of members identified with one church, I associated the entire class with that church. I have labeled two classes as highly likely to belong to John Street, and two as somewhat likely. I have labeled four classes as probable Bowery classes and one as somewhat likely. And finally, two classes remain ambiguous in their allegiance. In both, about half their members do not appear in the city directories.[34]

All five of the Bowery and Bowery-leaning classes contain more artisan members than any other occupational category. In each, artisans proportionately outnumbered both city and New York Methodist society averages. Four of the five classes, ranging from 55 to 90 percent artisan, included more artisans than individuals of any occupation labeled as Bowery by residence. In other words, even artisans who lived closer to John Street tended to join Bowery artisans for worship. For example, in class number eleven, the coppersmith Peter Peterson of George Street was the only one of twelve men who lived closer to John Street Church. Although alone by residence, Peterson was among friends occupationally, as he was one of seven artisans (the class also included two cartmen). In class number twenty, a John Street–area shipwright, baker, and shoemaker joined with nail-makers, carpenters, and coopers (as well as laborers and a grocer) who lived closer to the Bowery church. Bowery classes were, more than any other characteristic, artisan classes.[35]

In comparison, the John Street classes reveal a mixed occupational base. Merchants and retailers appeared in greater numbers than in any Bowery class, but did not numerically dominate any single class. In three of the four classes, retailers comprised roughly the same numbers as artisans, outperforming both the city and Methodist averages for retailers. For example, John Street's class number thirty contained five retailers—four of them grocers—and five artisans out of fifteen members. John Street class number twenty-eight, the only class led by a merchant, contained five retailers and seven artisans, out of a group of seventeen.[36] In that same class, John Wilson may have been a shipmaster, physician, or cartman (the city directory lists all three occupations for that name). In a class that contained no majority of any occupational group, however, Wilson appears more significant than he might in a class comprised of 80 percent artisans, as was the case in the Bowery church.[37]

Close to retail and wholesale shops on Pearl, William, and Broadway Streets, John Street attracted more merchants. The Bowery church drew artisans from nearby marine industries and artisan shops on Cherry and

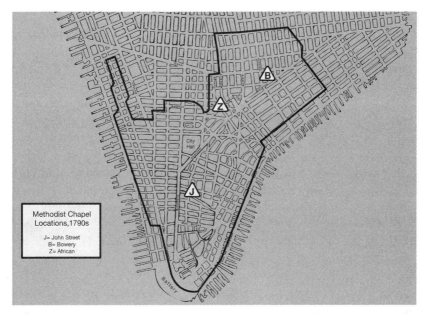

Figure 3.3. Location of Methodist churches in the 1790s, also showing expansion of settlement from colonial era. John Street lies near merchant homes, whereas the Bowery church encompasses laboring districts. The Zion Chapel, here in the rough Five Points neighborhood, would move west in 1800. (Map created by Alanna Beason, derived from map from United States Census Office, 1886.)

Second Streets. But statistically, artisans grouped together in even greater numbers than their places of residence suggested. On the other hand, retailers did not form a single class of their own, but joined with a minority of artisans and other occupational classes. At the Bowery church, occupation trumped other factors, suggesting a common identity based upon work, along the lines of the artisan republicanism described by historian Sean Wilentz.[38] At John Street, in contrast, the classes modeled what Methodist leaders wanted the church to be, by including rich and poor from all walks of life, revealing a unity in the body of Christ.

Most Methodist class leaders were artisans. But these leaders did not embrace a working-class consciousness, for they led meetings at both John Street and Bowery churches. Many leaders were older members of long residence in the city, the "Old Friends" whom Asbury described in his diary. Many were masters, often at odds with their journeymen coreligionists. Others worked in prosperous trades. For example, class leader Philip Arcularius of 11 Frankfort Street worked as a master baker during the Revolution. During the 1790s, city directories list him as a tanner, the occupation of his father-in-law, in which he also held master status. When journeymen shoemakers banded together to raise wages, Arcularius joined with fellow tanners in opposing their demands. Although he led a women's class in 1796, few rank-and-file journeymen, shoemakers especially, would care to be associated with Arcularius, and as such, they probably headed north to attend the Bowery church. Other class leaders worked in the building trades, where an expanding port economy and steady growth northward on Manhattan Island ensured continuous employment for masons, carpenters, and shipwrights. In contrast, shoemakers and tailors found that large-scale manufactories undercut the prices paid for their work, and they struggled to achieve competence, or comfortable subsistence, in the increasingly competitive market.[39]

It is easy to exaggerate the differences between artisans at this time, however, especially among Methodist leaders committed to unity. Although a shoemaker, Peter McLean led a class at John Street, probably alongside master tanner Arcularius. Elias Vanderlip, a shoe- and bootmaker, led classes at the Bowery alongside leaders who were carpenters, masons, and plaster of paris manufacturers. But differing class attendance patterns suggests that many of the Methodist rank-and-file detected a difference and voted with their feet.

John Street's classes contained merchants, artisans, unskilled laborers, cartmen, and tavern keepers, all joined in worship. The inclusion of all occupations suggests an organic social conservatism, in which the society of the class mirrored the city as a whole. John Street members apparently sought security and social stability in their class meetings: the revivals of this decade largely occurred uptown at the Bowery church, not at John Street. This religious conservatism also meant a greater willingness to associate with the new rich and entrepreneurial artisans and merchants who broke with older craft traditions. In contrast, more militant artisans went uptown to church. By bonding together, they highlighted the split emerging between social classes. As at Trinity, the upper-middling individuals who led John Street appear to have clung to the principle of a holistic, organic society.

Silent Struggles: Blacks in New York Churches, and Their Early Steps to Independence

Blacks had long worshiped at Trinity and John Street churches, where leading Episcopalians and Methodists had opposed slavery. This stance contrasted to some degree with most other churches in New York. During the 1790s, as both Trinity and John Street enjoyed increasing prestige and wealth, New York's free black community grew extensively. Most members of both churches did not welcome free blacks as equal members, and continued to associate free blacks with slaves. Consequently, while blacks in these churches did not break from the larger institutions, they carved out separate spaces for worship, where they might enjoy their new status and occupy positions of leadership. While in other northern cities African, Revolutionary, or reform identities may have predated the black church, in New York it appears that black men first acted in the public sphere largely as black churchmen. That is, for them religious, and specifically denominational, identity came first.

The Revolutionary rhetoric that condemned political slavery and championed the natural rights of all individuals did not translate into equality for African Americans. Republican political theory limited political rights to those men who held a significant stake in society. Consequently, neither women nor blacks received the rights of full citizenship, for women remained legally dependent upon fathers or husbands and most blacks remained enslaved or impoverished.[40] Both political parties enforced hierarchy, in differing ways. Federalist politicians often promoted manumission, but remained leery of propertyless laborers and favored keeping property restrictions on the franchise. In contrast, Republicans championed the common citizenship of all white men, but more strictly stressed the boundaries of race and the inferiority of blacks. During the 1790s, the two parties debated whether inequality should follow class or racial lines. New York State's Revolutionary 1777 constitution, one that lasted through the Federalist rule of the 1790s, limited voting rights to free men, black or white, who owned real property worth twenty pounds. In 1821, with Republicans firmly in charge, the state crafted a new constitution that abolished the property restriction for white men but retained it for blacks.[41]

The persistence of slavery in New York City in the 1790s illuminates the limits of political liberty. Expanded notions of political freedom did not translate into an increase in manumissions. New York City's slave population increased 22 percent from 1790 to 1800, and the number of slaveholders increased by 33 percent. The number of yearly city manumissions granted throughout the decade sometimes numbered only in the single digits. Statewide the number of free blacks doubled, to more than ten thousand. The free black population expanded not by manumission, but through in-migration from other states, for statewide the number of slaves decreased by only 2 percent in the decade. New York's slaveholders granted freedom only grudgingly.[42]

This grudging acceptance of a limited freedom for African Americans paralleled limited economic opportunity for New York's blacks. Legal barriers and capital requirements ensured that most African Americans worked in menial, low-paying positions. For both Trinity's and John Street's black males, even those who planted roots in the city remained in far more precarious economic position than nearly every white male at Trinity and most at John Street.

The only communicant information that survives for Trinity before 1845 is a partial list that Bishop Benjamin Moore compiled beginning in 1801. According to this list, Trinity's forty blacks comprised 10 percent of all communicants; black communicants existed in proportions roughly equal to their proportion in the city at large. Only eleven of the forty were men.[43]

Eight of the eleven male names have at least a residence or occupation listed in the city directories, a proportion higher even than those of Trinity's white pewholders. They were well-established residents, rather than transients. Of the eight listed in the directory, three names contain multiple listings, distorting the meager occupational information. Even with this limitation, the occupations spread evenly across categories—one to three individuals were in retail, one or two were artisans, one or two in service, and one was a laborer. In all cases, unskilled laborers and low-level artisans dominate. Four men possessed a certain occupational identity: Isaac Black was a cook, Peter Lee a stevedore, Anthony Maranda a confectioner, and Joseph Brown a sailmaker. John King was probably a carpenter or milkman. William Martin was likely a grocer.[44] Unlike Trinity's whites, who came from society's upper orders, Trinity's blacks' occupations were far less prestigious or lucrative.

Blacks in Methodist classes similarly occupied a marginal yet hard-fought place in the city's economy. Of the forty black males in the 1795 class lists, seventeen (43 percent) went unlisted in the city directories, a figure slightly better than in the poorest or youngest white male classes. Unlike the blacks at Trinity, where no occupational group predominated, nearly two-thirds of John Street's black Methodists were artisans, albeit in marginal trades such as hatter, baker, tobacconist, and shoemaker.[45] The seventeen unlisted individuals were probably unskilled laborers, who joined self-identified laborers George Moore and James Peters. Other individuals attempted to carve out a place in small-scale ventures and semi-skilled occupations, from John Southerland, who probably worked as a tea-waterman (peddler), to John Williams, who likely worked as a stevedore at docks on the East River, near his residence on William Street.[46]

The white churches pushed blacks to increasingly marginal spaces, outside the common worship areas shared in the colonial era. In the colonial period at Trinity, the church placed slaves in the gallery, out of sight of most parishioners and behind the poorest white congregants who rented the cheapest pews. In contrast to colonial-era benevolence, Trinity Church's subsequent records, which date from the second church building in 1790, make no mention of any place for slaves. The church reserved a few pews at the rear of most rows for "strangers" who did not have reserved seats—perhaps slaves took places in these seats if they were available on any given Sunday. Perhaps slaves sat in their owners' pews, especially if they worked as personal attendants to white family members.

In the 1790s, Trinity Corporation granted free blacks seats at Trinity's chapel, St. Paul's, six blocks north of the mother church. St. Paul's reserved seven pews in the gallery for "free blacks," left unnamed in the records, unlike all white pewholders. The annual rent of $2.50 was the lowest price in that chapel. Trinity's vestry built St. Paul's as a "chapel of ease" to deal with church overcrowding and geographic expansion in colonial-era New York, a summer chapel or retreat at New York City's northernmost extremes. During the 1790s, St. Paul's stood in the middle of a city rapidly expanding northward. It lay closer to the city's poorer neighborhoods, the almshouse, the jail, and centers of prostitution than did the main church.[47]

New York's black Methodists similarly occupied marginal positions in the church, recorded not in pews but via the organization of classes.[48] During the mid-1780s, New York Methodists began to specify race in membership records. In 1785, the Methodist secretary simply added the title "Negroes" to the end of the list of church members, an unnumbered addendum to the class lists proper. This black class consisted of seventeen names, only three of them male. Only seven individuals recorded last names; the other ten were probably slaves without family names.

The 1786 Methodist society records formally created a black class of twenty-five, plus nine additions that year. The thirty-four represented a doubling of black Methodist members over the previous year, with nine men and twenty-five women. Those with last names represented fully half the members, seventeen on the list recording family names and seventeen without. Only two of those without last names were male. In 1787, Methodist leaders standardized their organization of black members, placing them in three clearly defined classes. Unlike in the previous two years, Methodist leaders separated men and women into their own classes, with more-numerous women comprising two classes. Also new, white males led all three black classes (a black woman, Jane Barsary, had led the black classes earlier). Carpenter Cornelius Warner took charge of eight men, two of whom had no last names. David Canther led women's class seventeen, in which ten of seventeen listed no family names. Class eighteen, led by a Mr. Courtney, contained only seven women, including the demoted Jane Barsary; four of the seven had only first names.[49]

In the first black classes, then, black men suffered a double indignity. Methodist leaders grouped black men and women together, something typically not done in white classes.[50] Further, Methodists segregated blacks from whites, but grouped free blacks with slaves. Thus they denied free black males the separate identity that free white Methodist men enjoyed. Black male Methodists increased their membership by more than tenfold in a decade, and attempted to carve out their own occupational identity in New York, but remained among the lowest in society.[51]

Black Methodists included many from society's lowest orders—women and slaves. In many cases, the two groups overlapped considerably: from the Revolution's 1783 aftermath to the end of slavery in 1827, New York's slaves tended to be women, as more free black males entered the city and female manumissions lagged behind male. Thus the act of separating black male and female classes led to a de facto separation of slave from free.[52] However, even as black men entered separate classes, in the 1790s white Methodists tended to place all blacks in a category neither male nor female. Record-keeping ministers regularly listed new Methodists in three categories: men, women, and colored.

Given these slights, few black men formally identified as Methodists. During the 1790s, however, increasing numbers of blacks sought separate worship. Segregation allowed whites to keep their main meetings respectable in a society that increasingly found interracial contact suspicious. For black members, however, racial separation allowed the gifted leaders in the group a chance to practice organizational and spiritual skills. More militant members may have conceived of their separation as a victory, although the move also preserved implicit hierarchy and inequality in the church.

During the early 1780s, free blacks in New York organized the African Society. Similar societies appeared in other northeastern cities, paving the way for separate black churches and benevolent societies throughout the North. Through them, blacks established an African American community based on religion. In his work, historian Craig Steven Wilder posits that New York's African Society reflected black male solidarity and communitarian African cultural survivals. Alternatively, the African Methodist Episcopal Zion bishop and church historian William Walls claims that the society's members became leaders in the black Methodist church, a position that authors of a celebratory bicentennial history of Mother Zion also affirm.[53] Historical evidence suggests, however, that New York's African Society was a denominational group that consisted primarily, if not wholly, of Episcopalians and remained subject to Trinity's influence.

Wilder's main evidence for his interpretation of the African Society lay in drawing a parallel between the experiences of New York's and Philadelphia's black populations. The black church in Philadelphia had a clear institutional pedigree and well-defined origins. Its great antecedent lay in the formation of a pan-religious Free African Society in the 1780s, which united blacks across Protestant denominational bounds. This fraternal organization promoted acculturated, skilled black men, yet also offered broader cultural pride in invoking Africa as heritage. The society's members included Richard Allen and Absalom Jones, who took what they had learned into their congregations, an African Methodist and black Episcopalian church, respectively.[54]

Compared to Philadelphia, in New York City slavery remained legal and widespread. While individual African Americans in New York might have held universal aspirations, the reality was that 1790s New York gave blacks few outlets to build them. New York's African Society, despite a similar name to Allen's Philadelphia group, served a vastly different purpose. It was a denominational group, a gathering of black Episcopalians most of whom had been in the city for some time. Although its name clearly cherished Africa as a heritage, the group was African neither in its membership nor in a pan-African/black identity. Members of the African Society affirmed that Trinity patronized their undertakings. In 1795, members of the society approached New York City's Common Council in an attempt to procure a burial ground for the city's blacks.

The petition noted that Trinity Church Corporation had already promised to donate funds to aid them in their purchase of the burial ground.[55]

Trinity occasionally granted funds to non-Anglican groups, but other evidence shows that black Episcopalians led in the creation of the African Society. In a letter to Trinity Church written in 1826, St. Philip's rector, Peter Williams Jr., argued that his parish directly descended from the African Society. Williams described the African Society as "originally composed of about thirty colored Episcopalians." Williams asserted that all five survivors belonged to St. Philip's, and two of them served in the current vestry. Williams also stated that the African Society intended to erect an Episcopal church with the land granted from the 1795 petition.[56] Trinity's baptism and marriage registers lend credence to Peter Williams's assertions.

Most African Society members who signed the 1795 petition affiliated with Trinity parish via baptism and marriage. Of fifteen individuals listed, five married at the parish in the 1780s and 1790s; another two baptized their children there in that time. Another, John Farguson, sponsored a baptism in 1796. Also, African Society trustee William Hutson had namesake William Hutson baptized by brother and sister-in-law James and Flora Hutson in 1799. As many as 60 percent of known African Society members thus affiliated with Trinity Church. These included Isaac Fortune, who presented the petition and was the first name on the trustee list, and William Hutson, who signed the names for, and at the request of, two of his fellow trustees and seven of the additional witnesses. Hutson served as one of the first vestrymen at St. Philip's Episcopal Church at that black institution's founding in 1819. Another signer, Lewis Francis, served as St. Philip's first churchwarden. In his 1826 letter, Peter Williams referred to Hutson and Francis as African Society members who later served in St. Philip's vestry.[57]

The African Society favored acculturation, focusing on moral improvement and religious instruction. In 1784, the society invited Jupiter Hammon, a poet and slave, to address their meeting. Hammon urged slaves to obey their masters, in accordance with God's law—to do otherwise was a sin. He reasoned that whereas the submission of slavery was temporary, dishonesty and faithlessness would result in an eternity of hell. Besides, noted Hammon, as he was more than seventy years old, he did not wish freedom for himself, for at his advanced age he would not know how to care for himself. Hammon concluded with a few words to New York's free blacks, warning them that slavery was preferable to free lives spent in idleness, drunkenness, and thievery.[58]

Some scholars have argued that Hammon was no simple apologist for masters. Although he did not judge slavery a sin, he stated that freedom must be good, given whites' willingness to spend money and lives for their own freedom in the late war. Hammon begged his audience to learn to read, so that they could ponder the Bible on their own. He appealed to free blacks on the basis of their brotherhood with the enslaved, for he explained that free blacks' bad behavior would make it difficult for current slaves to earn their freedom. And Hammon explained that in heaven there would be no judgment based upon race or slave status. He noted subtly that because God chooses "the weak things of this world . . . there are no people that ought to attend to the hope of happiness in another world so much as we do." He implied that the powerful in this world (most whites) ought to fear for their souls.[59] Such moderate critiques, coupled with calls for literacy, paralleled the emphasis on morality of the Anglican missionary movement to the slaves throughout the eighteenth century.

In a 1795 petition to the Common Council, the African Society similarly expressed moral and religious purposes. Petitioners asserted that they had formed the society "for the laudable purposes of improving their morals, by promoting a Spirit of brotherly love, and a strict regard to the Laws of the State, and also with Intent to procure a place for the erection of a Building for divine worship and the Interment of people of Color."[60] The members assured the city government that they wished to promote socially acceptable behavior that would conform to the law. Both immediate and ultimate aims of the society expressed an explicitly religious theme. While the African Society initially sought only to purchase a burial ground, the overall vision called for the building of a religious community that would serve blacks in life as well as death.

The African Society thus realized, in part, the Anglican colonial-era vision for its black members. In the colonial era, Anglican elites had hoped to catechize blacks to ensure an organically connected society, and to make slaves more docile and harder-working. But blacks accepted instruction for their own aims, as evidenced by those in the 1712 revolt who used instruction to gain literacy, and hoped-for magical powers from baptism. By 1795, increasingly acculturated blacks had little connection to Africa, but used the name to identify themselves. Unlike their forebears, they formally aligned with the Episcopal Church, making sure to remain close to Trinity for the latter's patronage and support.

The African Society represented a minority of New York's free blacks. At its greatest extent, the society probably numbered only thirty souls, with little influence outside Anglican circles. The society's emphasis on moral conduct may have kept many blacks away, either because it demanded unwanted behavioral changes or remained silent on political issues. But blacks of other denominational affiliations shared the aim of erecting a black place of worship. In particular, black Methodists desired their own worship space.

While black Methodists ultimately appear more assertive than their Episcopalian cohorts, their first attempts at separation from the white church were partial and tentative. In 1780, white Methodist leaders had rejected black petitions to worship separately without white oversight. In August 1796, blacks again approached Francis Asbury to request the right to hold their own worship meetings. This time Asbury assented, provided that those meetings did not occur at the same time as the white-run services. Because the scheduling allowed for blacks to attend the John Street or Bowery chapels as well as their own meetings, the change did not affect the intent of the 1780 ruling. In October, the group rented a house on Cross Street, between Mulberry and Orange, where they would meet for the next four years.[61]

Later historians of the African Methodist Episcopal Zion Church relied on oral tradition to explain the petition for separate worship. According to their accounts, white discrimination drove the movement for separation. Bishop James Walker Hood's history noted that blacks attended church upstairs in the gallery, and could bring their children down for baptism only after the white children had been baptized. According to Hood, upon hearing the request of parents to christen their child George Washington, the white minister scoffed and baptized the child Caesar instead.[62] Benjamin Wheeler also suggested that Mother Zion developed out of grievances against the white-run church: white officials repeatedly denied preaching licenses to black applicants, and blacks received the Lord's Supper only after all whites had approached the table.[63] While these histories undoubtedly preserved the real experiences of black members, they could not explain why discrimination led to a break at this time, for such discrimination had long existed. Further, they cannot explain why the 1796 movement accepted Asbury's limitation to meet only when whites did not meet, and why blacks accepted continued white supervision.

In his account of the church's origins, AME Zion bishop Christopher Rush laconically stated that "the Colored members of the Methodist Episcopal Church in the City of New York became increased, and [felt] a desire for the privilege of holding meetings of their own, where they might have an opportunity to exercise their spiritual gifts among themselves."[64] Rush was not in New York in 1796, so he did not witness the formational events. Written closer to the founding than any other history, Rush's 1843 account focuses not on the negative effects of racism, which all blacks necessarily felt, but on a select group's positive desire for status. Rush echoed Wheeler's complaint that whites denied spiritually gifted blacks the prestige of leadership. The men who desired to "exercise their spiritual gifts" might be discovered from a look at the church records in the years before the black church's creation.

Most black separatists retained some connections with the white church. Between 1795 and 1796, the black male classes decreased from forty to twenty-nine members, a drop of just over 25 percent. Of the eleven names that Christopher Rush listed as the basis of the future African Methodist Episcopal Zion Church, nine remained in the white-run classes in 1796. One, Abraham Thompson, became one of the first three ordained black Methodist ministers. Thus most blacks did not consider the separation to be an absolute break. Two who left the white-run classes and stayed away—James Varick and William Hamilton—became prominent leaders in the black church, but in their militant separation they stood alone in 1796.[65] Most blacks who eventually joined Mother Zion remained in the white-run classes these first years. This first separation, then, did not create a new church. Rather, it added another layer of religious significance to the black men's lives, a black-run service in addition to class meetings and regular Sunday worship services.

Those who left with Varick and Hamilton were comparatively prosperous, and stressed their status as free men. Such can be discerned by examining the 1796 class lists, which record blacks who continued to attend the white-led groups. The percentage of unlisted members in the city directories increased to 55 percent, a figure up from the 43 percent unlisted rate of the previous year. The percentage of artisans in the black classes also declined in 1796, leaving a group dominated by low-paying service and unskilled occupational categories. Black artisans, like white artisans, felt entitled to self-determination in their church, and they had the legal freedom and funds necessary to set off on their own. Enslaved or impoverished blacks apparently felt compelled to remain at the white church.[66]

The 1795 and 1796 class lists confirm that the action for separate worship was primarily a male affair: whereas twenty-six women in the 1795 lists do not appear on the next year's lists, twenty-five new names appeared in 1796, a net loss of one. Given the much larger numbers in the women's classes (just over one hundred members), the drop in women is statistically insignificant compared to the men's 25 percent loss. Women attending the new meetings probably remained with the old group. Apparently few slaves attended the new meetings. By 1795, only one black male in the class lists, Sampson, had merely a first name listed; he remained in the white-led classes the following year. Eight women lacked family names in the 1795 list; seven of them reappeared on the 1796 list.[67]

Thus the creation of a black Methodist church in 1796 involved separation of not only black from white, but also black from black. The leaders of the new meetings reacted against their placement in a largely female and enslaved setting, by emphasizing their own masculinity and independence. Many blacks who followed them did not draw such a sharp distinction, and remained affiliated with the white-run group, and that group's insistence on the organic unity of the body of Christ.

Differences between black Methodists and black Episcopalians emerged during these years. Neither group attempted to overturn the concepts of social hierarchy or of limited liberty that permeated 1790s America. But the black Episcopalians appear to have been more willing to recognize the reality of slavery in their midst. For example, the African Society heard lectures from slaves such as Jupiter Hammon. Black Methodists, in contrast, had few slaves worship with them in their new surroundings. The difference may have been one of roots, for the Anglican Church had catechized slaves for almost a century. The high percentage of black Episcopalians listed in the directory suggests that they had lived in the city for some time. That meant they also lived with slavery within the church itself and for their own family members.[68]

The Methodist Church in New York, in contrast, had recently formed in the 1760s, as the Revolutionary rhetoric of natural rights surged. Many early Methodists called for slavery's end. As relative newcomers, black Methodists had little experience accommodating to slavery. Black Methodists also had more to defend, as they possessed more skills and better employment than black Episcopalians. But black Methodist leaders attempted to create their own niche in an inevitable hierarchy. In New York of the 1790s, no whites pushed for full racial equality. Blacks had little outside support beyond their own limited resources. The attempt to create a liberating, reforming environment through the black church remained a generation away.

Black New Yorkers' conservatism is most evident in comparing blacks' public presence in New York with blacks in Philadelphia. Historians who have studied New York blacks have assumed a direct parallel between the two cities, but differences in slavery and in black leadership meant differences in church structure, and in subsequent efforts at reform.[69]

Richard Allen and Absalom Jones headed black churches in Philadelphia in the 1790s, the most visible face of that city's community. Before that time they gained access to Philadelphia's public sphere through their writings. Historian Richard Newman has placed Richard Allen among the American Founding Fathers, highlighting Allen's participation in the Republic of Letters, the eighteenth-century tradition of high literacy and political rhetoric. Allen and Jones penned numerous letters, essays, and pamphlets, all directed at persuading a skeptical, educated white audience in the public sphere. Allen and Jones promoted their churches as centers of Christian charity, and, by implication, republican virtue. This aim clearly shone in their defenses of blacks against charges that Philadelphia's black community spread the yellow fever, an especially unjust charge against a group that had remained in the city when many fled, and nursed ill and dying citizens, white and black.[70]

In contrast, blacks in New York fail to appear in the written record through much of the 1790s. Why were they silent? Some, like Peter Williams, were illiterate. Others, like Jupiter Hammon, were elderly. And in New York, where black support of the British army's occupation remained fresh in the minds of many whites, it might not have been expedient to speak up. Whatever the reason, in New York the Republic of Letters remained largely closed to African Americans. Among those seeking entry, however, was William Hamilton, a young black man of twenty-three who penned a letter to recently elected Governor John Jay in 1796. A Methodist, that year he would join James Varick in the exodus to what would become Mother Zion.[71]

Hamilton's letter to Jay was more essay than epistle. General in tone, Hamilton's letter reads like a school exercise, although Hamilton would have been too old to attend the African school that Jay and his colleagues had established the decade before. In broad terms, Hamilton condemned the evils of slavery as unchristian and as acts of theft. As befitted an entrant to the Republic of Letters, he invoked biblical language, philosophical reasoning, and two quotes from William Cowper's 1788 poem "The Negro's Complaint." Hamilton begged Jay to consider, with Cowper, that critics of blacks "deem our nation brutes no longer."[72]

Hamilton's command over rhetoric was as yet uneven, confirming his shaky formal education. His sentence structure often rambled, and his florid language faltered awkwardly. Yet the letter achieved its basic rhetorical purpose. Hamilton revealed the fundamental contradiction of the new Republic: "how falsely and contradictory do the Americans speak [of] this land, a land of liberty and equality, a christian country[,] when almost every part of it abounds with slavery and oppression?" John Jay, a devout member of Trinity Episcopal Church, and a founding member of the New York Manumission Society, invoked similar ideas during the Revolution when writing to whites about slavery. To Hamilton, Jay had no ready answer.[73]

While the letter was forceful, it had little influence. William Hamilton's attempted foray into the Republic of Letters in 1796 came to nought. Hamilton never published his original letter, nor did Jay record a response. Although Hamilton would become one of Mother Zion's most prominent laymen, and a clear and forceful writer, in his 1796 letter to Jay he had not yet mastered form or style. Instead, that year Hamilton's actions spoke louder than his words, when he joined James Varick and other black men in taking early steps to separate from the white Methodist church.

Conclusion

By 1800, church leaders at Trinity and John Street could point to their own congregations as examples of harmonious and well-functioning communities. The Revolution's political infighting was long past, and both churches had grown. Furthermore, in both congregations wealthy individuals led each church. Although led by elites, both Trinity and John Street retained members from all occupations and all income levels. And both churches recruited African Americans, offering religion as a moral blueprint and a solace for their condition. Even so, blacks remained on the margins of the church, in a bow to the demands of social respectability. In the next decade, as Jeffersonian Republicans championed the equality of all white men, explicit racism also increased, and blacks took steps to assert their independence more forcefully.

Most worshipers at Trinity and John Street were common people with modest aspirations. Those least mentioned in public records, yet most numerous, were women. Fully two-thirds of all congregants were women; among black members, three-quarters were female. Those women would take different roles in the churches in the following decade. Elite white women attempted to bolster older practices of charity in a changing environment by focusing on the natural objects of charity—other women and children. Although blacks accorded women importance in everyday religious practice, black men led in forming interdenominational bonds and creating a new community centered upon abolition and benevolence.

4 / Stepping Up and Out: White Women in the Church, 1800–1820

As a new century dawned, New York City continued to grow. Between 1800 and 1820, the city doubled in population, from 60,000 to 120,000 inhabitants, as masons and carpenters skillfully erected new buildings northward on Manhattan Island. The city showed the strains of growth. A "householder" writing in the *Republican Watch Tower* complained:

> Maiden-lane is now itself a common sewer, or a receptacle of filth for a very extensive and crowded part of the city, reaching with few exceptions from John to Pine Street, and from Broadway to the East River. . . . [T]he waters of the marsh are not drained, the filth on the surface of it is not washed away. It stagnates, ferments, putrifies, and is finally decomposed upon the spot. If there is . . . poison in the exhalations which arise from this and from the marsh below . . . the inhabitants work, sleep, and move in the midst of it.[1]

This region included the houses of worship for white Methodists at John Street and black Methodists at Cross Street; not far away, black Episcopalians would gather in the next decade. Despite its health hazards, the area, situated in the Second Ward, was affluent, with considerable wealth accruing in merchant shops nearby on Pearl and William Streets. Just west of Broadway, Trinity rose above the Methodists, literally and figuratively. Its location on higher ground avoided the watery health nuisance. So did most of Trinity's merchants, whose spacious homes overlooked "the New World splendor of airy Broadway" and other major streets in the lower city.[2]

As the city grew, so did the churches. By 1800, both John Street and Trinity were full-fledged congregations. No longer did they ambiguously represent both denomination and congregation in New York City. In the 1790s, evangelically inclined Anglicans built two Episcopal churches distinct from Trinity, and Methodists added four meetinghouses apart from John Street. Both Trinity and John Street could thus begin to take on the distinct characteristics of their neighborhoods, rather than serve as the public face of their respective denominations citywide.

Both John Street Methodist and Trinity Episcopal were downtown churches; they might both be deemed merchant churches. Here some of the city's wealthiest and most established families worshiped. Their congregants' personal homes also showed signs of wealth, where families employed domestic servants and slaves, rooted to their masters by economic necessity, law, or force.

The merchant neighborhoods of Lower Manhattan were somewhat of an anomaly in larger New York City. Throughout this era, the Lower Manhattan wards voted for the Federalist Party, the party of commerce, hierarchy, and social order. These wards voted Federalist even in the years 1800–1806, when the rest of the city, the artisan and laboring classes, and most of the nation, defected for Thomas Jefferson's Democratic-Republican Party.[3]

Privileged families who lived near Trinity and John Street also fled the city when yellow fever epidemics raged. A mid-decade census reveals that as many as 80 percent of the inhabitants of the lower wards left the city in the summer, making Lower Manhattan a virtual ghost town. By contrast, in the poorer uptown wards, only one-third of the population had the ability or funds to leave. The disease originated and spread most extensively in these uptown wards, causing the greatest fatalities.[4]

In this downtown location, women worked and worshiped. Historian Christine Stansell has characterized antebellum New York as a city of women. Women held households together: wives as managers of the household economy, servants as the labor that put management into action. They worked in boardinghouses, markets, and shops. They cared for their children, with or without fathers present. City censuses reveal that women outnumbered men throughout the city, and especially in the lower wards. This gendered status was directly connected to the elite nature of the Lower Manhattan neighborhoods: wealthier individuals were more likely to forge successful families, with dependent wives and daughters, in contrast to the northernmost outlying wards, where single men dominated. And wealthier families employed more domestic servants, who were usually female.[5]

The churches, too, were worship houses for women. Institutional church histories have focused on the male clergy who led the churches and the wealthy male laymen who bankrolled them. Both types of records give the impression that men dominated worship.[6] Nearly the opposite was the case. Even more than in the city at large, women formed large numerical majorities of both Episcopal and Methodist churches, black and white. Nowhere was this more evident than in Trinity's and John Street's Lower Manhattan locations. A silent majority, women deeply influenced Episcopalian and Methodist church life.

Despite their numerical majorities, women's influence in the churches was indirect. Church leaders in both bodies, along with most Americans in the early Republic, assumed women's roles to be beneath those of men. An emerging literature reaffirmed women as supplementary and secondary; women's deep emotional and maternal instincts limited their effectiveness or desirability in public roles.[7] Given those strictures, women could not directly lead the churches.

Using the roles assigned them, Trinity's and John Street's women took greater steps into the public sphere, and into expressing deep forms of piety and religiosity. In so doing, they did not challenge gender roles, but their approved expressions of piety brought them into close contact with ministers. In a rapidly changing environment, with much social dislocation, some laity would question women's influence with, and connection to, church leaders. Such anxieties would eventually combine with social tensions to create ruptures in the churches.

Families in Faith: Differing Models of Women's Church Attendance

Both Trinity Episcopal and John Street Methodist were churches filled with a strong female presence. But the status of women in each church differed. A fundamental difference between Trinity and John Street lay in their respective denominations' attempts to define family life and women's roles. The Episcopal Church built its parishes around the nuclear family and assumed patriarchal authority as normative. By contrast, the Methodists viewed themselves as a new family. Old family ties broke when one heard the call to follow Christ, and all became brothers and sisters in the faith.[8] Consequently, Trinity's records tend to record individuals in terms of family units; wives came attached to husbands. John Street, in contrast, housed many individual women, and minimized matrimonial and household bonds. It is likely that some John Street women were servants in homes of Trinity-attending families.

Even though Trinity's structure assumed nuclear families to be the building blocks of the parish, records reveal that, behind the official public male face of the church, women may have attended and worshiped without their husbands. Trinity's pew rent lists record the parish's most prominent individuals, and therefore tend to list wealthy men. An examination of Trinity's communicants reveals a different image. Pew renters represented the public face of the church; pewholders might rent a space (and might or might not attend church) as a civic duty, to gain public exposure, or to provide a moral example to their social inferiors. In contrast, communicants represented the private, devotional side of church attendance. As members eligible to take the Lord's Supper, communicants to the Episcopal Church did not necessarily have public prestige, or financial means, but needed to exhibit a good moral character and approval of the presiding priest. While a pewholder could have deep religious convictions, a communicant probably held a deeper level of personal religious commitment than the average pewholder. The Episcopal Church did not set a high bar for participation in the Lord's Supper, but in 1801 Benjamin Moore recorded a list of communicants, perhaps to note who among his parishioners regularly participated in the sacrament. Moore's 1801 list reveals some overlap between pew renters and communicants: 16 percent of the pew renters from the 1790s list, men such as William Bayard and Matthew Clarkson, also appear on Moore's list.[9]

Male communicants may have been slightly less well-off than male pewholders, but in general little differed between the two groups of men. Communicants shared similar occupational standing, and thus similar socioeconomic status, with pew renters. Slightly fewer communicants gained listing in the directories, suggesting a less settled status, and fewer worked in the most lucrative government, professional, and merchant categories.[10] But generally, the men who took communion but did not rent pews at Trinity resembled those who rented pews.

The greatest disparity between the official pew rents and the unofficial communicant list lay in the category of sex. Women rented just over 10 percent of Trinity's pews. Almost all were older, propertied widows. Among communicants, however, nearly two-thirds, or 64 percent, were female. This suggests that, at Sunday services, Trinity Episcopal appeared more like its evangelical rivals in gender composition. If male heads of households did attend, many remained content to watch their wives or daughters approach the communion rail by themselves.[11]

The women at Trinity generally did not appear wholly alone; family connections did play a role in church participation. Unlike Methodist class lists, which were rigidly sex-segregated, male and female names jostled together in the Episcopalian communicant list, with husbands and wives, like Robert and Lucy Bird or Jane and John Ferrer, often listed on the same line. In a few cases, Moore listed only a family name, such as Jarvis or Rutledge, suggesting all members were eligible communicants.[12]

But according to the communicant lists, most Anglican women participated in church life by themselves. Many women took communion alone—only 17 percent of the female communicants shared a surname with a male communicant.[13] The probability of relationship increases slightly when comparing communicant surnames with pewholder surnames—nearly one-quarter of female communicants shared a surname with a pew renter. Many of Trinity's female communicants, then, if not single or widowed, had husbands with no affiliation to Trinity, and approached the communion rail alone.[14]

A similar majority of women attended John Street Methodist Church. The New York City Methodist class lists reveal that women regularly outnumbered men by a ratio of two to one, a figure slightly higher than the sex ratios among Methodists in other northeastern cities. Within the city, more women would have attended John Street than the newer churches, for city censuses reveal that the older, established wards contained greater percentages of women. The newer chapels uptown, conversely, contained a larger share of men, because of the male predominance in the northernmost wards. A merchant church in its leadership, John Street's laity were women.[15]

In organizing their chapels, Methodists generally deemphasized family affections. At traditional churches like Trinity, pews arranged seating by household. Husband, wife, children, and, in the colonial era, attendant slaves sat together in one location. Early Methodists, however, eschewed pews, because pews could lead to rents, which symbolized an unwelcome hierarchy and preference for wealth. Methodists went a step further in symbolically removing the household from the center of church life. In Methodist meetinghouses, men and women sat on opposite sides of a center aisle, separating wives and husbands along with single men and women. Children and blacks typically sat at the rear (and blacks retreated upstairs to the gallery, where one existed).[16]

The symbolic separation of families in seating accompanied real differences in the composition of the Methodist society. Many single individuals attended Methodist meetings, drifting in and out of the city as opportunities allowed and tragedies dictated. Dee Andrews's analysis of the city society records in New York, Philadelphia, and Baltimore suggested that the typical Methodist woman in a city society was young, unmarried, childless, and often bound in domestic service. But when new Methodists arrived in the city with friends or relatives, women attended with other women. Andrews has demonstrated that a literal sisterhood connected many Methodist women in kinship, as women tended to share surnames with other women in the society, to a degree not existing among male members. Like Trinity's communicants, John Street's women may have largely attended church without men, but they were not alone, as they did appear with other women.[17]

Churchwomen in Early Reform Movements

While their respective views of familial authority differed, both Trinity's Episcopalians and John Street's Methodists assumed women's roles should be auxiliary to men. Gendered assumptions labeled women emotional, pious, and (ideally) silent. Yet those very assumptions afforded women in both denominations a wedge into the public sphere. In this time of economic and demographic growth, and also great poverty and need, women in both churches joined organizations that put them in contact with others: either for benevolence for the poor, or for the education and evangelization of the unchurched.

City and church officials struggled to adequately support the city's poor, as population pressures strained traditional means of charity. Republican theory had branded women as dependents unsuitable for citizenship, but the strains of the Revolution forced some theorists to allow women a role in the cultivation of patriotic virtue in sons and husbands, promoting women's natural abilities as maternal nurturers. Married women could participate in public life indirectly in exhibiting the proper roles of wife and mother. The city's dramatic growth forced city and church officials to allow elite women greater public exposure by distributing relief.[18]

Elite white women who attended churches like Trinity began to participate in New York benevolent organizations that focused on the natural objects of women's concern, widows and children. Modeled largely upon colonial-era assumptions about poverty, these benevolent societies did not change the way poor relief was administered. But even as they restricted women's actions to a narrow arena, they paradoxically carved out a space for elite women in the public sphere. Women Methodists at John Street, by contrast, included a component of evangelization, keeping a recognizably Methodist identity to their efforts.[19]

In 1797, the widow Isabella Graham, who had run a girls' school in New York during the previous decade, organized "a number of ladies" to form the Society for the Relief of Poor Widows with Small Children. Many of the same women who founded the Widows' Society then organized the Orphan Asylum in 1806. In both cases, the elite women founding the organizations limited their aid to women and dependents.[20]

The Society for the Relief of Poor Widows with Small Children understood that women held a special right to receive relief, provided they met the proper character requirements. The charter statement of the Widows' Society explained that, although they had until now no institution devoted to their benefit, widows with children held "peculiar claims on the public beneficence." The society's members established regulations to ensure that the women who received assistance were of the worthy poor. Widows had to be legal city residents, and of "fair character." The directors refused aid to women who begged, sold spirits, or practiced any "gross immorality." The society managers also barred assistance to widows who refused to allow their children to work in a trade or service.[21]

The society's women overwhelmingly came from long-standing traditional churches, the Presbyterian, Episcopalian, and Dutch Reformed. Many of Trinity's elite women participated in the society. Indeed, of the Widows' Society's original officers, only the first director, Isabella Graham, joined a Presbyterian church. The second director, Sarah Hoffman, treasurer Elizabeth Seton, and secretary Lucy Bird all attended Trinity. In the organization's first twenty years, Trinity's women supplied at least half of the officers.[22] John Street's women remained absent, focusing instead on their internal religious world and possibilities of sanctification within the structure of the class meetings. The society's connections with churches remained broad and ecumenical, as the women asked for, and usually received, funds from ministers of many different denominations throughout the city.[23]

The society's women also mostly came from the upper classes. The demands of charity work, which included regular visits to families and the procurement of such items as firewood and food, precluded lower-class women from participating. Isabella Graham was the exception, a middle-class widow whose daughters both married wealthy merchants. Even so, as a schoolteacher she enjoyed contacts with high society: then-president George Washington had attended her school's annual exams, which were open to the public. Benjamin Moore, Trinity's rector and New York bishop after Samuel Provoost, regularly attended those exams.[24]

In forming societies to aid widows and orphans, Trinity's women continued the public charity that their male relatives had performed in the colonial era. These women assumed with colonial elites that society's betters would dispense charity. They limited aid to the worthy poor, and restricted the amount of funds dispensed to nominal relief. Like their forebears, they relied upon a network of churches for aid; the society often requested that charity sermons be preached at Trinity and elsewhere, the proceeds from which aided poor women and children. But unlike colonial-era relief, widespread poverty encouraged women to be the agents as well as the objects of charity. Without elite women's involvement, the city's meager resources allocated for poverty would not stretch far enough to meet the needs of even the worthy poor.[25]

The widows and orphans societies thus generally looked to the past, not the future. They were conservative institutions that adhered to the existing order. Within two decades, some women would enter public space to promote more far-reaching reform agendas, but they differed in emphasis. As historians of the antebellum era have noted, the first groups were benevolent, not reform, organizations. They willingly accepted the relegation of women into a private sphere, and limited the objects of their charity to other women and children. Devoted to relief, they did not attempt to end poverty, or attack the social structures that created it. Few of these women in benevolent organizations later joined reform societies; reformers came from entirely different populations.[26]

Methodist wives did not generally occupy the same social stratum as Trinity's Episcopalians, and thus did not appear as prominently in early benevolent efforts. Further, the Methodist emphasis on individual conversion and personal transformation did not immediately lend itself to movements with larger social ramifications such as poor relief. But because John Street housed more women than the other Methodist chapels, and because its generally wealthier women were better able to pursue reform efforts, John Street women tended to dominate the early female Methodist efforts at relief. And by the 1810s, Methodist women did support evangelization efforts that, like Episcopalian benevolence, affirmed women's auxiliary status and supporting role.

The first of these was the Female Assistance Society, which like the ecumenical Widows' Society assumed that the natural weaknesses of women rendered them worthy objects of charity. Isabella Graham joined several John Street Methodist women in providing aid to poor women who suffered from illnesses that prevented their employment. Among them were Ann Disosway and Pamela Lamplain, Methodist matriarchs whose grown children were already prominent in New York chapels, and Sarah Hall, whose husband, Francis, was publisher of the *Commercial Advertiser*.[27]

Mary Morgan (later Mason) joined Isabella Graham and her Methodist sisters in these efforts, but soon turned to more explicitly evangelizing aims. Morgan was an exception in Methodist women's early benevolent efforts, as she was young and single.[28] Daughter of Irish immigrants, Morgan left her family in Philadelphia as a teenager to teach at a Quaker school in New York. She attended John Street Chapel along with the well-established Disosways, Halls, and Lamplains. Morgan's greatest concern lay in instructing her students in religion, which she could only inadequately do during the week.

With the permission of the Quaker board, Mary Morgan opened her classroom for Sunday School use, instructing a new set of students, including an increasing number of Catholics. She taught these laboring and immigrant children how to read and write, using the Bible and catechisms as aids, and included regular doses of religious instruction and prayer when she could do so without censure. As the closing bell rang, so did the church bells, and Morgan walked alongside all students (and parents) willing to join her at John Street's services.[29]

Morgan's interest in Sunday Schools placed her on the cutting edge of evangelical reform. British evangelicals had created the Sunday School program late in the previous century, and American evangelicals sought to bring the model to New York. Mary Morgan wanted to provide more religious instruction than the Quaker school board desired, and she joined with other Methodist women to plan a Sunday School under the care of New York Methodists. After some initial resistance, Morgan successfully implemented her vision. By 1820, she had taught hundreds of New York children, mixing instruction in literacy with religious doctrine and prayer.[30]

Women also supported denominational-specific ministries. In 1816, Methodist women formed the Asbury Female Mite Society, which combined poor relief and religious aims by providing for the wives of nonsalaried and retired Methodist ministers. Originally a cause of the now-deceased Francis Asbury, women took up the role of temporal support that male ministers had once promoted.[31] The women who led Methodist benevolent efforts differed in degree from their Episcopalian counterparts, but not in kind. Most tended to be older wives of well-established husbands. And although less explicit than the Widows' Society, the Sunday School and Mite Societies assumed that aid should go to the worthy poor, particularly to women.

John Street women tended to dominate among New York Methodist women involved in public affairs. A merchant church, it allowed merchants' wives like Ann Disosway to pursue benevolence. Younger women like Sarah Hall, whose husband was a publisher, and Mary Morgan, a teacher, had somewhat better prospects than the average single laboring woman. Methodist women's activities represent an early shift to reform, however sectarian they appear in their connections to ministry. While still connected to the ethos of individual conversion, their exhortations to the poor ultimately led to movements grander, and more coercive, in their aims.

Piety Unleashed: The Example of Elizabeth Ann Seton

While few women took part in the formation and function of the benevolent societies, many more participated in the churches using acceptable forms of private piety and devotion. Just as republican theory dictated women's proper role as that of wife and mother, so did churches tend to funnel women's roles toward marriage and motherhood.

The merchant culture at Trinity and, to a lesser extent, John Street, offered elite white women greater influence than women held elsewhere. As historian Edward Pessen revealed in his study of antebellum urban wealth, elite families largely married into other elite families, and wealth overwhelmingly married wealth.[32] The higher beginning status of women in merchant marriages also meant they held a more privileged place in the household, and were less likely to suffer neglect, with wealthy kin observing the match. In general, merchants could preserve the extended household in a way that emerging professional and artisan families did not.

Oral and popular histories reflect wealthy women's prominence by sketching the beginnings of high society life in New York, in which female hostesses skilled at entertaining furthered their husbands' and families' reputations. Such was the case of Sarah Livingston Jay, wife of John Jay. Sarah's father, William Livingston, had fought against High Church pretensions in the King's College case of the 1750s, signed the Declaration of Independence, and served as governor of New Jersey. In marrying Jay, Sarah joined with another prominent politician and important public figure (who like his father-in-law would oppose Trinity's High Church clergy). While John served as a diplomat, the Jays lived in Madrid, Paris,

Figure 4.1. Sarah Livingston Jay, model of colonial refinement. (From Martha Lamb, *History of New York*, vol. 2 [1880].)

and London. Upon their return to New York, visitors praised Sarah's elegant and stylish parties, which furthered her husband's political reputation and kept the Jay family within the ranks of the elite.[33]

Sarah Jay's own words minimized her role. In a letter to her sister, after a passage containing a passionate defense of liberty, she retreated: "But whither, my pen, are you hurrying me? What have I to do with politicks? Am I not myself a woman, & writing to Ladies? Come then, ye fashions to my assistance!"[34] But such protests artfully hid the influence elite women wielded in their households. The demands of republican politics forced elite politicians especially to rely upon their wives as partners in a new type of household economy. Historian Catherine Allgor describes how the First Ladies in the presidential administrations from Jefferson to Jackson played leading roles in promoting their husbands' careers, in ways ranging from the decoration of the White House to securing audiences for purposes of political patronage.[35]

Sarah Jay's hospitality may have promoted her husband's political career, but her public presence in church and society appears to have operated under an older, more conventional role. Jay focused her energies on her household. She did not take part in the limited benevolent aims of the Widows' Society, nor did she appear to take a leading role in worship at Trinity Church, where her family attended while in the city.

By contrast, Elizabeth Ann Seton applied the traditional understanding of women's roles as meek and passive in order to gain a form of spiritual superiority. A communicant at Trinity Church, Seton served as the first treasurer of the Society for the Relief of Poor Widows with Small Children. Her activities in the years after 1800 reveal an increasingly pietistic sense of religion, marked not by public performance but by private devotion. The turn from public faith to private, however, was not toward quietism or acceptance of the existing order, but rather reflected a subtle challenge to public displays of formal religion.

Elizabeth Seton's path ultimately led her to convert to Roman Catholicism. Seton founded the Sisters of Charity religious order, and in the late twentieth century she became the first U.S.-born saint in the Roman Catholic Church. Thus her story stands as exceptional, both in its trajectory outside Protestantism and in its intense spirituality and extreme devotion. But her relationship to her husband and her minister may reveal some of the tensions that accompanied deep, heartfelt faith for female Episcopalians.[36]

Buoyed by family wealth, Elizabeth's husband, William Seton, had been a successful merchant, but in the latter 1790s his business ventures began to fail, and he went bankrupt in 1800. William had always been weak from what was thought of as biologically inherited consumption, and as his business failed, his health worsened.[37] The Setons traveled to Italy in the autumn of 1803, in a final desperate attempt to recover William's health. Upon landfall, Italian authorities quarantined the ship, because yellow fever had raged in New York that summer. A dying William and his young wife found themselves confined to the drafty rooms and cold stone walls of a military barracks. There Elizabeth poured her thoughts and fears upon the pages of a journal she kept. In those barracks, William died of tuberculosis in December 1803, before Elizabeth turned thirty.[38]

Elizabeth's memoir repeatedly focuses on the mortification of the flesh, of the sweetness of death when accompanied by the promise of

Figure 4.2. Elizabeth Ann Seton, as a young wife,
before her conversion and sainthood. (Courtesy:
Archives Sisters of Charity of New York.)

eternal life in heaven. In this regard she served as a spiritual midwife for
her husband, to birth his soul into heavenly realms. William recognized
Elizabeth as spiritually superior, relying upon her as religious guide and
mediator in his last days, and repeatedly asking her whether she believed
he would be accepted in heaven. She continually assured him of his salvation, and even encouraged him to welcome death's approach.[39]

William's submissive attitude compelled Elizabeth's certainty. She
did not claim assurance of his salvation from her own spiritual knowledge, but in William's meek acceptance of grace: "I always tried to convince him that, when the soul was so humble and sincere as his, and

submissive to God's will so uniformly as his had been through his trials, it became sinful to doubt one moment of his reception through the merits of his Redeemer." Yet humility had its limits: when he faltered, Elizabeth chided William for wavering in his hope in Christ.[40]

Elizabeth wrote that William's spiritual growth, and the beginnings of his salvation, began when he renounced his business accomplishments and any public prominence. His illness gave him opportunity to prove his patience, to wait for God with faith, and to think on the status of his soul.[41] Elizabeth Seton could claim a spiritual advantage in her household because her life lay largely outside the public arena. Elizabeth naturally occupied a secondary, lowered place, and thus paradoxically attained spiritual superiority. As William's stance in the world worsened, Elizabeth grew stronger.

In this time of personal turmoil, Elizabeth's faith deepened. Her strength derived from her connection to Trinity Episcopal Church, a cradle of solace for her. During her Italian confinement, Seton cherished the visual signs of religion. While held offshore, Seton recalled a comforting dream of being back at Trinity "singing, with all my soul, the hymn at our dear sacrament." Her devotions consisted of reading through the liturgy and practicing an ersatz, lay-instituted Eucharist, along with continual prayer. Elizabeth thus re-created a High Church setting in her cell.[42]

Trinity's assistant minister, later bishop, John Henry Hobart assumed the leading mantle of the High Church party among New York City's Episcopalians in the early nineteenth century. High Church theology championed Episcopalian uniqueness, separating it from the errors of Roman Catholicism on one hand and other Protestant denominations on the other. The theology emphasized the apostolic succession of the church's bishops, that is, the continuity of church leaders from the time of Christ to the present day. In contrast to the colonial era, during which SPG churchmen championed the church-state relationship, High Church theology after the Revolution emphasized spiritual and sacramental purity, and retreat from public affairs.[43] Unlike his colonial-era predecessors, or those High Churchmen and Oxford Movement priests who followed him after 1830, Hobart was known for his passionate, fervent presentations. He used two major bulwarks of evangelical practice—Scriptural study and prayer—to support his theological position. The results electrified many at Trinity.

Hobart's presentations aroused a passionate faith in individuals like Elizabeth, blurring the standards of feminine roles in the early Republic.

As William grew sicker, Elizabeth's matrimonial role grew less sexual and more motherly: her language reveals maternal concern in discussing her husband's slow, childlike faith. But her relationship to others, her sister-in-law and her pastor, assumed a greater passion.

Elizabeth's relationship to her sister-in-law Rebecca Seton reveals a spiritual sisterhood, united by a fevered faith, much like young Methodist women experienced in their class meetings. But Elizabeth's and Rebecca's relationship to Hobart added another, nearly sexual, dynamic in its intensity. Upon missing a Hobart sermon while away, Elizabeth wrote to Rebecca, "Give HH[obart] a look and a sigh for me, such as you will for yourself."[44] Both Elizabeth and Rebecca cherished the celebration of communion, an important High Church rite that Hobart stressed in his preaching. On communion Sundays, Elizabeth recounted running alongside Rebecca from Episcopal church to church to chapel, unwilling to miss receiving another portion of the sacrament. Such parish dashes, accompanied by sighs and looks, suggest youth, impetuousness, even passion. Her religious intensity allowed Elizabeth to blur feminine roles, even though they all remained feminine: as a wife she appeared older and maternal, but as a congregant she grew younger, even flirtatious.[45]

Elizabeth defended Hobart against all detractors, solidly grasping the theology of his High Church principles. In one letter she regretfully noted that she had attended St. Paul's on a day Hobart had preached at St. Mark's. She complained to Rebecca that the minister (Cave Jones, with whom Hobart would clash in the following decade) preached a sermon of "schism," which she knew Hobart would never do.[46]

Elizabeth's feelings for Hobart were mutual. While the Setons were in Italy, Hobart watched their belongings. Using the sentimental language of the day, Hobart wrote:

> Your furniture we gladly preserve as memorials of you, I never cast my eye on the escritoire without thinking of its inestimable owner, nor on the piano forte without having my soul in imagination enlivened and soothed by the chants of praise and consolation which it was my delight to hear burst forth from it. The sacred portrait of the Redeemer recalls to my mind the ardent piety of her who before this endeared memorial poured forth the emotions of holy love and gratitude.[47]

In his letter, Hobart combined the genteel appreciation of fine consumer goods with the appreciation for Seton's friendship. Hobart's florid language heightened the sense of intimacy between the two.

Elizabeth Seton's religiosity, which strained the traditional bounds of marriage and the typical relationship between parishioner and priest, ultimately proved incompatible with the more traditional conceptions of family and women that existed at Trinity Episcopal. After her husband's death, Elizabeth converted to Catholicism and became a nun, eschewing Protestant female norms entirely. But before her conversion, her relationship illustrated the tensions in High Church theology, particularly with John Henry Hobart. Hobart had a strong personality. He encouraged strong faith in others; such were often women, whose private devotions trumped their husbands' public displays of religious identity. This connection created strong ties on the congregational level, but would soon lead to resentment, as public-minded men with little inclination for private devotions would balk at Hobart's High Church vision. Theological disputes would also contain social, and thus gendered, dynamics.

Methodism Domesticated: The Example of Catherine Livingston Garrettson

Methodism created a more complicated role for women in the church. Wealthy Episcopalian women attempted to preserve the prestige of their households, and kept family connections intact, even as they participated in the piety and devotion of church ritual to a far greater degree than their husbands. By contrast, Methodists accepted that the gospel message would sear souls, and separate father from son, mother from daughter, and husband from wife. Methodists created a new family that deemphasized traditional households, even as it re-created new nuclear families that placed converted and sanctified Methodist men at their heads.[48]

Methodist women were, like Elizabeth Seton, spiritually influential. Whereas Methodist women's conversion narratives recounted family opposition, Methodist men often entered the church with the support of female relatives. Numerous autobiographies by Methodist preachers credit a mother or sister for the individual's conversion, and often his subsequent entrance into the ministry. According to John Street oral tradition, Barbara Heck goaded Philip Embury into continuing the lay preaching in New York that he had done in Ireland. Nathan Bangs credited a "pious and devoted" sister with his conversion and subsequent entrance into the ministry, as well as his brother John's conversion. And African Methodist George White explained that his daughter taught him to read using passages of Scripture, making his ministry possible. To signify the importance of women, at every white-run Methodist church the preacher's class, assuming a prominent place, was female. Often, this class included a number of ministers' wives.[49] Methodists thus memorialized their respect for religious women, those who called their wayward men back home, to the family and true religion.

English Methodism had been born with aristocratic support; the Countess of Huntingdon, Selina Hastings, had befriended the Wesley brothers and helped fund the upstart group. New York Methodists could point to their own benefactresses in their origins. Mary Barclay, widow of Trinity rector Henry Barclay, had been one of the original supporters of Methodism in New York, providing the fledgling group with the property upon which they would build the John Street meetinghouse. In the early Republic, one of Francis Asbury's strongest "Old Friends" came in the form of a member of America's aristocracy, the Livingston family. Catherine Livingston joined in matrimony with Freeborn Garrettson, a fiery circuit preacher. The marriage of Catherine Livingston and Freeborn Garrettson not only illustrates the generally ignored upper-class structures underlying city Methodism, but also the gendered dynamic in which matriarchs allied with ministers to create a semi-aristocratic ethos.[50]

The Livingston family straddled religious and cultural worlds even as they embraced their aristocratic pretensions. While upstate in Rhinebeck during the summers, family members attended the Dutch Reformed Church of their mother, Margaret Beekman Livingston. Winters in New York City included services at Trinity Episcopal or its chief chapel, St. Paul's. Catherine Livingston's brother Robert R. Livingston rented a prominent pew at Trinity.[51]

Catherine Livingston's conversion invoked traditional Methodist accounts of family opposition. She chafed at the strictures of family obligation; Livingston recounted having an early romantic interest denied by both her parents, and her would-be beau's family. Consequently, Livingston could well have remained unmarried had she never encountered the Methodists in her late thirties. Catherine reported having feelings of isolation and loneliness throughout her adult years, broken only by the moments of peace she felt in various church services. Like Elizabeth Seton, the sacrament of Communion celebrated at St. Paul's Episcopal in New York touched her deeply, and one might imagine her converting to Catholicism like Seton, where her celibacy would be rewarded as a spiritual virtue.[52]

The Methodists' arrival in Rhinebeck in the late 1780s transformed Livingston's world. The genteel and generally agnostic tendencies of her brothers (most prominently the politicans Robert and Edward) tended to be comic in their resistance, but nonetheless revealed horror at any connection with the uncouth sect. One brother reportedly stated, "Catherine, enjoy your religion here at home all you please, but for heaven's sake don't join those Methodists; why, down at the ferry, nobody belongs to them only three fishermen and a negro."[53] But the joke revealed strong underlying social tensions: Methodists condemned slavery, forsook family wealth to further the gospel, and demanded rigorous personal behavior. Freeborn Garrettson, the first itinerant to gain entrance to polite society in Rhinebeck, personified such opposition. From a genteel Maryland slaveowning family, Garrettson freed his slaves and divided his family's patrimony among them. With little salary and no worldly status, Garrettson was beaten for his pacifism during the Revolution. Catherine's conversion to Methodism coincided with Garrettson's regular passages through their Rhinebeck estate.[54]

Livingston's most intense religious emotions occurred in the first decade after her conversion, before her marriage. Like many early Methodists, Livingston valued the divine power of dreams and visions, and was firmly convinced that God intended that she marry Freeborn Garrettson. Catherine's mother, Margaret Beekman Livingston, refused to approve of her marriage, and Methodist leaders like Francis Asbury, who moved in elite circles and remained committed to social propriety, refused to intervene.[55]

The opposition of Catherine's siblings soon melted when her seriousness became apparent to them; they provided a softening intermediary to Margaret and Catherine. Eventually Margaret relented, and Catherine and Freeborn married in 1793. Over forty at the time of her marriage, Catherine had one daughter, who herself remained sickly and never married. Catherine's connection to Freeborn Garrettson, unlike Elizabeth Seton's with John Henry Hobart, contained real eros, as Livingston and Garrettson were joined in matrimony. But their long courtship and joint commitment to leading others to Christ, and becoming more holy in the process, meant that their love at times appeared more platonic than erotic.[56]

Despite the early narrative of persecution, Catherine Livingston Garrettson soon reassumed her higher social station. In between Freeborn's circuit assignments, the Garrettsons built a mansion on the Hudson River on Livingston family property. The humble Methodists thus could boast of a lavish country retreat for their ministers, virtually worlds away from the hot and crowded city streets. The Garrettsons named it "Wildercliffe," in homage to the region's Dutch and Indian pasts; Francis Asbury, who took comfort there for nearly two decades, called it "Traveler's Rest," and repeatedly voiced his appreciation for the genteel hospitality he enjoyed there.[57]

The circle of hospitality extended to merchant families with evangelical inclinations. Garrettson befriended Catherine Rutsen Suckley, who was a Rhinebeck neighbor to the Livingstons and whose husband was a prominent New York merchant. Catherine and Freeborn were eventually joined with the Suckleys in their (im)mortality, as the two couples shared a tomb in Rhinebeck. Catherine apparently influenced one already religious brother-in-law, Episcopalian John Jay, toward a more evangelical direction in his last years, and Methodist tradition also records her converting her brothers Robert and the notoriously scandalous Edward Livingston to a more heartfelt faith. By her death in the 1840s, Methodism was no longer the refuge of social and racial outcasts it had been during Catherine's conversion.[58]

The Garrettsons provide an example for the domestication of Methodism before many historians have located it.[59] Freeborn eased into semiretirement, working in nearby New York City to build a seminary to train ministers, as well as a Methodist missionary and Bible society. Freeborn and Catherine both entered the city regularly as honored guests, grand statesman and stateswoman of the church. The preacher's class, the class meeting where local ministers led pious women in devotions and prayer, was filled with preachers' wives like Catherine Garrettson. While many women attended Methodist churches and chapels, older and married matriarchs, joined in matrimony with ministers and merchants, wielded the most power in the city churches.[60]

Catherine Livingston Garrettson's life thus highlights the tensions women felt in joining Methodism. Early in their faith many women defied natal family expectations for marriage and motherhood, but eventually most Methodist women embraced family life. Guided by religious convictions, they chose their own spouses, married later in life, and had fewer children; such changes revealed a compromise between early Methodist rhetoric that obliterated old family bonds and the realities of a movement that allowed social connections to remain after conversion.[61]

As with later conflicts among New York Episcopalians, New York's Methodists would also divide, as some would chafe at the innovations that ministers, and presumably their wives and female supporters, would

Figure 4.3. Catherine Livingston Garrettson as a
Methodist matriarch, after her spiritual and familial
crises had passed. (Reproduced with permission from
the Methodist Collections at Drew University.)

introduce to the churches. Mary Morgan's successful effort to introduce
a Sunday School ministry to New York Methodists provides an early
example. As in many Methodist narratives, Morgan encountered family opposition to her religious choices; as in Catherine Livingston's case,
maternal opposition burned hottest, since Morgan's mother was an
ardent Deist opposed to organized religion. A Methodist uncle encouraged her faith, but Mary had to defy her parents to gain an education
and to attend class meetings. After a particularly intense conversion
experience, Mary especially roused her mother's opposition in wearing
plain garb and refusing to adorn herself with jewelry. Before she turned

twenty, Mason moved to New York City, accepted a job as a teacher at a Quaker school, and joined John Street Church.[62]

Morgan desired to create a British evangelical-inspired Sunday School for New York Methodists. She joined six John Street Methodist women in the effort, including two daughters of local preacher William Phoebus, and Mary's friend Sarah Hall, the wife of publisher Francis Hall. This small group met resistance when they promoted their idea at the Second/Forsyth Street Church, as Methodists there feared the added expense of supporting a Sunday School, when Methodists already paid to support weekday instruction. But support from pastor Phoebus allowed the women to push their vision through.[63] The alliance of ministers, ministers' female relatives, and well-off women promoted a new ministry that a body of Methodists opposed. Such tensions would eventually boil over, showing that theological conflicts included social and gendered dynamics.

The intimate connections between elite churchwomen and their ministers, coupled with the large proportion of women among Trinity's communicants and John Street's class lists, suggest that Methodist and Episcopal clergy held significant power in both bodies. Several studies on colonial and nineteenth-century America have posited that a gender imbalance in the churches reflected a strong clerical presence. When clergy held greater power, and more ability to discipline, male laity attended church in fewer numbers, and women dominated.[64] Consequently, when clergy spoke of themselves as pastors of a flock, the biblical imagery also took on gendered implications of femininity: a male shepherd tending a group of female sheep. As such, disputes with clergy often implicated conceptions of gender.

Conclusion

By entering the public sphere through benevolent societies, white women promoted an older vision of organic hierarchy. In undertaking public acts of charity, elite white women attempted to reassert their high-status households' prominence and the colonial vision of unity. While influential, their power rested in the paradox that they were weak. Only by embracing gender norms did they gain support.

Most women, elite or not, embraced a vision of unity in more mundane ways, primarily by attending churches that preached that there was neither male nor female in Christ, spiritually speaking. In actual experience, women who did not defer to their husbands did defer to their ministers. Because of this deference, the church conflicts that arose in the following decade would contain a gendered component.

Concerns of gender cut across other forms of identity. Social concepts of femininity carry within them implied messages about masculinity. Even more striking, society's ideas about what is feminine and what is masculine bleed into ideas about racial identity. Black men in the churches found themselves fighting against ideas of femininity imputed to them. As they formed their own benevolent societies, black church-men stressed a heightened, even exaggerated, masculine leadership in their churches.

5 / Gendering Race in the Church: Black Male Benevolence, 1800–1820

Peter Williams, former sexton at John Street Methodist, later a successful tobacconist on Liberty Street, never learned to read or write. What words we have from him come from memories of white Methodist ministers who celebrated his piety, or from his son, Peter Williams Jr., who became a minister of St. Philip's African Episcopal Church.[1]

Late in life, Peter Williams commissioned a portrait of himself from an unnamed French West Indian painter. This work, as with all early modern portraits, attempted to balance some sense of Williams's physical likeness with what he and the artist wanted the audience to see about him. In this work, we might hear Williams's voice, if only softly. The painting of Williams, however, is an exercise in restraint. Peter gazes just to the right of the painter, with an earnest yet calm expression, the soft background and lighting displaying little drama. The painting contains no allegorical devices, nothing to indicate Williams's profession, property, or lineage. Williams's simply cut, dark suit and lack of jewelry, lace, or ruffles reflected the early Methodist penchant for simplicity. Methodists and other evangelicals used dress as a marker of righteousness, in which their plain, unadorned bodies proclaimed earnestness in seeking salvation, in contrast to the trifling fashions of the day.[2]

So Williams may not have been stylish (although a family member remarked that Williams was bald, and vainly wore a wig for the occasion); and he certainly appeared devout. But primarily, Williams portrayed the image of a gentleman. Only a gentleman commissioned a portrait, and displayed his self-assured confidence for all visitors to his

Figure 5.1. Peter Williams Sr., variously slave, patriot, sexton, tobacconist, freeman. Here, a gentleman. Williams consistently attempted to
move between black and white religious worlds. (Collection of The New-
York Historical Society.)

home. Peter Williams's image depicts him as he would have us see him:
steady, dependable and, above all, successful.[3]

The portraits of other black churchmen, in New York and beyond,
display a similar sense of simplicity and sobriety. They are all gentlemen;
some are also men of the cloth. None wear loud or flamboyant cloth-
ing, or betray anything that hints of a bicultural life mediated between
African and American worlds. Their public faces contradict the picture
of a vibrant working-class or Africanized culture that historians such

as Shane White have uncovered among other black New Yorkers in the early Republic.[4]

The development of black churches in New York after 1800 reveals the aspirations of this class of men. Women numerically dominated the black church and often provided the impetus for their sons and husbands to attend, but men who aspired to middle-class status assumed the church's public face. As the city grew, they would divide: Peter Williams's vision of biracial Methodism clashed with increasingly separatist inclinations of the men who formed Mother Zion. But these men had more in common than not. All adopted the language of unity or inclusivity that white churchmen had done before. But the ideal of unity had to paper over deeper divisions: divisions between white and black churches, between black men and women, and between middling and laboring blacks.

Black Churches as Foundations of the Black Community

New York's 1799 emancipation law guaranteed that slavery would die in New York, albeit slowly, for the law only directly affected children born after July 4 of that year. Blacks took matters into their own hands to speed the process. New York City's African Americans continued to work with the New York Manumission Society to sue for the freedom of slaves unlawfully held; further, many blacks negotiated early manumissions with their masters, combining their labor and money to accelerate what was only guaranteed to their children. By 1810, New York City's free blacks outnumbered its slaves by a ratio of seven to one.[5]

As such, after 1800 a free black community emerged more fully into the public sphere. Churches were central to that identity. In 1801, the African Methodists established a new institution, incorporating their chapel separately from New York's white-run Methodist society, albeit under white oversight. By the end of the decade, a black Episcopalian consciousness also emerged. After 1800, the African Society disappears from the records, but the first black Episcopalians, distinct from catechized slaves, began to meet on their own in 1809. A decade later they would form St. Philip's parish.

In 1807, a European visitor to New York assumed churches were the primary institutions in black life. Consequently, he described the black population in terms of religious affiliation. From the presence of Mother Zion, he assumed most blacks in the city were Methodist. The European traveler was mistaken, on two fronts. Many blacks attended no church:

African American laborers mingled with white workers in oyster bars and dance halls, to the consternation of white elites and blacks with middle-class aspirations. And increasingly, those who were churched were not exclusively Methodist, as Mother Zion was no longer the only game in town. In the two decades after the gradual manumission bill passed, blacks formed three more Methodist, three Episcopalian, two Presbyterian, and two Baptist congregations.[6]

But the European visitor was not wholly wrong. In terms of the public sphere, where individuals entered in order to expand rights and gain recognition of citizenship, the black churches were central.[7] And among all the churches, the Methodists generally, and Mother Zion specifically, stood out. In the two decades after emancipation, Mother Zion's leaders—joined by black Episcopalians who would form St. Philip's—promoted a vision of male middle-class respectability. They spoke the language of unity that the white churches had used before the Revolution, in this case invoking racial solidarity. But that vision of unity ironically separated them from whites, who remained suspicious of black abilities. That vision also provided less space for black women's leadership than did the white churches. Finally, it spoke in the name of, and for, laboring blacks who did not share the same assumptions about character building, morality, and cultural attainment that black churchmen invoked.

Separated, but Unequal: Continued White Control over Black Churches

In the first two decades of the nineteenth century, neither New York's African Methodists nor black Episcopalians completely separated from their white-run church establishments. Black Methodists increasingly disagreed over the level of connection to have with white Methodists, but their presence under white leadership indicates that unity in Christ remained a significant ideal. Black Episcopalians gained greater presence publicly, but their very existence remained connected to the white church. As New York's Episcopal Church, headed by Trinity, increasingly moved in a High Church direction, the importance of staying institutionally connected to the mother church remained.

In 1800, the black Methodists who had begun separate worship five years earlier built a new church at the corner of Church and Leonard Streets. The location lay west of their former location on Cross Street, physically distancing the group from the growing infamy of the rough laborers in the Five Points neighborhood. The following year, church leaders applied to city officials for incorporation as a distinct religious body, separate from the white church. This separate status did not grant the African Methodists full autonomy. The articles of incorporation provided that a white minister would regularly officiate at the black church. As no blacks had risen to the level of deacon, a white minister would also officiate when the congregation celebrated the sacraments of baptism or the Lord's Supper. For the next two decades, Zion, or the African chapel, as it was often called, would represent African Methodism, yet remain under the discipline of the New York Methodist society, with its white ministers.[8]

This intermediary status highlights the uneasy, anomalous place of Peter Williams in New York's Methodist churches, black and white, for Williams served as a founding trustee for Zion, and presented the articles of incorporation to the city. A well-known figure in the popular history of New York City, Williams is celebrated for his devout Methodism, political patriotism, and industriousness in business. Most historians champion him as a founding father of Mother Zion. Williams's relationship to that church is more complicated, however, and reveals the tensions within the black church community and its relationship to the white church.[9]

Upon gaining his freedom, Peter Williams left John Street's employ and set out on his own as a tobacconist. His business nearly went up in smoke when an anonymous arsonist attempted to set fire to his property. Williams discovered combustible items and firemaking tools outside his shop, which he reported and had posted in the newspaper. Although white assailants may have targeted Williams as an unwanted example of free black success, the paper did not mention Williams's race. The editors warned all citizens to be on the lookout for similar attacks on property. The simple lesson from the attempted arson was powerful enough to be circulated in other newspapers, outside New York.[10]

Shorn of context, the news item reveals Williams as an alert, even patriotic, businessman: this message may have been what Williams hoped to portray, and the message readers outside New York received. For New York City inhabitants in the 1790s, the racial dynamics of the event would have resonated more strongly. Arson had long been a favored tactic of slaves in colonial rebellions. The 1741 conspiracy, which elderly New Yorkers might have remembered in 1796, focused on mysterious fires. Further, mid-decade witnessed the influx of French refugee slaveholders from San Domingue, along with their human property. These Haitian slaves had just witnessed an open, successful rebellion. In this fevered environment, white fears ran high. In 1796, city officials posted watches to stop suspected arsons; no major conspiracies ever material-ized.[11] In such a setting, then, Williams proved exceptional. No friend of disorder, Williams served as a hardworking, observant businessman who preserved his own property, but also aligned with the existing order. In a decade that contained more silences than words from New York's blacks, Williams's actions stood out.

Peter Williams also remained distinct from the brotherhood of black men who founded the African Methodist church in New York. A regular Methodist class attendee from 1786 through 1796, Williams attended the lone black class that Jane Barsary had led; the stigma of slavery and anomaly of female leadership had kept many black men away from the white-run church in the 1780s. In 1796, when black leaders first began separate worship, Williams did not attend class number thirty-one, with James Varick and William Hamilton. Half of the members of class thirty-one left the white church that year. Instead, Williams attended class twenty-eight, which contained no prominent future leaders of Mother Zion, and from which fully two-thirds of the members remained with the white church the following year.[12]

To white Methodists, Williams represented ideal African American piety. Even after his service as sexton (and slave) ended, Williams and his wife continued to entertain white Methodist ministers who traveled through town. He also remained loyal to the Methodists as a denomi-nation: in one case he chided ex-Methodist minister Thomas Lyell for his unfaithfulness, when Lyell had gained more secure employment as a priest in the Episcopal Church.[13]

Peter Williams attempted to straddle black and white Methodist worlds that were splitting by 1800. Williams had experienced slavery, the upheaval of war, and female religious leadership. He worshiped with blacks and whites alike. Williams and his wife hosted not only white ministers, but also black leaders, for when Mother Zion's new leaders pushed for independence in the late 1810s, Williams hosted both groups in his home during their negotiations. When his wife died, Williams called for guests to call upon him "without distinction of colour." As such, Williams represented biracial Methodism, a belief that the church could connect both races in deep and pious worship.[14]

Fewer black Methodists emulated Williams's model of worship over time. Even Williams appears to have had no clear church home by the end of his life: while numerous histories assert that Williams gratefully remained at John Street his whole life, his name disappears from the class lists after 1796. Often black Methodists new to the city would start at John Street before going to the African church; such was the case of Isabella Van Wagenen, who would rename herself Sojourner Truth. But with the establishment of Mother Zion, the number of those who remained fully connected to biracial worship by staying at John Street dwindled.[15]

After 1803, John Street typically contained two or three black classes. Women numerically dominated these classes; the church recorder often listed two or three male members. And these women were older: when preacher Nathan Bangs inaugurated the new chapel at John Street in 1818 with a sermon, he championed the Methodist Church's efforts to evangelize blacks and to oppose slaveholding. Bangs briefly recognized the gallery to note the "sooty" faces of those blacks in attendance. He suggested that some had first heard the gospel message even before the previous chapel had been erected, forty years before. If Bangs based his statement on visual evidence, the blacks who remained at John Street were elderly. They were more likely to remain slaves. And as the class records reveal, they were women.[16]

While John Street and Peter and Molly Williams represented a declining, and mostly feminized, biracial religious environment among the Methodists, it was unknown in the city's other Methodist churches. In 1817, only two other white Methodist chapels—Duane and Forsyth Streets—had any black classes at all. By 1818, that was down to one, Forsyth Street, the second-oldest Methodist chapel in the city. Ninety percent of the city's black Methodists worshiped in the black churches. The average Methodist, white or black, had no communion with members of another race.[17]

One particular African Methodist's journey led to changes for New York's black Episcopalians. Peter Williams's son, Peter Williams Jr., joined Mother Zion as a new member in 1803, but within four years had become an Episcopalian. Scholars have surmised that the younger Williams had befriended Thomas Lyell, the Methodist preacher who sought more secure employment in the Episcopal Church. When Lyell left John Street Methodist for Christ Church Episcopal in 1804, the younger Peter may have followed him. If that was the case, Williams did not remain there long. The most numerous, visible group of black Episcopalians were not at Christ Church, but attached to Trinity Church, where they received religious instruction and worship on Sunday afternoons. If he indeed began at Christ Church, Williams appears to have made a quick transition to Trinity.[18]

In 1809, Trinity's blacks acquired a meeting place of their own. Fittingly, it was at the African Free School, which typified the complex relationship between Episcopalians, Federalists, and the black community. The school, a creation of the New York Manumission Society, had been connected indirectly to Trinity, as many elite Episcopalians, especially prominent statesmen, had taken the lead in promoting gradual manumission. In 1809, however, the NYMS had recently dismissed John Teasman, the black principal popular with the families who sent their children there. Even before Teasman's dismissal, black New Yorkers had increasingly searched for other schools to send their children. While many black families chafed at the paternalistic restrictions of the manumission society, black Episcopalians lived in the shadow of their patrons at Trinity Church. Their first steps toward independence were therefore limited. On a different level, education resonated strongly, especially with this group: as Episcopalians, the blacks who worshiped at the school valued formal liturgy, and thus literacy.[19]

Black Episcopalians nonetheless desired to worship under their own leaders, and petitioned the state diocesan convention that one of their members could undertake training to receive religious orders. The group presented four candidates; the convention chose Peter Williams. The following decade is largely silent on the group that would become St. Philip's Episcopal Church. The group moved twice before settling into a house of worship its members built. Williams served as a lay reader, which allowed him to lead services in the absence of an ordained priest. He received instruction from Trinity Church's John Henry Hobart, and in 1819 would lead the black Episcopalians into St. Philip's. From their inception, though, New York's black Episcopalians relied upon Trinity for patronage and protection, a living embodiment of the ideal of organic connectedness and unity. Although the younger Williams followed a different theological trajectory than his father, the two men shared a willingness to associate, and attempt community, with white coreligionists.[20]

In this, the Williamses were not unusual. With the exception of Baptist churches, which remained autonomous on the local level and thus allowed for de facto black control, many black churches in the early Republic began and remained a part of larger, white-dominated denominations. This was true even of Mother Zion through 1820. But while black Methodists and Presbyterians might count on northern allies who would promote abolition, black Episcopalians were part of a church whose hierarchy (and unity with southerners) tended to minimize any emphasis on racial equality. Further, other black Protestants could theoretically devise ways to secede from their white parent bodies, but the Episcopal Church's emphasis on religious order made such attempts nearly inconceivable.[21]

New York's Middle-Class Black Men Enter the Public Sphere

A decade after Philadelphia's Richard Allen and Absalom Jones entered the public sphere by writing pamphlets defending their community against unfounded charges, New York's black men took to the Republic of Letters. They represented a generational transition in black New York. Jupiter Hammon, an old man in the 1780s when he counseled piety and patience to New York's blacks, was dead. Peter Williams, now approaching sixty, had never learned to read or write. But William Hamilton was now in his thirties, having practiced rhetoric and argument for the past decade. And Williams's son, Peter Jr., had emerged as the NYMS African School's prized pupil, a new, young voice for antislavery reform. These men spearheaded the public processionals that celebrated the end of the Atlantic slave trade and the future end of slavery in New York, and called for greater emancipation and equality.

Some scholars have posited that African cultural connections bound together this fraternity of black leadership in the public arena. Others have focused on the common educational environment of the African Free Schools in New York and the Northeast generally.[22] In New York City, religious affiliation provided a striking connection between nearly all major participants. In the first public processions, most leading figures were Methodist, and nearly all either Methodist or Episcopalian.

The United States Constitution provided that Congress could not regulate the slave trade for twenty years. After much debate, a coalition of abolitionists and slaveholders in Congress passed laws to end the trade, to be effective on the New Year 1808.[23] Northern blacks took advantage of this legislation to plan their entrance into the public sphere. In December 1807, a committee of twelve black men met to plan the first public celebrations of the end of the Atlantic slave trade. Black Presbyterian John Teasman chaired the proceedings, but accompanying him were at least five men connected to Mother Zion, and another four to Trinity Episcopal. Peter Williams Jr., now aged twenty-seven, served as the group's secretary. Since these men "formed the nucleus of those who would become the intellectual, religious, political, and social leaders of early black New York," as scholar Robert Swan has argued, the black church appears as the primary connection among them.[24]

Black Methodists assumed the primary role in the first public displays celebrating the end of the slave trade, held on New Year's Day 1808. The African Methodist church on Leonard Street—then called Zion Chapel or the African Church—hosted the events. All of Mother Zion's leaders took part in the proceedings. Abraham Thompson, the oldest black minister, opened the morning service with prayer, and William Hamilton, Mother Zion's leading layman, directed two hymns. Exhorter Thomas Miller Sr., closed the morning events with prayer. In the afternoon service, June Scott, another senior preacher, prayed, and Hamilton led another hymn. James Varick, Mother Zion's most prominent minister, preached a sermon and closed with prayer that afternoon.[25]

The only non-Methodist speaker at the event had Methodist roots. Peter Williams Jr. had entered Mother Zion as a new member only five years before, but now stood as the lone example of ecumenical, nonsectarian cooperation among black men. Now a black Episcopalian with as yet no clear congregational home, he delivered an address in the name of all sons of Africa. Black Methodists did not reach far beyond their community, keeping much of the event within their denomination.

African Methodist Henry Sipkins, like Williams a recent graduate of the African School, provided a short introduction. In Sipkins and Williams, New York's black leaders placed youth at the heart of their ceremonies. Sipkins's introductory oration, verbose, florid, and soaring, was nonetheless an excellent concise model of elaborate prose. Sipkins called for thanksgiving at the slave trade's end, but also for a renewed hope that the injustices slavery wrought would now be more clearly seen and destroyed.[26]

Peter Williams's address was even more elaborate than Sipkins's. Williams contrasted an Edenic vision of Africa as a place of "simplicity, innocence, and contentment," with the horrors of the slave trade, which he deemed "the unnatural monster inflict[ing] gross evils on the human race." Williams's telling reduced naïve Africans to simple victims, drawn into ever-expanding cycles of war and kidnapping. He urged his listeners to imagine fields "bedewed with blood" and "mangled carcasses," as well as the sorrows of seeing families and friends forever ripped apart. Williams then called for rejoicing at the cessation of such horrors. Although he invoked the American Revolution's ideals, he spent more time praising the British abolitionists John Woolman, Anthony Benezet, and William Wilberforce for their efforts across the Atlantic. Williams closed with a call for his audience to be worthy of the liberty for which their white allies fought. In "a steady and upright deportment" and in "strict obedience and respect to the laws of the land," blacks would shield their white benefactors from criticism, and themselves be immune from attack from their opponents. Williams opened his piece with moral indignation, but concluded it with calls for moral conduct.[27]

The published proceedings included testimonials from white men as to Williams's identity. All reflected the religious connections to race and reform in New York. Methodists and Episcopalians again revealed their influences on the free black community: the first two signees were Benjamin Moore, current bishop at Trinity, and Methodist minister Ezekiel Cooper. Accompanying the two clergymen were John Murray Jr. and William Slocum, Quakers who had taken an active role in the African School. White approval served to validate black ability. By including white patrons in the certification, the participants demonstrated no desire for full separation by race, but attempts at inclusion in finding a place in the public sphere.[28]

The following year the celebrations on the end of the slave trade expanded, but also showed signs of strain. The black men moved their ceremonies to January 2 to avoid conflict with white revelry, a clear sign they were not fully welcome in the city streets. Blacks held three different celebrations, representing three different institutions. Such reflected perhaps greater participation than before, but also the beginning of fissures or differences between black leaders.[29]

Most distinct of the three were the celebrations of the Wilberforce Philanthropic Association. The procession to the Lyceum on Warren Street included badges and banners worthy of a political rally, fitting trappings for the oration delivered there. Joseph Sidney's speech skipped the horrors of the slave trade, for he explained that numerous other orators had thoroughly covered the topic. Instead Sidney focused on the horrors of Democratic-Republican rule, as Jefferson's Embargo Act of 1807 had severely damaged the city's commerce. Sidney replaced the idea of an Edenic Africa with an Edenic era of Federalist rule, and called his listeners to support the embattled Federalists with their votes.[30]

The Wilberforce Association appears to have been not only explicitly Federalist in politics, but largely Anglican in religious makeup. Two-thirds of the standing committee, as well as Sidney, had either married or baptized children at Trinity Church. This mostly younger generation of Anglican blacks was less conciliatory than the African Society of the previous decade, but still closely connected to white benefactors, in this case the Federalists. The young Peter Williams, having grown up Methodist, would thus represent a shift in Anglicanism, for he later steered other black Episcopalians away from deferential Federalism toward different expressions of reform, including, eventually, immediate abolition.[31]

In contrast with the Wilberforce Association, the African Methodist Church and African Society for Mutual Relief held celebrations similar in tone to each other. At the church, Henry Sipkins continued in the train that Peter Williams had established the year before, intoning a florid address that contrasted the "blissful" and "innocent" Africans, precontact, with the evils of the slave trade. Sipkins praised a series of British abolitionists: Quakers John Woolman, Anthony Benezet, and William Dillwyn, and Anglican Granville Sharp. In his address for the relief society, held at the Universalist Church, African Methodist William Hamilton briefly condemned the trade, noting that the term "fiend" was too sacred a name for the "man-stealers" who pillaged the African coast. He also praised the members of the New York Manumission Society, who helped to pay the African School's debts from their own funds.[32]

Hamilton paused to defend black mental facilities. He extolled Peter Williams and Henry Sipkins for their addresses at the previous year's celebration, praising them as excellent models of rhetoric and reason. Hamilton favorably compared their work to Phillis Wheatley's poems, which he deemed as limited. Hamilton's emphasis on literary achievement would mark future black attempts at uplift, paralleling their middle-class aspirations.[33]

All celebrants expressed gratitude to white benefactors. Sipkins's and Hamilton's unwillingness to engage in Federalist electioneering, however, suggests that many African Methodists had distanced themselves from too close an identification with the NYMS and its Federalist Episcopalian leadership. By this time, the Manumission Society's restrictions on black parents and the firing of a black principal had led to greater discontent among New York's African Americans. In fact, John Teasman, a mentor for Sipkins and Hamilton in the previous year's celebration, was active in New York's Democratic-Republican Party, suggesting perhaps a new model for black political action divorced from the deferential demands of Federalism.

Hamilton's address marked a shift in the black community, for it inaugurated a new black-run institution, the first in New York not devoted explicitly to religious purposes. Given its name, the New York African Society for Mutual Relief (NYASMR) appears to be a source of benevolence for the poor. But the NYASMR turned the concept of benevolence on its head, highlighting the bourgeois and productive aims of its founders. Instead of emphasizing charity to the worthy poor, it emphasized fraternal bonds to the productive young men who joined it.

Formed in 1808, the African Society for Mutual Relief first met in a black school on Rose Street. As with the first slave trade abolition celebrations, the society appeared to be a nearly completely Methodist undertaking. William Hamilton served as the institution's first president, Henry Sipkins as secretary, and James Varick as chaplain. The Reverend Miller (whether Thomas or William, unknown, but Methodist in either case) offered a closing prayer at one of the early meetings. The biggest exception to this Methodist dominance, as with the 1808 celebrations, was Peter Williams Jr., now Episcopalian, who replaced Presbyterian John Teasman as the society's vice president in 1809.[34]

The New York African Society for Mutual Relief limited its membership to fifty men between the ages of twenty-one and forty, seeking only those individuals at their physical and productive peaks. The main aim of the society was to establish a fund to temporarily aid unemployed or sick members, or for dead members' widows and orphans. The society required a one-hundred-dollar initial fee and subsequent dues of twenty-five cents per month. Members had to pay into the fund for a year before applying for aid; widows would receive a modest fifteen-dollar death benefit and twenty-dollar annual pension. The initial fee and subsequent dues would necessarily have limited participants to only the wealthiest blacks in New York; historian Robert Swan has calculated that the initiation fee represented a half year's earnings for a typical laborer. Society members expected the resulting fund of five thousand dollars, representing hundred-dollar initiation fees from fifty members, to be enough to last in perpetuity.[35]

Black Methodists soon established other funds that aided blacks who were not as well-off as those in the NYASMR, but who nonetheless had some property to defend, or dependents for whom to provide. In 1810, New York blacks founded a marine fund to aid orphans and the poor whose male relatives had been killed while working in the maritime industries. The group's constitution explicitly noted that "the elder ministers of the African Zion Church in this city" would preside over and approve the election of the fund's officers and trustees. Mother Zion's ministers June Scott and Abraham Thompson signed the charter constitution of the organization in 1810.[36]

In public processions and in expressions of benevolence, black men held much in common. They generally stressed the unity of their communities and their solidarity with white reformers, including their benefactors in the New York Manumission Society. All recognized the evils of the slave trade, and promoted black achievement and morality as a cure for their community's ills. All were propertied, to some degree, and all were men. Most were Methodist, all were churched. Despite the unity that they invoked, this did place them in a minority in their churches and community.[37]

White Attacks on Black Masculinity

Despite their achievements, the black men involved in public processions and displays of benevolence faced an uphill battle to establish themselves in New York City. Their white coreligionists, men one might expect to have greater sympathy than the typical New Yorker, looked upon them with suspicion. White Methodists and Episcopalians considered the typical black to be dependent, unworthy, immoral, impoverished, enslaved, or feminized. Consequently the black response heightened independent, worthy, moral, and male conduct.

Philip Arcularius, a trustee and member of John Street Methodist Church, was also a Republican politician. A German immigrant, Arcularius arrived in New York shortly before the Revolution. According to family records, Arcularius had labored as a master baker during the war, but worked with his stepfather as a tanner thereafter. As a Republican he was committed to retrenchment and frugality in government expenditures, including relief to the poor. When Republicans swept into office in New York City in 1800, they awarded Arcularius the position of almshouse superintendent.[38]

In October 1805, in the wake of a yellow fever epidemic that killed hundreds, Arcularius reported to the city council on three classes of "improper objects of public charity." The first group consisted simply of "imposters," those who presented themselves as needy to swindle the public funds. The second group consisted of New York City's unofficial residents, "of whom the free Blacks, make a Considerable part." Arcularius suggested that such individuals be returned to their places of legal residence, although he noted that it must be soon, for the city could not justly undertake deportation during the winter. The third group consisted of wives and children of mariners gone to sea, and left without support.[39]

Other than his comment on free blacks, Arcularius expressed a traditional stance toward treating poverty, similar to what the Widows' Society women advocated. Arcularius suggested that families who received aid must bind their children to employment. The superintendent promoted the old idea of forcibly imprisoning society's debtors. Arcularius also embraced older notions of city citizenship in attempting to deport nonresidents. He apparently did not know that eighteenth-century city officials had already deemed it impossible to deport most of the city's poor to their former residences.[40] Almshouse employees could not keep track of the nonresidents among the thousands who received relief, and could not determine the places of origin for the many poor who moved regularly. Finally, Arcularius revealed that he believed women should receive aid, but not if their husbands refused to support them. Male guardians held primary responsibility to care for their wives and children.

Arcularius only briefly mentioned race, for he labeled most free blacks as nonresidents and thus ineligible for aid. As almshouse commissioner, Arcularius might have encountered many impoverished blacks, for they numbered among the poorest in the city. Blacks, however, generally avoided institutional forms of poor relief and preferred to rely upon mutual assistance, as they were consistently underrepresented on the almshouse rolls. The few blacks whom Arcularius saw, and to whom he wished to deny further service, therefore did not typify the black community.[41]

Arcularius linked race and poverty through the medium of residency, because he considered most free blacks to be nonresidents. By 1805, Arcularius apparently had little contact with blacks in his church. As a Methodist trustee, Arcularius should have seen many blacks, for among New York City Methodists, blacks comprised about one-fifth of the church's population, double that of the city population as a whole. As a member of John Street Church, however, Arcularius perceived the black population in a skewed manner. In the lower wards, slavery kept a hold on the black population. City slaves lived with or near their wealthy masters. The city's wealthiest citizens congregated in the older sections of the city.[42] Free blacks, on the other hand, typically lived to the north, in the same wards where laboring whites congregated in ramshackle housing. Not legal residents of the city, transients and new emigrants failed to qualify for aid under Arcularius's assumptions.

When Arcularius filed his report, many free blacks were indeed nonresidents in a legal sense. Before the 1799 law established gradual emancipation in New York, few city residents manumitted their slaves. Thus most free blacks in New York City had recently arrived, some from New England, most others from the Upper South. As recent arrivals to the city, these free blacks could not claim legal residency. Soon Arcularius's assumption would be incorrect, however, for faced with the prospect of defiant or runaway slaves, New York slaveowners increasingly freed their human property ahead of schedule.[43] With increasing numbers, free blacks gained a critical mass in forming new and lasting institutions.

A gender dynamic shaped Arcularius's perceptions of black slavery and black poverty. Arcularius targeted free blacks who used public relief, not slaves whose masters provided their board. Female slaves outnumbered the male in every ward but one. Further, the rate of female manumissions lagged far behind the male. Largely employed in domestic service, black women had fewer cash-earning opportunities to purchase their own freedom than black men who worked in trades or as maritime laborers, and they worked in occupations where whites still desired help and saw slaves as prestigious objects.[44] Arcularius's offhand comment directed at the free black community thus hit black men hardest.

Others shared Arcularius's suspicion toward free blacks. Federalist politician and Trinity vestryman John Jay, a founding member of New York's Manumission Society, expressed private reservations about the fitness of the black community. In 1805, upon answering an inquiry about the African Free School, Jay worried that the school's graduates would not get proper supervision after they completed their studies. "To me it appears important," Jay wrote, "that they not be left entirely either to their parents or to themselves, it being difficult to give them good morals, manners, or habits in any other way than by placing them under the care and direction of persons better qualified for those purposes than their parents generally are." Jay suggested that such graduates be bound in trades, or placed in service in "decent families," to counteract the baneful influence of their own relatives.[45]

For Arcularius, blacks were either slaves or shiftless nonresidents; for Jay, free blacks practiced bad morals and habits. Arcularius's and Jay's own churches welcomed blacks to worship, yet they saw fewer blacks after 1800, with increasingly segregated worship; instead the blacks in the city they viewed did not exhibit acceptable behavior. Hence both men remained skeptical about free blacks' progress, and both suggested restrictions—upon movement, on behavior, toward bound labor—to adequately mold their charges.

Black Methodists and Episcopalians walked a delicate line. They were minorities of a minority: most New Yorkers were not black, and scorned black elites' calls for uplift, and most blacks in New York were not churched, and despised black leaders' attempts to uplift them. In this climate, the processions and relief organizations gain greater clarity. The language of black unity in celebrations masked attempts to preserve status. Issues of status even concerned members of the New York African Society for Mutual Relief. Society members were critical of chimney sweeps, for that profession often subjected children to dangerous work conditions. As orators like William Hamilton implied, children were to receive classical educations, and not toil in cramped and hazardous places. The sweeps, however, were among the most visible black laborers in New York, and could earn a considerable income with hard work. Perhaps unsurprisingly, no sweeps joined the NYASMR.[46]

Quiet Strength: Women in the Black Church

The black men who joined churches and led benevolent societies were doubly exceptional. First, despite being the public face for the black community, these men represented a small minority of that community. And second, despite being the public faces of their churches, these men constituted a minority even in there. In terms of attendance, the black church was a woman's church.

In the colonial and Revolutionary eras, Africans in the church were far more likely to be women than men. Black Episcopalian and Methodist women attended their churches in greater numbers than did white women, at least when one compares male-female ratios of church attendance. In both black groups, women brought and kept men in the church. But despite their preponderance in bringing men to church and dominating the church numerically, women did not have a place in the emerging black public community. The men connected to churchwomen were also men attracted to middle-class values and concerned with uplift, for they had others to provide for.

According to Benjamin Moore's 1801 communicant list, Trinity's forty blacks comprised 10 percent of all communicants, a number roughly proportional to the African American population in the city at large. Before the Revolution, Samuel Auchmuty reported thirty adult blacks regularly appearing for catechetical instruction on Sunday afternoons, so the numbers reflect a modest growth, albeit not in line with that of the city as a whole.[47]

In the colonial era, female slaves had always been more likely to receive Anglican catechization. Trinity's first catechist, Elias Neau, recorded twenty-eight women and eighteen men attending his lessons in 1705, and fifty-eight women compared to forty-two men in 1707.[48] By the turn of the nineteenth century, with church attendance increasingly voluntary, black Episcopalianism had become even more a woman's affair. Bishop

Benjamin Moore recorded only eleven men as communicants, to twenty-nine women. Men represented just over a quarter of all Anglican blacks. Almost all black men came to church with family attachments. Eight of the eleven men shared a surname with a female on the list, suggesting that wives brought their husbands into the church, or that most black men at Trinity were there with family ties. In general, black Anglicans probably attended as families to a greater degree than their white coreligionists. Just over half of Trinity's blacks (twenty-one of forty, or 53 percent) share a surname with another black.[49]

Later baptismal records from St. Philip's, which began in 1819, confirm this women's involvement. Women probably formed a significant numerical majority in the black Episcopal Church, as they did in almost every antebellum house of worship, black or white. Of the adult baptisms recorded between 1819 and 1829, fifty-five of sixty-six individuals—over 80 percent—were female. Few men joined the church unless they had grown up in the church.[50] The strongest indicator of female religious activity comes indirectly through those same baptismal lists. Almost all parents appear as couples. Out of more than 170 baptisms, only 13 women presented a child for baptism alone. The men who would later serve in the vestry and spearhead black reform movements appeared at the baptismal font as fathers and husbands. Almost without exception the leading men in business and church affairs married women in the church, continuing the pattern begun in the late colonial period at Trinity. The family provided the main base from which the church's leaders emerged.[51]

Strikingly, black women also dominated among the city's early Methodists. Only three black men appeared on the first surviving Methodist class lists in 1785. Ten years later, the number of black men on the rolls increased to forty, but men still comprised less than one-third of all black Methodists at this 1795 high-water mark. Some scholars have suggested that this reticence lay in the racism inherent in the white church structures.[52] While early Methodists separated white men and women, they kept black men and women, and slave and free, together. In the church, there may have been no difference between male and female, slave and free, but only free black men experienced a negative reality as the consequence of that ideal, in being grouped with women, and slaves, ostensibly lower in status than they.

As with black Episcopalians, many of the black men who began to attend Methodist classes in greater numbers probably did so through the influence of a female relative. According to the 1792 class lists, over 40 percent of the men shared a last name with a black woman on the class lists. By contrast, the numbers of black men who shared surnames with other black men, and black women who shared surnames with other blacks, male or female, ranged from 19 to 29 percent. As the number of men increased, so did the proportion that shared family names with female Methodists. In 1795, 55 percent of the men had a last name identical to a black woman in the class lists, compared to 30 percent who shared a surname with another man. In contrast, just over one-quarter of the women shared a name with a man, and one-third shared with another woman. In 1796, the year after black men left to worship at Cross Street, 48 percent of the men still had identical surnames with a woman in the class lists, whereas less than one-third of the black women shared a name with another black woman or man.[53]

In 1796, when James Varick and William Hamilton organized separate services for blacks, the number of black men involved in the white-run classes decreased to less than one-quarter of all blacks. Fewer black women attended these new meetings, or at least fewer attended them to the exclusion of their older commitments to the white-run church. Some female reticence may have been due to the bonds of slavery. Throughout the city, female slaves outnumbered the male. Although manumissions accelerated, women were less likely to be freed, in part because male slaves could more easily acquire employment to purchase their freedom. Further, while slavery declined in artisanal and laboring positions, it remained strong for domestic service, where most women were employed. While many white masters may have not minded their female slaves getting religion, many more would have balked had their slaves attended a church whose trustees were limited to those of the African race, and which barred slaveholders from membership, as Mother Zion did.[54]

African Methodist minister George White's memoir closes with a funeral sermon and an account of the death of Mary Henery. She was only twenty when she died in October 1809, a slave to the Post family in New York. Henery had been converted just two years before her death, and had attained sanctification the previous year at a Croton Camp Meeting that White conducted. George White thought little of the behavior of most enslaved blacks, as he remarked that Henery was "modest, decent, sober, and diligent; in short, she possessed all the embellishments of the most chaste female character, to a degree seldom equaled, especially by those in a state of slavery." White added, however, that some of Mary's good behavior might have been attributed to her master and mistress for

Figure 5.2. James Varick, first bishop of the African
Methodist Episcopal Zion Church. (Reproduced with
permission from the Methodist Collections at Drew
University.)

their "indulgence" and "kindness" to her in both health and sickness. They
had, after all, allowed her to attend camp and class meetings. Henery's
example induced her father to join the church after her death, and greatly
affected her mistress and mistress's son. White's funeral sermon presented
the standard consolation that, although Methodists could lament the loss
of one so true in the faith, they could rejoice that they, too, could hold the
hope of eternal life that Mary Henery would certainly enjoy.[55]

Unlike many of his brethren in the black church, George White spoke
little about slavery or political rights in his narrative. In Mary Henery,
he chose a congregant who embodied the ideas that black religious

involvement was passive, resigned to slavery and service, and apolitical. While black men increasingly gained freedom, the typical black woman remained a slave, perhaps because her work lay outside a cash economy, making the purchase of her freedom more difficult. The association of black women with the church therefore associated slavery with the church. As such, to church leaders like James Varick, only an explicitly free church, run by men, would convey the proper image to the outside world.[56]

The place of women within the black church thus held a couple of ramifications for the future development of that church. First, because women represented enslavement and passivity, the black men who led the church assumed a greater public presence to counter or minimize any negative associations. However, the men who led the church were sons and husbands of the women who numerically dominated. They were thus family men, connected by kinship and obligation to others. They depended upon proper behavior—industriousness, frugality, sobriety—to provide for their families. So while black churchmen assumed a strong presence to counter negative assumptions about their masculinity, their association with women family members meant their public presence would necessarily tend toward a middle-class identity.

Male black church leaders projected status and strength to minimize their association with slavery and with feminized leadership. At Mother Zion, leaders turned Methodist gender identity on its head. White Methodists assigned their ministers to lead women's classes, offering women a prominence of place and the spiritual protection of their most esteemed leaders. In contrast, the African chapel's preachers, deacons, and exhorters led the male classes, establishing a fraternity of male leadership. Lay ministers James Varick, Samuel Pointier, George White, Abraham Thompson, and June Scott all led male classes, leaving female prayers and devotions to less prominent men.[57]

The black-run church appears to have defeated some of the associations of feminization or enslavement that apparently plagued perceptions of white-run Methodism. Under white leadership, black male members lagged. But once African Methodists established their own chapel, the situation adjusted. One-third of all incoming members at the African chapel in its first years, between 1802 to 1804, were male (32 of 100). This gender ratio was comparable to white Methodist figures, and represented significantly more black men entering the church than the previous two decades under white control.[58]

Conclusions

African Americans rarely occupied New York's public sphere, often appearing only at the first of the year to publish their orations and ceremonies on the slave trade's end. Even these modest steps faced opposition. After the first year, blacks who celebrated the end of the slave trade moved their ceremonies to January 2 to avoid white antagonism; they would later do the same regarding the end of slavery in New York, moving their events from July 4 to July 5. The Wilberforce Association eliminated its processional in 1809 ostensibly because of the large, enthusiastic crowd, but given that group's Federalist message and black leadership, the crowd might easily have mixed hostile with friendly faces. City officials ominously warned blacks celebrating the NYASMR's anniversary that they could not guarantee the safety of the participants. And, over time, whites hostile to any black improvement would mock the celebrations with satirical, racist taunts in their own publications.[59]

The churchmen behind these celebrations did not have complete autonomy in their own churches. The home of many black leaders, Mother Zion submitted to regular white oversight as Methodist clergy regularly oversaw services and performed sacraments for the African Methodists. Black Episcopalians waited a decade for that privilege, having a white layman officiate their services until at least 1810. They would wait, uneasily, for a priest of their own for more than another decade.

White New Yorkers' racism, and white churchmen's strictures on black churches, shaped the way black leaders presented themselves. African New Yorkers' colonial-era celebrations regularly featured women; the church records suggest that the pews at Mother Zion, and at the African Free School where black Episcopalians worshiped, were dominated by women. Working-class blacks were prominent in oyster houses and dance halls, and black laborers swept chimneys, peddled goods, and worked at the docks. Black leaders' presentation of their churches, parades, and assemblies in the first decades after 1800—as male and middle-class—did not reflect a full community. Rather, a group of black male leaders within the church enhanced their status and established connections with other black men throughout the city.[60]

White women's participation in benevolent societies had affirmed a holistic vision of social cohesion, while in similar roles black men broke with that vision. Like white women's benevolent organizations, black men promoted signs of unity, for their societies and processions mirrored the same civic ideals proclaimed in the white churches. But their place in the public sphere signified a widening fissure over race in both church and society. Whereas white women appeared representing the elite men who supported them, black men appeared independently, without masters or sponsors. And they did so affiliated with church bodies comprised solely of other blacks. The appearance of black benevolent societies paved the way for the independent black church during the 1810s, and the continued white reaction to that church in the following decades.

The city's growth increased the social strains that led to the introduction of elite women and black men into the public sphere. As economic struggles continued in the century's second decade, church members clashed over disputes ostensibly framed in theological terms. These ecclesiastical battles mirrored conflicts in other denominations nationwide. But in New York the causes behind each struggle had local and social roots, tied to the city's growing pains. These battles ultimately led to a privatization of church life, in which local experience washed away the colonial vision of a larger churched society.

6 / Preacher Power: Congregational Political Struggles as Social Conflicts, 1810–1830

In his journal, Francis Asbury recorded that delegates to the 1812 Methodist General Conference, held in New York, hotly debated the issue of elder ordination. Some participants disputed the bishop's exclusive right to appoint all elders. Others critiqued the promotion of local ministers, who had not displayed the dedication of itinerants, to any elder positions. Ultimately the conference maintained the status quo, and upheld the bishop's right to appoint all elders, including local preachers. That evening Asbury ate dinner with seventeen ministers, some of whom had fought for the losing side. Asbury commented, "We should thank God we are not at war with each other, as are the Episcopalians, with the pen and the press as their weapons of warfare."[1] A great pamphlet war had engulfed New York's Episcopalians, dominating events at Trinity Church.

But Methodist harmony proved short-lived. By decade's end, Asbury was dead, and the New York Methodist society suffered a schism. This conflict among whites contributed to the departure of the city's African Methodists, who achieved denominational independence in 1822. Only black Episcopalians escaped sectarian conflict during this decade, for they secured patronage from Trinity's High Church leaders to form St. Philip's parish in 1819.

The conflicts in New York's churches paralleled church conflicts nationally. Some historians attribute such religious battles to the effects of the American Revolution, noting that political struggles wracked religious societies.[2] While the Revolution contributed to the proliferation of pamphlet wars and denominational splits, within the city social tensions exacerbated by expansive urban growth played a greater role. Those tensions shattered the ideal of unity that leaders within the churches had advocated.

During the 1810s, New York's economic fortunes swung from growth to recession. A disastrous embargo and a botched war hampered New York's economy through mid-decade; postwar growth slammed to a halt with the Panic of 1819 as overextended banks and businesses failed nationwide. New York City's overall population continued to grow, however, adding thirty thousand individuals between 1810 and 1820. Impoverished foreign immigrants and rural refugees often settled in the city seeking charity. In the severe winter of 1817, the city almshouse provided aid for fifteen thousand people, or one in every seven residents. By 1820, the city's almshouse expenditures had doubled from its 1800 levels, to over $100,000 of the city's budget. Receiving little public assistance, many free blacks left town, and the city's black population declined, even though manumission rates decreased and those remaining slaves were compelled to stay.[3]

Opportunity accompanied the city's growing pains, as social elites pooled their physical and spiritual capital to promote improvements. During the 1820s, private investors joined with New York State to undertake the most audacious economic project in the country to date: the construction of a canal to link the eastern seaboard with the Great Lakes interior. Such grand aspirations matched equally grandiose attempts among churchmen to convert the entire society. Evangelical churches, particularly, supported aggressive missionary efforts. These visions, however, met fierce internal resistance. This context of social opportunity mixed with social unrest frames the ecclesiastical conflicts that wrenched apart the churches.[4]

Asbury described an Episcopalian pamphlet war over the appointment of an assistant bishop. Although apparently trivial, the fierce and wide-ranging debate revealed deeper root concerns. In 1811, as Bishop Benjamin Moore's health failed, New York Episcopalian leaders nominated Trinity assistant minister John Henry Hobart to serve as Moore's assistant. Hobart's Trinity colleague, Cave Jones, published a pamphlet objecting to Hobart's election. Jones wrote that he did not object to Hobart's qualifications, but to his character, which he labeled as small-minded and vindictive. Jones advocated a more experienced, better-tempered, and less partisan candidate for assistant bishop than Hobart.[5]

Trinity's vestry censured Jones for publicly voicing his complaints, and John Henry Hobart ascended to the position of assistant bishop

Figure 6.1. John Henry Hobart, electrifying champion of a renewed High Church position. (From Morgan Dix, *History of Trinity Church*, vol. 3 [1905].)

on May 29, 1811. Hobart then organized a vestry meeting, and subsequent council of ministers, to fire Jones. Bishop Moore heard the case in November 1811, and released Jones from his contract with Trinity. Jones refused to resign, and published another pamphlet that questioned Moore's authority. Jones argued that, since Samuel Provoost was still alive, Benjamin Moore was effectively an assistant bishop, with no right to hold termination hearings. Ignoring his retirement, Provoost jumped into the controversy, and wrote Jones a letter counseling him to disregard his dismissal.[6]

Rejecting Hobart's actions as punitive, some parishioners took Jones's side. From the summer of 1811 to the spring of 1812, Episcopal clergy and laity held a flurry of public meetings and penned scores of pamphlets. In April 1812, Jones's legal counselors agreed to arbitration with Trinity's vestry to settle the matter. The following October, New York's Supreme Court heard the case. The court upheld Jones's termination but awarded him $7,500 plus his salary through his dismissal date on November 5, 1811.[7]

During these events, pamphleteers debated a range of issues related to the location of authority in the church. They debated who was truly bishop; the relationship between Trinity, its chapels, and the city's other Episcopal churches; the right of parishioners to protest clerical actions or clergy to hold termination meetings; and the efficacy of Hobart's own ordination.[8] To modern sensibilities, the voluminous exchanges seem a tempest in a teapot, for many concern legalistic details over contracts, elections, and theological phrases. Indeed, church historians have dismissed the Hobart-Jones dispute as a mere conflict of personality.[9] But the battles reveal larger divisions over social privilege and clerical control in the church.

Hobart led Episcopal scholars in formulating a High Church theology, which championed Episcopalian superiority and separation from other Protestant denominations. In the early nineteenth century, High Church theology encountered a unique historical context. The American Revolution irrevocably severed ties between church and state. The church thus rejected all trappings of establishment, and instead attempted to act as a sacramental haven in a lost world. Hobart's vision broke with the eighteenth-century practice that allowed leading laity to largely run the church. In return, the church made few claims on the secular world in which the laity worked and lived. Although politically quietist, the High Church vision demanded that the laity eschew social activities that polluted the apostolic church's purity. High Church clergy specifically denounced ecumenical missions, because they entailed cooperation with other denominations deemed impure.[10]

Hobart's theology carried social ramifications, for groups in the Jones case took sides based upon their reactions to the High Church platform. Most clergy supported Hobart. Clergymen comprised nearly half of the witnesses for Hobart in his court case. These included Thomas Lyell, rector of Christ Church, whose Methodist background did not prevent him from taking an anti-Methodist High Church position. Trinity's notable exception, Abraham Beach, was an older minister who had served under Provoost during the 1780s.[11]

Hobart also garnered much female support. Jones's lawyers asked witnesses to provide the names of pro- and anti-Hobart congregants. No witness recalled a female congregant supporting Jones, whereas half of Hobart's known supporters were women. Peter Augustus Jay wrote that a majority of Trinity's rank-and-file congregants refused to hear Jones preach. According to the communicant lists, women dominated among the disgruntled congregants. Hobart's High Church vision attracted pious women, including Elizabeth Seton, to a deeper faith. Seton had praised Hobart's sermons, and grumbled about Jones's, well before any conflict had surfaced.[12]

By contrast, as a forceful proponent of a robust High Church theology, Hobart may have unwittingly discouraged male membership. Wealthy and prominent Episcopalian men led the opposition to Hobart. One-quarter of the men who signed public resolutions supporting Jones also appeared on Edward Pessen's list of the two hundred wealthiest New Yorkers in 1828, with property assessments of at least fifty thousand dollars. Many belonged to Episcopal congregations with more evangelical leanings than High Church Trinity. For example, Peter G. Stuyvesant helped found St. Mark's, the city's second Episcopal Church incorporated separately from Trinity. Stuyvesant's family was one of the city's oldest, most distinguished, and wealthiest, and he owned vast tracts of land just north of town. Another Jones supporter and prominent non-Trinity Episcopalian vestryman, Nicholas Fish, had married Stuyvesant's sister Elizabeth and also held great wealth in real estate.[13]

Other anti-Hobart partisans served on Trinity's vestry in the 1780s and 1790s, when the connections between a compliant clergy and strong laity had been secure. These included Thomas Farmar and James Farquhar, who organized a rally on Jones's behalf, and John Jay, who wrote a public letter supporting Jones. Their working relationship with Samuel Provoost differed enormously from their dealings with Hobart. Provoost became Trinity's rector because he was the only Whig priest in post-Revolutionary New York, a position that won him lay support. Kinship networks connected Provoost, the son of a prominent merchant, to many of his congregants, including Jay. And he had offered theologically orthodox and emotionally unchallenging sermons. From old and established Episcopal families, many leading laymen preferred Provoost's easygoing brand of authority.[14]

Although charged with protecting the church's interests, Trinity's vestry suffered divided loyalties and only tepidly supported Hobart as assistant bishop. After Frederick de Peyster and Francis Dominick signed the petition on Jones's behalf, both lost in the vestry elections of 1812. Garrit H. Van Wagenen testified on Jones's behalf at the trial, and ended his term of service in 1812. Other vestry members remained neutral in their sympathies, unwilling to wholly support Hobart. John Jay's son, Peter Augustus Jay, wrote to his father that he believed Jones should not be "sacrificed to Hobart's resentment." And although Rufus King testified on Hobart's behalf, his fastidious legalistic testimony indicated a judiciously moderate position. Throughout the controversy, King remained friends with Jones, and fulfilled his duty to dismiss Jones only with great reluctance. King's patronage later secured Jones employment as a naval chaplain in Brooklyn.[15]

After the Jones case receded, another pamphlet battle renewed the social fissures opened in the Hobart-Jones controversy. The issue concerned Episcopalian involvement in evangelical reform societies. After 1800, Protestants of differing denominations joined together to organize benevolent societies. They sought to evangelize the nation's large unchurched populace. Such societies promoted ostensibly nondenominational ways for Christians to unite in action. Bible societies printed and distributed copies of the scriptures. Tract societies disseminated religious and moral reading materials to schools, churches, and interested individuals. Sunday School and educational societies funded ministers and teachers, and provided them with religious instructional materials. These benevolent societies began as local chapters, but in the 1810s, proponents called for national organizations to centralize their scattered efforts.[16]

In 1816, the American Bible Society (ABS) formed, uniting disparate state-level Bible societies in a national organization based in New York City. New York had become America's publishing center, and most ABS board members resided in or near the city. Trinity vestryman Peter Jay praised the revived Protestant unity that the organization promised:

> When we consider the multiplied divisions which exist in this extensive country; the animosities of political parties, the multitude of our religious sects, the local interests and jealousies, that have so often impeded or defeated the most salutary undertakings, we have reason to be astonished at the perfect unanimity, which has, in this instance, prevailed among delegates from widely distant parts of the union, and of various political and religious denominations.

Jay argued that the ABS's central tenet, distributing "the Holy Scriptures without note or comment," could soothe the nation's many political and religious divisions. Distributing "the Holy Scriptures without note or comment" would create a new unity.[17]

Hobart supported evangelization efforts only if they remained explicitly Anglican. He established the Bible and Common Prayer Book Society in 1809, which distributed the standard Episcopalian church liturgy with the Bible. In a message to New York's Episcopalians, Hobart opposed his laity's participation in the ABS. He argued that support for the ABS drew limited funds away from his denomination's missionary efforts. Further, ABS support indirectly aided anti-Episcopalian Presbyterians and Congregationalists, who joined the society in far greater numbers.[18]

William Jay replied to Hobart's open letter with his own public response. Son of John and brother of Peter, William lived outside the city and attended a parish in Bedford that his family long patronized. In a scornful pamphlet, Jay mocked Hobart's contention that Episcopalians needed the Book of Common Prayer, a liturgical order of worship, to interpret divine Scripture. He argued further that support for the Episcopalian society diluted the value of every dollar donated, for the cost of including prayer books with Bibles effectively cut donations in half.[19]

As in the Jones case, pamphlet skirmishes continued into the 1820s. As in the Jones controversy, the rhetoric turned personal and ugly. But unlike the Jones case, Hobart's adversaries did not withdraw from the church, and Hobart could not simply expel them. Both sides claimed victory, and ultimately both won some church historians to their respective sides. Outside the narrow confines of ecclesiology, however, few other historians found significance in the debate.[20]

Social tensions at Trinity connect the seemingly unrelated battles in the Jones case with the disputes over joining benevolent and reform societies. Laity who supported Jones in his complaint against Hobart openly broke with the High Church attempt to limit interdenominational involvement. They eagerly participated in the benevolent organizations.[21] While few in number, Trinity parishioners who joined the ABS were important church and community leaders. John Jay served as the society's nominal president in the 1820s, and Peter A. Jay served on its board of directors. Former Trinity vestrymen and Jones supporters Frederick de Peyster and George Warner also served on the board. A parishioner who had remained neutral in the Jones case, Matthew Clarkson, also joined the American Bible Society, as did John Watts, who served on Trinity's vestry and the American Bible Society board at the same time. The explicitly evangelical goals of the American Bible Society attracted ministers who had remained on the sidelines in the Jones case, including the former Methodist Thomas Lyell, and James Milnor, who later led Low Church opposition to Hobart's theology from St. George's parish.[22]

Ultimately, however, most of Trinity's ABS participants became marginalized in their own parish. Many, such as Frederick de Peyster or John Jay, came from the older Revolutionary generation, and died by 1830. Others joined new parishes, alternatives to Trinity. These included George Warner, who helped erect Trinity's first evangelical rival, Christ Church, and Peter Stuyvesant, who built Saint Mark's on family land. Thus Hobart's attempt to centralize church control under a High Church model of clerical supremacy met with partial success. Most of Trinity's parishioners conformed to the High Church example that their rector set. But Trinity did not offer an example that all New York City parishes emulated. Ministers and parishioners remained in control of their local parishes, and refused to submit to the authority that Trinity's leaders expected. Most parishioners gave little attention to the issues in the pamphlet war. Hobart complained to Trinity merchant William Irving that although Jones's case fully occupied his energies, "You gentlemen only think and converse on this matter occasionally."[23]

Uptown, Downtown Methodists Clash over John Street

In contrast to Episcopalian clerical battles, Methodist disputes directly involved the laity. Methodist lay discontent drove the Stilwellite schism. As with Trinity, social tensions colored theological concerns. The conflict included issues of class resentment, for Methodists feared privilege and worldliness as signs of sin and spiritual decline.

American Methodists struggled to balance the extremes of liberation and control, via the revival and class meeting, respectively. Ministers welcomed the influx of new converts at camp meetings, but also insisted upon strict behavioral controls once converts joined a class and took steps toward regular membership.[24] In New York City, some ministers and many wealthy members preferred control over liberty, for they worried about improper conversions and excessive emotional displays in the revival.

In 1810, young Methodist minister Nathan Bangs arrived in New York City. Presiding elder Joseph Crawford appointed Bangs to take charge of the city circuit. As preacher-in-charge, Bangs served as the first among five equals who rotated through the city's seven churches. Bangs had recently returned from a circuit in Canada, where he presided over great backcountry revivals. New York represented a different

Figure 6.2. John Street Methodist Triptych. The image on the left, the famous colonial-era church. In the middle, the infamous neoclassical church, the erection of which would contribute to the Stilwellite schism. On the right, the current building, symbol of urban decline (see chapter 8, conclusion). (Collection of The New-York Historical Society.)

problem, for Bangs viewed the emotional excesses in the city's Methodist services with alarm: "I witnessed a spirit of pride, presumption, and bigotry, impatience of scriptural restraint and moderation, clapping of the hands, screaming, and even jumping, which marred and disgraced the work of God." Bangs called a citywide meeting at which he read sections of the Methodist Discipline to the society. These passages insisted upon order and decorum at worship services and class meetings.[25]

Bangs held the disciplinary meeting at John Street, a church where fewer revivals took place. John Street's downtown location meant that it was comprised largely of women, who as in the Episcopalian example tended to support the clergy. The church's location in the lower wards also meant that the Methodist society's wealthier individuals, including most of its merchants, called it home. In short, John Street members welcomed a message that stressed order and discipline. Bangs later wrote that the older preachers and older, more established members backed his actions.[26]

Bangs's biographer wrote that he succeeded in calming the society. Opposition proved to be brief and ineffectual, for nearly all the church's ministers backed his efforts. But not all of the church's laity felt the same. In fact, the disagreement over orderliness in the church grew into a greater dispute over wealth and worldliness in the church. In this latter conflict, Bangs's victory grew ambiguous.[27]

The new dispute began inauspiciously. By 1818, the old John Street Chapel needed repair. Led by wealthy members who attended John

Street, the Methodist city trustees decided to erect a larger building with greater ornamentation on the site. The call for ornamentation strikes the modern observer as modest, for the new building's neoclassical design presented simple angles and straight lines. But to some primitive Methodists, who gloried in the stories of Wesley's followers meeting in homes and in rigging lofts in the 1760s, the erection of a new building appeared presumptuous. So, too, did hints that the new edifice would contain a carpeted altar. Most distressing to these opponents were rumors that the church would hold pews instead of seats. If the trustees charged pew rents, these Methodists feared the wealthier members would grow puffed up and become unable to heed the gospel, while poorer congregants might be forced to the margins or outside the building completely, unable to hear the message at all.[28]

While making plans for John Street's rebuilding, New York Methodist leaders proposed a change in the society's accounting structure. Previously, congregations collected offerings for local expenses. Whatever was left they sent to the trustees, who distributed it to the ministers as salaries. In 1819, trustees requested that the churches send collections directly to a board of stewards, who forwarded the money to ministers' salaries. Because the New York Methodist society ran a deficit, the new arrangement required local congregations to request loans from the central board of trustees for their expenses.[29]

Many Methodists outside of John Street discerned a sinister combination in the trustees' proposals. While their congregations pinched pennies, the trustees and ministers increased the society's debt to rebuild an old chapel in grand fashion. One group of dissenters feared that Methodist preachers aimed to control all property, and to deed the titles of the churches to the ownership of the General Conference. When Methodist leaders attempted to force a bill through the state legislature to reorganize their proposed property arrangements, the discontented members left, denouncing the resort to secular laws as a "step toward popery."[30]

Nathan Bangs labeled those departing discontents "uptown" members, because of their geographic distance from John Street. They also acquired the name the Stilwellites, after the minister who led them, William M. Stilwell, and his prominent lay uncle, Samuel. In 1820, they incorporated themselves as the Methodist Society of New York. The very name elicited memories of primitive Methodism. The parent church's title "Episcopal" reflected an unwelcome hierarchy. Even the title "Church" referred to an institutionalism, formal and dead, that Stilwellites rejected in favor of the more organic term "society." The stress on society instead of church invoked Methodism's early years of meeting in homes, other denominations' churches, and chapels formed from rigging lofts.[31] The calls for simplicity and purity in the church resonated with many.

About three hundred individuals joined the Stilwellites, including two former Methodist Episcopal Church trustees. Although no Stilwellite class lists appear to have survived, Methodist bookkeepers recorded Stilwellite class leaders who left in 1820.[32] In addition, class lists reveal a group of Stilwellites who originally defected but rejoined the Methodist majority in the mid-1820s.[33] The names of known Stillwelites are therefore biased toward class leaders, and toward more established Methodists who remained in the city for several years. Even so, the lists do not reveal great wealth or prestige in occupation. Stilwellites appear to have been composed largely of the lower orders.

The list of known Stilwellites resembled the composition of the uptown Methodist classes of the 1790s. Nearly 90 percent of the group worked in the artisanal, cartman, or unskilled occupational categories. The only professionals, a minister and a doctor, both served as the society's preachers. The only retailers were small dry goods or grocer operations; no one occupied the upwardly aspiring merchant category. Although working-class, Stilwellites had long resided in the city. Over 85 percent of the male Stilwellites appear in a directory. Few were so destitute or transient as to pass from the eyes of the directory tabulators.[34]

The group's geographic organization was equally striking. The overwhelming majority of Stilwellite leaders came from two churches: Forsyth Street and Allen Street. Both lay close to each other, as Allen Street formed in 1810 as an outgrowth of Forsyth. Two other leaders attended churches north of the city, James Demorest at Greenwich and Joseph Piggot at Duane Street. None attended the John Street Church downtown.[35] Like their leaders, the group's rank and file lived near these same streets: Allen, Stanton, Forsyth, Division, Spring, Bowery, and Rivington.

The Stilwellite working-class identity rejected licentious behavior. The group's discipline revealed a moral stance that called for hard work and limited consumption. The group forbade drinking "spirituous liquors," or participation in the slave trade. The discipline banned fighting or violence, speaking ill of another Methodist, or monetary loans given at "unlawful interest." The rules attacked unnecessary luxury in fashion or worldly "diversions" like secular songs or books that distracted one from pious thoughts. When the Stilwellite discipline counseled ministers to work hard, that advice apparently sprang from the laity's experience:

Be diligent. Never be unemployed; never be triflingly employed. Never trifle away time; neither spend any more time at any place than is strictly necessary. Be serious. Let your motto be, *Holiness to the Lord*. Avoid all lightness, jesting, and foolish talking. . . . Be punctual. Do every thing exactly at the time. And do not mend our rules, but keep them.[36]

Thus, although the Stilwellite group rejected attempts at social control from the downtown Methodist ministers, they preached a self-control that required similar behavior.

Stilwellite polity recalled an older Methodist vision of lay leadership. The laity worked closely with ministers to govern the society. The lay community chose new ministers, and class members chose their own leaders. The church order dictated that no rules could be altered without the consent of a majority of lay individuals. Peers, not ministers, solved internal disputes. Geography, not ministers, determined class composition.[37]

Stilwellite policy also reformulated women's roles, hearkening back to early Methodist equality of all believers. Women were allowed to vote for new ministers, and in lay disputes women served in peer juries over other women. Husbands and wives also attended classes together, ending the rigid sex separation that had marked American Methodist practice since the Revolution.[38] Such measures toward women appear progressive, but the Stilwellites held an ambiguous stance toward women in the church. When the Methodist Episcopal Church segregated men and women in classes, it placed women, including preachers' wives, in a prominent place in the "preacher's class" at each church. This minister-women alliance subtly undermined the independence that artisan heads of households had exercised. Stilwellites placed women alongside their husbands, subject to closer observation and supervision.

The Stilwellites could point to recent innovations at John Street that illustrated the dangers of a women-preacher alliance. Mary Morgan joined with the daughters of preacher William Phoebus to support a Methodist Sunday School system in New York. The women attended John Street and understandably had the preachers' support. Members of the Forsyth Street Church, where the Stilwellites garnered their greatest support, balked, citing the expense of supporting a new movement not directly connected to the gospel message. With ministerial support, Morgan's sisterhood won out.[39] When John Street's ministers also collected funds to remodel their church or pay preachers' salaries, Stilwellites could fume that Methodist women backed ministerial advances against laymen.

A few Stilwellite leaders believed that the political steps toward more democratic meetings should translate to greater economic parity. In 1823, William Stilwell and local preacher James Covel became founding members of the New York Society for Promoting Communities. The society's leader, Cornelius Blatchly, a radical Quaker, penned a work entitled *Essay on Common Wealths*. Blatchly advocated implementing a biblical jubilee. Based on passages from the Old Testament Bible, Blatchly's jubilee called for an end to permanent foreclosure on real property. Every fifty years, owners of real estate could reclaim their lands lost by debt. This measure would mitigate the effects of capital accumulation. This Society for Promoting Communities advocated legislation to enforce this peculiar vision of property rights. The Stilwellites criticized the main body of Methodists for resorting to legislative intervention in religious matters, but they did not have a problem with inserting religious matters into legislation.[40]

Although the Stilwellite Methodists occupied a vastly different social space than did Hobart's opponents at Trinity, both groups blurred denominational boundaries. Both opposed the clergy's aims toward greater ministerial oversight. At Trinity, leading men joined with elites from other churches in ecumenical ventures to evangelize the lower orders. The uptown Methodists supported their own versions of ecumenicity: the Stilwellites balked at Methodist Episcopal Church attempts to limit the use of Methodist church buildings only for Methodist services. Stilwellites also held a close affinity for others outside orthodox Christian faith, particularly the Quakers. In an account of the group's origins, Samuel Stilwell praised the early Quakers for having "the piety and the simplicity of the Gospel." And in the *Friendly Visitor*, William Stilwell stressed the common bonds uniting Christians of different denominations, including those between Quakers and Methodists. By comparison, orthodox Methodist Francis Asbury judged that the Quakers' unorthodoxy barred them from true salvation in Christ.[41]

Historians have offered conflicting views on the Stilwellites' significance. Methodist church historians argued that the Stilwellites amounted to little, and quickly passed from the scene. Abel Stevens recounted that in 1825 three class leaders and the seventy members under them approached Bangs and admitted their error in leaving. Bangs quickly welcomed them back to the mother church. Samuel Seaman noted that the Stilwellite movement lasted only a generation, with most of its members returning to the Methodist Episcopal Church. Labor historian William Sutton disagreed with such assessments. Sutton wrote that the Stilwellite movement grew from three hundred to eight hundred souls from 1820 to 1825, with perhaps two thousand Methodists part of the regional movement outside the city limits. The group did not falter until it attempted to hold a June 1826 conference to unite populist Methodist groups in a larger connection. For unknown reasons, shortly after the conference the primitive Methodist union shattered. William Stilwell continued to lead his congregation as an independent example to the rest of the world.[42]

The Stilwellite–John Street controversy illustrates the local nature of political and theological church battles. Churchgoers determined their identity from congregational location as much as from biblical arguments. The uptown attempt to keep purity within the church against ostentatious displays of wealth and fashion and aggressive ministerial authority found a willing audience in a specific geographic space. That space contained a self-conscious community of laborers whose ethic blended Methodist and laboring assumptions. Outside of that space, however, the Stilwellites gained little support and could not sustain a lasting denomination. Those who wished for local control of churches lost out to a ministry committed to greater centralization.

Black and New Yorker: Mother Zion Defines Herself

Fears surrounding church centralization also touched the black church. From 1800 to 1810, black Methodist leaders erected their chapel and achieved separate incorporation from the white church. During the 1810s, black church leaders divided over the course their congregation should take. White New York and black Philadelphia Methodists each appealed to Mother Zion's ministers to join them. Although some individuals found these appeals attractive, the allure of autonomous spiritual leadership swayed most of Zion's leaders toward independence. Wishing to exercise their spiritual gifts without outside oversight, Zion's African Methodist leaders steered a course toward institutional autonomy, befitting their occupational status as independent producers and their aspirations toward middle-class uplift.

New York's African Methodists confronted the same internal tensions regarding individual conversion and social obligation that white Methodists did. All Methodists championed the individual's right to choose his soul's fate. Yet having exercised this spiritual freedom, new believers bound themselves to church authority. This collective discipline sometimes defied the larger society's institutions, as when early Methodists condemned slavery. Yet these same leaders allowed many moral imperatives to fall silent in the face of the larger aims of conversion and sanctification. Methodists both submitted to and defied the established powers in the world.[43] These ambiguities help explain why black Methodists disagreed with each other over the course the church should take.

In the two decades between Mother Zion's creation and independence, the church contained no clear locus of authority. Black Methodists did not immediately repudiate the charter for their institution. For two decades, they submitted to regular white preaching and oversight. During that time, three main breaches developed among factions within the congregation, the last of which led to new denominational status. The politicized battles thus represented an attempt to determine who would rule at church. Occupational culture helped to shape the debate, as a middling artisan group ultimately took charge of the congregation.

The first dispute occurred shortly after 1810. Two preachers left the Africans to build a new church with John Edwards, a white scale beam maker. Abraham Thompson and June Scott had been senior ministers at Zion. They were the first blacks to receive their preaching licenses from the white church, before blacks had gained separate incorporation. They had also actively aided in the formation of black benevolent organizations. The venture soon collapsed, apparently because Edwards grew mentally unstable. Shortly afterward, Thompson returned to Mother Zion, while Scott left the African Methodists for good.[44]

This dispute shows that the black church struggled over issues of financial independence and racial identity. As was the case with many poorer Methodist churches, Mother Zion could not afford to pay its ministers. In 1803, Zion contributed $25.70 to the Methodist society in donations, compared to $608.88 total for the conference as a whole. Edwards promised Thompson and Scott regular salaries. The offer of pay tempted those balancing duties to family and the ministry, especially those with limited prospects of employment, like Thompson and Scott. Abraham Thompson appeared in the 1796 city directory as a laborer, and June Scott did not even appear in the 1795 or 1796 class lists. In addition to the promise of pay, Edwards may also have promised interracial worship. A former member of the Society of Friends, Edwards had no qualms in approaching blacks to take leadership positions in the church. An interracial church may have achieved more solid financial footing than an all-black one, since even poorer whites often held better job prospects.[45]

Interracial worship also offered the men a chance to return to the Methodist church of a previous generation. Perhaps Thompson and Scott, older men who had once experienced interracial worship, wished to recapture that earlier unity in the new church. Abraham Thompson was probably the first black man to join the earliest recorded Methodist classes at John Street in 1785. As other blacks left the white church, Thompson lingered. When Francis Asbury granted James Varick and William Hamilton the right to worship separately in 1796, Thompson remained in the white-run classes.[46]

Racial unity had largely disappeared from the city churches. Philip Arcularius assumed that free blacks were nonresidents, which suggests that he knew very few of them. City churches separated black and white classes. The creation of the African chapel meant that worship space, as well as class space, divided into white and black sections. By the 1810s, only three black classes in the city met regularly under the auspices of white leadership; two of them were at John Street, downtown.[47]

Reminders of the older vision remained nearby. When black Methodist exhorter George White traveled to Long Island, whites challenged his right to preach, citing opposition from another African Methodist minister. When White showed his preaching license to the presiding elder, however, the Long Island Methodists admitted him. The license, not his skin color, had been the deterring factor, and White then ministered to both white and black classes.[48] This example highlighted a fluid racial situation in the countryside, where black membership remained low but stable. But in the city, segregation became the norm. Having no other biracial options in Manhattan, Abraham Thompson limped back to Mother Zion.

A specific community within Mother Zion pushed for full institutional independence. In the original 1796 separation, an artisan occupational identity drove the movement toward separate black worship. This impulse influenced Zion's leaders for the next two decades. George White's example is instructive, for he remained on the margins at Zion. Three times White approached the white elders to request a promotion from the position of exhorter, which only allowed him to share his testimony, to the position of local preacher, which enabled him to interpret Scripture passages in his public pronouncements. With little support from black leaders, however, White struggled to gain a foothold in the Methodist ministry. Unlike native New Yorkers James Varick and William Hamilton, White hailed from the South, having been freed in Virginia at his master's deathbed conversion. Unlike many other African Methodist leaders, White held no skilled trade. As an itinerant preacher he gathered fruits from outside town to peddle upon his return to the city. He also worked as an oysterer, which required little initial skill or investment. In contrast, many of Zion's other ministers and lay leaders held skilled occupations: Varick was a shoemaker, Hamilton a carpenter. William Miller, who headed Zion's daughter church Asbury African Methodist, worked as a cabinetmaker.[49]

Black artisans possessed a greater confidence and stronger financial position than their unskilled colleagues, which translated into bolder political stances. Occupational differences did not automatically create differences in creed or ideology—tobacconist Peter Williams Sr. did not share the same radical faith as his artisan brothers. But the insecurity of laboring led some African Methodists away from institutional independence. The promise of security in biracial worship tempted Abraham Thompson, a laborer. Another unskilled worker, George White, avoided political questions. White's unwillingness to grapple with slavery may have led to a divide with leaders like Hamilton, who joined mutual aid societies and later promoted antislavery measures. Hamilton strongly identified with his status as a carpenter. When neighbors prosecuted Hamilton for the "nuisance" of working in a wooden building, thus creating a fire hazard, the court defended him as being in the same position of a "generality of mechanics." In this instance, Hamilton's artisan status won him an innocent verdict in court.[50]

Two outside parties exploited the differences within New York's African Methodist community to pull the church in different directions in the late 1810s. Richard Allen's vision of a pan-African Methodist alliance attracted many Zionites. Second, the emerging Stilwellite schism caused many of Zion's members to reconsider their church's status in the white Methodist society. Zion emerged from these struggles with a new corporate independence and institutional identity as a center of African Methodism in New York. This identity depended on established ministers, however, and caused others to leave the church. As in the case of Trinity's opponents of Hobart and the Methodist Stilwellites, social position helped influence religious allegiance.

Richard Allen founded Philadelphia's Bethel Church, the nation's first independent black Methodist church. Seeking to expand his denomination, Allen used Zion's discontented members to enter New York's mission field. In 1819, former Zionite William Lambert traveled to Philadelphia, where Allen ordained him as a traveling preacher. Lambert had unsuccessfully applied for the ministry from his New York brethren. Upon returning, he established a church under Allen's authority. George White aided Lambert in setting up Bethel Church on Mott Street. Because White and Lambert had been Zionites, New York's African Methodists took the affront personally. Zion's leaders ordered that none of its ministers preach at Bethel, and denied any Bethelites preaching privileges at Zion. The prohibition extended to Asbury, Zion's daughter church.[51]

Black Methodists temporarily forgot Allen's machinations when William Stilwell approached the Zionites with news of his group's departure in July 1820. Stilwell had been the white elder in charge of the African churches that year, and he hoped to induce the black churches to join his fledgling denomination. Stilwell explained that the Methodist Episcopal Church had turned to the New York state legislature in an attempt to give the ministers more control over the church's property. The warning resonated with the African Methodists. Zion's charter held that church property belonged to its lay trustees, who were limited to members of the African race. If white ministers successfully seized Zion's holdings, it would completely destroy any power the African Methodists had built in the previous quarter century. The white church continued to hold spiritual primacy: its ministers determined which men could be ordained to preach, and its white elders periodically presided over black services. Black Methodists controlled church property, but little else.[52]

Mother Zion's leaders then met with the Methodist Episcopal Church elders to confirm Stilwell's story. Peter Williams acted as liaison, holding a meeting between white and black Methodists at his home on Liberty Street. Their fears confirmed, the Zionites explored options that would allow their ministers, deacons in Methodist hierarchy nomenclature, to be elevated to elders. Once raised to the status of elder, Mother Zion's leaders could ordain ministers on their own, not requiring approval from outside clergy and creating a self-perpetuating ministry. In the meantime, the Zionites asked Stilwell to preside over their church services for the next year. Even so, the break with the white church was not absolute; Zion's leaders continued to consult with the Methodist Episcopal Church for the next two years. Although the senior Peter Williams no longer served as Zion's trustee, he held a position of trust with the other African Methodists, and perhaps counseled a cautious approach in their tactics.[53]

While working with Williams, Zion's leaders also temporarily relaxed their animosity toward Richard Allen's group. Several Zion ministers attended Allen's Bethel Church services. Some sat near the altar behind the pulpit, lending Allen an unspoken yet powerful support. Zion's leading minister James Varick introduced Allen at a meeting, notwithstanding his earlier resolve to withhold fellowship to the Allenites.[54]

The collegiality with Allen's group soon dissipated. The Zionites approached Allen to request that he promote their deacons to elder, but Allen refused, unless they placed their church under his authority. As with Zion's initial break in the 1790s, New York's male African Methodists wished to "exercise their spiritual gifts," to hold positions of prestige in, and control, their own church. In a subsequent congregational meeting, the people rejected both union with Richard Allen's group and continuing under the authority of the white Methodist Episcopal Church.[55]

Some Zionites considered leaving Methodism, and approached Bishop Hobart at Trinity Episcopal Church to request ordination for their deacons. Abraham Thompson particularly opposed this move. Christopher Rush attributed this opposition to Thompson's belief that the Africans should not go to a white bishop given Allen's availability. Thompson, however, had gone to a white artisan in his earlier attempts to form a new church. Thompson's strongest loyalty was to the Methodist discipline. Zion's oldest minister, Thompson held the longest ties to Zion's Methodist roots at John Street.[56]

The white Episcopalian leadership hesitated to support an independent black ministry, especially as they had their own preaching candidate, Peter Williams Jr., taking the helm of St. Philip's that year. Episcopal priest Thomas Lyell, himself a former Methodist, suggested the Zionites turn to Methodist William Stilwell. Mother Zion's leaders returned to Stilwell, who had retreated from his earlier attempt at union with New York's black Methodists. Now Stilwell only wished to persuade them that his status as elder was sufficient to ordain them as elders. Stilwell argued that no bishop, whether Methodist or Episcopal, was required. Nonetheless, the Methodist Episcopal Church reentered the picture, as Bishop William McKendree stated that he could not ordain elders immediately, but promised to study the matter and formally answer the Zionites at the next annual conference. Zion's members proceeded to elect Abraham Thompson and James Varick as elder candidates after the Sunday service on October 1, 1820. The two men then began their service as elder, yet awaited official ordination "by the hands of a proper authority." The Methodist Episcopal Church stalled for another two years, until the African Methodists had enough. Three Stilwellite ministers finally ordained Zion's elders in June 1822, thereby creating an independent African ministry.[57]

Mother Zion remained firmly Methodist in its steps toward independence, and embraced a hierarchical understanding of Methodist church polity. Mother Zion's leaders insisted upon gaining proper ordination from other ministers of the gospel, preferably bishops, to become independent. Even in separation they followed an order and a discipline that implied an acceptance of spiritual hierarchy. Zion's independence differed from the Stilwellite vision of a democratic, egalitarian Christianity.[58]

Zion's leaders remained committed to a specific, traditional brand of theology and order. Unwilling to shed their denominational identity, they retained a hierarchical ecclesiastical structure. Their actions reflect neither African cultural survivals, nor democratized strivings for independence. Rather, Zion's independence demonstrated the ecclesiastical maneuverings of an acculturated, male, artisan leadership to retain its power within a recognizably Methodist tradition. Christopher Rush's description of the service that elected Varick and Thompson could apply to the entire episode: "The whole process was conducted with much apparent solemnity and satisfaction."[59]

Zion's congregation made several attempts to find proper religious authorities willing to ordain Zion's ministers yet not insist upon any control over the church. The group that ultimately did so, the Stilwellites, shared an occupational identity with the Zionites. Artisans dominated the ranks of both Stilwellite and African Methodist leaders. All early Republic artisans cherished their independence, especially self-employment and freedom from coercion. These artisans faced palpable social stresses, with spousal abuse and heavy drinking endemic in the working community. Often white artisans jealously defended their prerogative against blacks, sometimes violently attacking them as economic rivals. As plebeian Christians, however, the Stilwellites held the Zionites to be their brothers, and aided them in their separation. At the least, such support tweaked the Methodist hierarchy whom the Stilwellites opposed. Blacks' ability to control their own churches paralleled the Stilwellite desire for local control over the church.[60]

The African Methodist example demonstrated the triumph of black clergy who steered a path between white control over their church and union with other black Methodists. Zion's ministers excluded black laity committed to interracial worship, including Peter Williams and the two black classes who remained at John Street. Abraham Thompson similarly found himself on the outside when he considered interracial cooperation in the 1810s. Zion's leaders also rejected black Methodists who sought a pan-African connection with Richard Allen's group, including clergy or potential clergy like William Lambert and George White. The desire of Mother Zion's existing ministers to preserve their own prestige and independence ensured a separate denominational status for the African Methodist Episcopal Zion Church. Such status remained orthodox, disciplined, and hierarchical.

Exceptional St. Philip's: A Need for Patronage

Alone among the churches studied here, St. Philip's Episcopal Church projected little outward turmoil during the 1810s and 1820s. In these years, St. Philip's achieved formal institutional existence, coalescing from small groups of catechized blacks at Trinity. Black Episcopalians achieved separation far more smoothly than black Methodists because the congregation moved in tandem with white leadership. Lacking in funds and unable to exist as a wholly independent parish, African American Anglicans embraced Bishop Hobart's High Church theology, thereby ensuring Trinity's patronage.

Black Anglicans who had worshiped in New York City for more than a century assumed different guises over that time. Early in the eighteenth century under Elias Neau, some Africans used Anglican instruction to their own ends, apparently seeking literacy, and baptism, for the powers it gave them to resist their bondage. In a similar way, some black Anglicans leveraged connections to the British to leave New York with the British army at the end of the Revolution. But black Episcopalians' actions in the early Republic diverged from these past actions, moving closer to the goals of some whites. The African Society of the 1790s had emphasized moral conduct and religious order, and the Wilberforce Society in 1810 had served as a pro-Federalist wing of black political involvement. Both groups worked closely with white patrons, whether church vestrymen or Federalist politicians.[61]

Black Episcopalians structured their activities around the requirements that white churchmen set. In the first decade of the 1800s, they worshiped on Sunday afternoons, just as they had in the colonial period, to avoid conflict with white services. Because the Episcopal Church demanded proper training and ordination for its ministers, a white lay reader, John McCombs, officiated blacks' services. McCombs's position was the lowest in an extensive hierarchy within the Episcopal Church, but he remained above his black charges. In 1809, they moved to the black school on William Street, a site offered to them by paternalistic members of the New York Manumission Society.[62]

McCombs's death in 1812 marked a turning point for the group. That year St. Philip's blacks left the school on William Street for a loft over a carpenter shop on Cliff Street. They also petitioned Trinity for the right to train one of their own to lead them in worship. The man white church leaders chose for the black Episcopalians was Peter Williams Jr., a rising star in the black reform movements. These modest moves toward independence attracted new followers; perhaps two hundred blacks attended services the second decade of the century, a significant increase over the thirty souls who attended Samuel Auchmuty's lessons in the late colonial era.[63]

Trinity's blacks gained an important figurehead when Peter Williams Jr. emerged to lead them at St. Philip's. The son of John Street Methodist's former sexton, a young Peter had entered Samuel Pontier's black Methodist class in 1803, but reappeared in the public record as an Episcopalian by New Year's Day 1808. Oral histories, and historians since, have connected Williams's conversion with minister Thomas Lyell's defection from Methodism to Episcopalianism when the latter took charge of New York's Christ Church Episcopal in 1804. Despite his background as a presumably low-church Methodist, Lyell subsequently affiliated closely with Bishop Hobart's High Church wing, including leading the charges against Cave Jones. Lyell repeatedly stayed close to powerful church leaders (before departing the Methodists he had secured the blessing of Francis Asbury); so would Williams.[64]

Williams was a gifted writer and orator. Unlike previous black Episcopalians, whose place in the public record remained muted and sporadic, Williams clearly promoted moral improvement for blacks, and followed that commitment to support immediate abolition by the 1830s. For a decade he was a lonely non-Methodist voice among New York City's black community leaders, often joining many of his father's associates, black Methodist ministers, to take part in antislavery and moral reform efforts.[65]

Williams's statements remained characteristically moderate. Like his father, Williams negotiated among differing black factions. He remained cordial toward, if not supportive of, blacks who promoted colonization, the attempt to transport free blacks outside the United States to escape racism. While blacks led early colonization efforts, later white control over colonization raised suspicions in the black community. Avoiding ideological conflict, Williams's public pronouncements focused on positive accomplishments and rarely criticized opponents, white or black.

Williams had to walk a careful line in pursuing his ministerial training. Bishop Moore waited a year before agreeing to train him as a lay reader and catechist. Williams was barred from a seminary education, so had to read privately with then-assistant bishop John Henry Hobart. Hobart's High Church theology continued the expansive SPG-era vision of a church that met the needs of everyone in society, but in the post-Revolutionary disestablishment that same tradition shied away from public statements on political issues, including slavery and racism. When Hobart rose to bishop in his own right, he recommended that Williams be ordained as a deacon.[66]

In remaining close to the High Church party, black Episcopalians shunned the Low Church, evangelical Episcopalians who otherwise might have been their natural allies. Many Low Churchmen such as John Jay were also Federalist politicians who promoted gradual manumission and supported black rights, however muted; as the century progressed, the Low Church group included immediate abolitionists. In order to gain training for their own clergy, though, St. Philip's blacks needed Bishop Hobart's High Church support.

They also needed High Church funding, and white financial patronage generally. In 1814, Lewis Francis and William Turner applied on behalf of the black Episcopalians to Trinity's vestry for $260 to settle arrears on the rent of their worship space, which the vestry granted. An Anglican layman also aided the black congregation. George Lorillard, tobacconist, shared the artisan trade of Peter Williams Sr. Lorillard offered a generous lease of land on Collect Street in what amounted to a de facto mortgage. The church was to pay $250 a year for sixty years, after which time it would own the land. Following Lorillard, Trinity granted an additional $3,000 to build a church, provided that it remain Episcopal and "under ecclesiastical authority," that is, under the bishop's authority and within the diocese, per High Church designs.[67]

Building commenced in August 1818. Among St. Philip's congregants were artisans who erected the building. Even so, the African Episcopalians again turned to Trinity's vestry in April 1819, unable to secure the necessary funds to finish the building; Trinity provided a loan of $2,500, requiring repayment within three years and the purchase of fire insurance for the building. On July 3, 1819, Bishop Hobart consecrated the building; on October 20 of the following year, diocesan leaders elevated Williams to the order of deacon.[68]

Most of St. Philip's congregants did not rock the boat. They included former members of the African Society, who had professed a commitment to moral order and respect for the laws of society. Later St. Philip's church historians praised it for its "superior respect for ecclesiastical order and authority." Such characteristics meshed well with the High Church theology of Hobart and his associates. Hobart praised the African church's congregants for being "remarkably orderly and devout in the performance of the service."[69] From its inception, St. Philip's displayed discipline by consistently following High Church forms. This acceptance displayed St. Philip's orthodoxy and order, much as Mother Zion's leaders insisted upon regular Methodist church forms in its quest for institutional independence.

At St. Philip's, the stress on order and decorum continued through the nineteenth century. Observers viewed the church as a site of proper and genteel activity. This could lead to subtle protests, as black men embraced uplift as a model of resistance. But St. Philip's tenuous financial position, and their dependence upon the bishop's good favor for their leader's advancement, assured that St. Philip's members would defer to Trinity's leadership.

Ultimately, both Mother Zion and St. Philip's sided with parties of order and discipline. In a larger society that viewed the black race in general as immoral or hopelessly childlike and unstructured, a regimented, orderly, moral form of governance and worship challenged white assumptions. It also favored leaders within those churches who valued acculturation to Euro-American ways and championed male authority in an exaggeration of the white-run church actions. Such a network formed the base of later reform movements, but also provided radical-minded reformers with a critique of the same black church as limited.

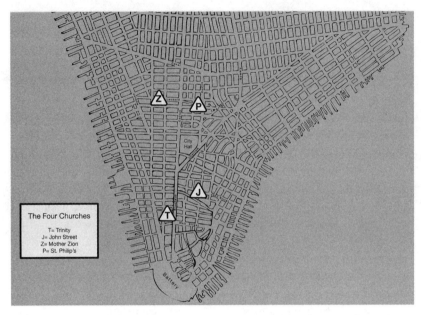

Figure 6.3. The Four Churches. (Map created by Alanna Beason, derived from map from United States Census Office, 1886.)

Conclusion

All the churches resolved their conflicts over authority, authenticity, and prestige around 1820. Hobart's High Church vision, which divorced the social and spiritual connection of the Federalist-era church, won out at Trinity. A silent majority of middle-class men and middling- and upper-class women sided with Hobart and his High Church clerical allies, against tepid resistance from elite men who had previously dominated the city's Anglican churches. Methodists rejected the antiformalist urges of their primitive branch by bidding farewell to the Stilwellites. Those who wished to expand into further education programs and larger financial projects won out over those who proclaimed a humble simplicity in the church. The African Methodists used the uptown schism as a launching point for their own independence, but did not accept the democratized vision of the Stilwellites. Rather, African Methodists adhered carefully to forms of order in their church, as did the newly formed black Episcopal church of St. Philip's. African Methodists specifically identified race as a prerequisite to lead, but black Episcopalians did not, as they remained institutionally under the white Anglican communion. Both churches' leaders borrowed from middle-class, acculturated norms to gain authority, for they formed mutual aid societies and stressed learning as signs of their legitimacy.

In all these cases, victory went to the groups with greater clerical support and a more focused denominational identity. The victors excluded those acting in the name of lay interest and those who promoted a more nebulous sense of interdenominational or interracial cooperation. These losers, however, would gain an indirect victory in the coming years by associating with another force of localization. That force arrived in the proliferation of neighborhoods segregated by class, and the embrace of the ideal of domesticity through the nuclear family.

7 /   Neighborly Refinement and Withdrawal: 1820–1840

New Yorkers confronted a changed world during the 1820s. The completion of the Erie Canal in 1825 began a new era in New York's economic development. The canal transformed Upstate New York from forested hinterland into agricultural settlements and proto-industrial mill towns. Beyond Buffalo, the Great Lakes connected New York to the Old Northwest. As the market link between Europe and the American Midwest, New York City captured the lion's share of new trade, rapidly surpassing its colonial superiors, Philadelphia and Boston.[1]

Feeding from this boom, New York grew spatially and demographically. The grid pattern of streets north of old New Amsterdam allowed for rapid expansion. No longer a country village, Greenwich abutted the city in the mid-1820s. The pace of the city's growth accelerated after 1820, as northeastern farms continued to decline and immigration from abroad increased. The city population numbered more than two hundred thousand in 1830 and more than three hundred thousand in 1840.[2]

Economic development rapidly changed New Yorkers' living patterns. Many wealthy residents moved uptown and out of town. They preferred the amenities of new construction and clean neighborhoods outside the city. Conversely, poor laborers squeezed into smaller quarters, as landlords subdivided homes and shops with greater frequency. Slums developed in the streets east of Broadway and north of the old city. The Five Points—the intersection of Cross, Worth, and Anthony Streets—drew international attention as a notorious location of poverty and vice.[3]

The separation of rich from poor profoundly shaped city church life. All four churches grew wealthier, but these changes affected white and black churches differently. The white churches lay in the lower wards, where old wealth still resided. The black churches stood near the Five Points, but their leaders and congregants aspired to middle-class status that called for a pan-racial uplift that nonetheless distanced themselves from their neighbors. When the churches had included poorer members, leading congregants had espoused ideals of community, binding all members in mutual concern. As congregations became homogeneous in racial and class composition, churchmen promoted refinement, and education and respectability grew more important.

The specifics of change varied in each congregation. In the African churches, wealth led to refinement. At St. Philip's, a few prominent service workers attained great prosperity. Many of these well-off members joined the growing abolitionist and reform movements that linked blacks nationally. At Mother Zion, a process of gentrified domestication reiterated male leadership, which preached bourgeois standards of education, respectability, and rationality in worship. But New York's black Methodists stepped back from leadership in national movements, appearing less frequently in the emerging abolitionist efforts. In the white churches, domesticity promoted the elusive ideal of secluded households. As wealthy members fled to exclusive enclaves, Trinity's outlying chapels increased in stature. Among white Methodists, the nuclear family gained a greater prominence. Earlier Methodists had conceived of their society as an extended family, but, as the city expanded, New York's Methodists embraced their private families as havens of purity. Primitive Methodists had viewed education and cultural refinement with ambiguity, if not outright hostility. Now both represented paths toward church leadership. All four churches took steps to privatize religious experiences, withdrawing individuals and families from each other and from the larger community as a whole. In this context, reform movements offered no quick transformation of the world but one key to manage it. Bureaucratic, rational order, an essential part of this task, placed pious acts squarely within limits.

St. Philip's Upwardly Mobile, and Uplifting, Identity

Changes in the black churches registered dramatically as white support for slavery eroded. Seeing manumissions increase, the state legislature revised the gradual manumission law to end all slavery in the state on July 4, 1827. With blacks no longer internally divided between slave and free, New York's black leaders expressed hope that their legal equality would lead to social respect and economic opportunity. They discovered that changes in legal status did not stop whites from employing race to bar blacks from full citizenship. The same whites that had acquiesced on manumission barred blacks from the franchise. In 1821, a special state convention drafted a new constitution that granted universal white male suffrage, while retaining restrictive property requirements for black men.[4] White racism did not prevent blacks from advancing materially, however. As St. Philip's and Mother Zion's congregants grew wealthier, they also promoted cultural improvement.

Character, respectability, uplift: these concepts infused black protest writing and orations in antebellum America. Such concepts revealed a process where elite black men interacted with, assumed, and corrected white American cultural assumptions. Historian Patrick Rael has persuasively argued that black leaders advocated notions of elevation in an attempt to unite blacks under a single banner, to avoid class-based divisions or splintering.[5] But blacks who voiced concepts of uplift necessarily did so from a masculine and elite perspective. The language of unity was voiced from a group that was socially more well-off, and nearly universally male. Black Episcopalians meshed well with the larger black community's concern with moral behavior and social advancement. Many of their lives exemplified, nearly exactly, the natural and social laws, and ideals, that black leaders expected would vanquish racism.

Evidence of St. Philip's improving material status can be found in church records. Lists of baptisms performed at St. Philip's survive for the years 1819 to 1829. In the sacrament of baptism, young parents promised to raise their children in the Christian faith, indicating a devotion to the church beyond mere attendance. Several of the fathers who baptized their children in the 1820s served during the 1840s and 1850s on St. Philip's vestry. The sacrament of baptism intertwined family and church life, and allowed black families to put down roots in the Episcopal Church.[6]

Changes in the composition of the black Episcopalians at St. Philip's illustrate larger changes in the black community. Over time, St. Philip's blacks gained a greater presence in the public record: in later years, more names appear in the city registries. Also, in later registries more names appear with an occupation listed, rather than simply an address. Both facts suggest greater stability and wealth over time. The directories also record that, as slavery faded out, race achieved greater prominence in the public record. Especially by 1840, entries that formerly made no mention of race noted blacks as "colored."[7]

Unlike at Mother Zion, where artisans dominated the church leadership from the beginning, the occupational makeup of St. Philip's was mixed. The 1819 city directory reveals that St. Philip's early parishioners held a range of occupations. Like the African Society two decades before, the new church contained a mix of service workers, like a coachman and hairdresser, and small artisans, like a shoemaker and mason. Two mariners and one ship carpenter made the marine category marginally larger than any other.[8]

Few of these individuals enjoyed wealth. Only a handful of parishioners appeared in the 1819 directory. Of these, nearly half listed only an address, suggesting unskilled laboring status. Black Episcopalian families sometimes shared lodgings to limit expenses. In 1819, William and Sally Ann Brown and Aaron and Ann Grey shared a tenement at 10 Theatre Alley. In 1825, Alexander and Harriet Polston and Peter and Mary Lawrence lived together at 132 Duane Street.[9] Both locations stood in poor working neighborhoods among other laborers, white and black.

Despite the early indications of poverty, a handful of black service-oriented workers profited from the expanding economy. As mass production squeezed many smaller artisans into poverty, service trades remained stable if modest forms of income, especially in jobs that traditionally employed blacks, such as coachmen or barbers. A few of St. Philip's blacks moved beyond stability toward modest wealth.[10]

One of St. Philip's wealthiest congregants, Thomas Downing, charted the most successful ascent in service employment. Downing arrived in New York City in 1819, and began to gather oysters in the Jersey Flats along the Hudson River.[11] Born on the Virginia island village of Chincoteague, Downing was the son of black Methodists. Their master, Captain John Downing, freed the elder Downings upon his own conversion to Methodism. In his honor, Methodists named the Downing Meeting House in Oak Hill. Downing was the most prominent citizen and landowner in the small village. According to Thomas Downing's son George T. Downing, elite white families made social calls on Downing's parents, because the latter were caretakers of the meetinghouse. More likely, they visited the captain, who gave his last name to his slaves.[12]

These early Virginia connections remained with Thomas Downing. According to Downing's son, Virginia governor Henry A. Wise had been a boyhood friend of Thomas, and later visited him in New York. More important, Thomas viewed displays of refinement firsthand, for the prominent Wharton, West, Taylor, and Custis families regularly visited his parents' former master. When Downing moved north, first to Philadelphia, and then settling in New York, he made his establishment a place for whites to eat. He also offered a range of oyster-based dishes to satisfy refined culinary tastes. This stood in great contrast to the rough-and-tumble nature of lower-class oyster houses found in ramshackle tenements farther uptown.[13]

Downing's memory paints a dubious picture of exaggerated refinement. In fact, the prominent white Downing family hailed from Northumberland County, not the Eastern Shore. Any Eastern Shore Downings would have been a minor, less influential branch.[14] Accounts of the Eastern Shore suggest that as a minor hamlet Chincoteague had no great families or plantations, and few slaves. Henry A. Wise was fifteen years younger than Downing; their connection may have been distant, even coincidental, as Captain Downing, upon freeing Thomas's parents, sent Thomas to the same tutor under whom Wise would later study. Further, any connection to Wise was less than genteel; although elected governor of Virginia, Wise was an unpolished character, known for his shabby clothes, streams of tobacco juice, and foul language. And Wise was an ardent proslavery politician, eventual secessionist, and Confederate general, one whose postwar visit to Downing, who died in 1866, would have been strange indeed. In relating his life story to his son, Thomas Downing refashioned his childhood to strengthen his adult identity. By placing his youth within the wealthy and prestigious society of the Old South, Downing staked a claim to status as a man of elegance and refinement. Despite his parents' affiliation with the Methodist church, Downing became an Episcopalian, the socially elite denomination par excellence.[15]

Downing quickly ascended from oysterman to restaurateur. By 1825, Downing purchased an eating establishment in the basement of 5 Broad Street.[16] Within another decade, Downing no longer raked oysters, but procured the highest-quality specimens from oystermen at the docks. During the 1830s, Downing leased the basements surrounding his restaurant to expand the dining area and space for food storage. Near the city's merchant, banking, and political centers in Lower Manhattan, Downing's refectory catered to the wealthiest New Yorkers.[17]

Thomas Downing's service business required expressions of deference, rather than assertions of independence that artisans practiced. Downing outfitted the oyster house with plush furniture and elegant surroundings. Downing welcomed oyster boat captains into his restaurant because their good graces ensured his continued success, but his eatery drew mostly wealthy merchants and government officials. Except as employees, blacks did not enter the oyster house.[18]

A few other prominent men at St. Philip's joined Downing in his business success. Peter Ray benefited from the Anglican Lorillard family's patronage and supervised their tobacco factory. Ray kept the company's "secret recipe for snuff." Henry Scott's pickle manufactory grew into a wholesale organization. Anglican connections in the maritime trades worked in Scott's favor, for he supplied ships in New York harbor. Both men served with Downing in the vestry; Ray and Scott were the first two men to represent the parish at the diocesan convention in 1853. In addition to these very public and well-known stories, less successful and less prominent parishioners proved to be upwardly mobile. Listed as a mariner in the 1830 directory, John Carter acquired enough capital to be listed as a grocer in 1840. Peter Van Dyck worked as a waiter in 1830 and moved to a cook's position by 1840; he later became a well-known caterer.[19]

Over time, more St. Philip's parishioners appear in the directories. As young families with children grew more established, they also put down roots and built businesses. Parents in middle age typically had a greater earning potential and likelihood of appearance in the directory than they did before. St. Philip's occupational blueprint also diversified to include a range of artisanal, service, and marine workers seeking niches in the expanding city economy. Fewer members appear to have been unskilled or unlisted: by 1840, three individuals appear in the directory with only an address, outnumbered by workers in all other major categories.[20]

Over time, black Episcopalians appeared with greater frequency in the marine industries. In artisanal trades, white mechanics militantly blocked blacks from work. In unskilled or service positions, white laborers often refused to work alongside blacks. Others insisted upon titles that distinguished them from black coworkers, even when employed at the same position. By contrast, seafaring offered a comparatively egalitarian environment because the dangers at sea demanded a color-blind adherence to ability. By 1825, the marine trades employed as many as one in six St. Philip's parishioners. In that year, mariners ranked as the parish's second-largest single job category, behind only hairdressers and barbers. Although white laborers forced blacks out of some artisanal and laboring positions, blacks found space in skilled and semi-skilled marine positions. These jobs were often low-paying and dangerous, but they offered an identity and status that unskilled work could not.[21]

Like its barbers and restaurateurs, St. Philip's mariners and marine-trade artisans did not enjoy the absolute freedom of self-employment. In fact, their status as Episcopalians may have earned them jobs, at the price of social deference. Many of New York's ship captains were Episcopalian, including a number of prominent pewholders at Trinity and Trinity's chapels. Captains held near-absolute authority over their charges at sea. These men appear to have hired many of their coreligionists, white and black, for several lesser pewholders at the white chapels also worked in marine-trade artisan positions like caulking and shipjoining. Religious identity offered opportunity, but also reiterated dependence.[22]

By the 1840s, the service elite dominated St. Philip's leadership positions. Episcopal historian Craig Townsend's analysis of the social composition of St. Philip's vestry during the 1840s and 1850s uncovered a preponderance of service laborers. Few artisans won leadership positions. A black professional class emerged in this era, for teachers and two doctors held vestry seats, yet even they remained far less numerous than the barbers, porters, and waiters.[23]

St. Philip's parishioners thus modeled the ideal of uplift that black elites hoped would put the lie to racism. Consequently, St. Philip's congregants occupied important positions in New York's abolitionist and reform communities. Earlier deference, as exemplified in the African Society in the 1790s and Wilberforce Society in the 1800s, had dissipated. Rector Peter Williams was one of only three blacks who served on the first executive committee of the American Anti-Slavery Society, alongside black Presbyterians Theodore Wright and Samuel Cornish. Soon black Episcopal laymen would join Williams on the rolls of the organization, men such as Thomas Jennings, Thomas and George T. Downing, James McCune Smith, and Alexander Crummell.[24]

As elite blacks, St. Philip's parishioners supported concepts of uplift as a means to combat racism. The reality of their uplift meant that many depended upon white economic patronage for their success. Their religion, no less, demanded interactions with white benefactors. The Episcopalian tradition stressed a cultural Anglophilia that served blacks' literary aspirations well. But the support of high culture and literary achievement generally came from the High Church wing, which demanded obedience as much as it required morality, especially when the church hierarchy issued orders. And in the 1830s, the High Church vision would increasingly retreat from politics, as a way to keep the church unique and united.

Despite the increased wealth of St. Philip's parishioners, black Episcopalians submitted to white leadership. St. Philip's vestry repeatedly appealed to High Church Trinity for financial support. The church also took collections for High Church benevolent societies that promoted an explicitly Episcopalian identity. As a High Church parish, St. Philip's parishioners believed that the church retained its authority because of the apostolic succession of its bishops. Hierarchy was central to the church's uniqueness and authority. Thus black Episcopalians remained under white church leaders, even as those leaders refused St. Philip's representation at the diocesan convention.[25] Consequently, St. Philip's parishioners supported abolition and reform, yet rarely offered the public pronouncements that other black reformers offered.

This hesitance is clear in considering Rector Peter Williams's stance toward colonization, an issue that reappeared periodically throughout the antebellum era. Colonization variously represented early forms of black nationalism or Western colonialism. It optimistically appealed to those momentarily lifted in millennial promise; and, conversely, it pessimistically served as a measure of last resort when race relations grew especially grim. Finally, colonization became a flashpoint for black resistance when whites of dubious motives advocated it.[26]

The American Colonization Society (ACS) formed in 1816 as an ostensibly charitable way to deal with the problems of racism and slavery in America. ACS officials held that only by removal to Africa could free blacks avoid the stigma of racism and fully develop a healthy society. Supported by prominent slaveholders in the Upper South, the ACS trumpeted a series of conflicting positions on race. Supporters argued that blacks were too degraded to thrive in white America but that American blacks could uplift and civilize pagan African society. They held that severe racism in America required removal, although presented themselves as benevolent friends of the Negro. They also hinted that colonization would induce slaveholders to manumit their slaves in greater numbers. In fact, the ACS did little to increase manumissions. Instead, the organization provided slaveholders with a rationale to remove free blacks from American society. Thriving communities proved that free blacks were not hopelessly degraded. Slaveholders feared that free blacks inspired slaves to run away or rebel. They also suspected that free black organizations surreptitiously aided runaways.[27]

Before the American Colonization Society formed, many African Americans accepted Africa as a cultural heritage. They willingly took the title African throughout the late eighteenth and early nineteenth centuries. In their public orations celebrating the end of the slave trade many black leaders, including St. Philip's future rector Peter Williams, publicly hailed Africa as an Edenic home. A black ship captain, Paul Cuffee, led an early attempt to plant an African colony in 1815. Such efforts contained within them millennial dreams of transforming their home continent, and serving as a shining example to all Christians, white and black. The ACS's aims, however, provoked full-scale opposition in the black community. Widespread black opposition convinced some reform-minded whites to support immediate abolitionism as a more effective and just solution to America's racial problems.[28]

The free black response to the American Colonization Society was so vociferous and united that some scholars of abolitionism have portrayed colonization as an inherently suspect undertaking.[29] Many black leaders viewed the subject with greater ambiguity. When pessimism over race relations increased and blacks' social or legal status eroded, some black leaders considered colonization very closely.

St. Philip's rector Peter Williams steered a middle road between activism against the ACS's racist claims and acquiescence to its goals. Williams delivered the funeral oration for Paul Cuffee in 1817. In 1824, Williams chaired the New York chapter of the Haytian (Haitian) Emigration Society of Coloured People, and addressed emigrants in the Zion African Methodist Church before their departure.[30] When Haiti became an unattractive destination for emigration, colonizationists turned to British Canada. Williams again supported their efforts. On the Fourth of July 1830, Williams preached a sermon in support of black emigrants to Wilberforce, a town in Canada.[31]

On one level, Williams's support reveals only strong fraternal bonds with blacks who had made up their own minds to leave America: in a speech supporting a Canadian colonization group, Williams contrasted the ACS's tortured aims with the clear reasoning behind the émigrés decision. But Williams also remained friendly with such procolonization voices as John Russwurm. Cofounder of the first black periodical *Freedom's Journal*, Russwurm made an abrupt about-face toward colonization in 1828 that earned him scorn from the black leaders who had worked with him; he became an agent for the ACS. Russwurm's cultural elitism placed him in a similar place as many of St. Philip's parishioners. Perhaps compromised by the need for financial support from the white church, St. Philip's Episcopalian identity steered its parishioners to a different course from other New York blacks. That course placed them in greater contact with ostensible benefactors in institutions like the ACS, a tactic most other blacks in the city rejected.[32]

Middle-Class Morality at Mother Zion

Unlike black Episcopalians, New York's African Methodists could not readily turn to their white coreligionists for financial support. The Methodist Episcopal Church in New York had little money at its inception, and continually operated at a financial deficit. Further, many of the white ministers who most sympathized with the blacks joined the artisan-heavy ranks of the Stilwellites. They took with them religious fervor but few hard assets.[33]

Zion Church sought institutional independence when Stilwellite leaders hinted that white ministers would confiscate the black church's property. For New York's black Methodists, control over their own modest resources trumped the benefits of association with a larger, wealthier body. During the 1820s and 1830s, African Methodists preferred freedom over financial security. The lack of white patronage allowed Zion's blacks to speak and act freely in the face of white racism. But with the end of slavery in New York, black Methodist leaders drew new status lines within their community, placing acculturated male leaders above Africanized, common, and female sources of influence.

Mother Zion's blacks knew poverty firsthand. Black churchmen had nearly all been slaves early in their lives; their wives, who were less likely to be freed early, may have been slaves as late as 1827. Even middle-class blacks lived in neighborhoods subject to the nuisances and dangers of poverty. Throughout the 1820s, the city inspector noted that outbreaks of yellow fever, consumption, and smallpox hit blacks disproportionately, as much as ten times above their rate of the population. Mother Zion lay near the Five Points neighborhood, the working-class slum that attracted increasing notoriety as the century progressed. Zion's members entering their church would see a brothel next door. They would also pass the homes of other black churchgoers, such as the home of Henry Highland Garnet, who would become a prominent Presbyterian minister and abolitionist, and Alexander Crummell, who would become an Episcopal priest. These juxtapositions were not incongruous: radical reformers who entered the neighborhood accused ministers of attending houses of prostitution. The jumble of what one might consider high and low, bourgeois and proletariat, respectable and criminal, highlights the mixed spatial layout of the early Republic city throughout the antebellum era. Elite whites who could move uptown would consider uplift differently from elite blacks, whose status was more precarious, and more enmeshed in the community around them.[34]

Black leaders thus did not breezily offer hard work and morality as a cure for all social ills. But after 1827, Zion Church leaders emphasized the importance of middle-class moral standards, similar to those that white Methodists promoted. And the leadership of the black church remained more patriarchal than the white. The language of respectability intended to apply to all blacks, but it had enmeshed within it a clear elite and male perspective.[35]

In a July 4, 1827, address at the church, Zion's most prominent layman, William Hamilton, praised the abolition of slavery in New York. Echoing the show speeches that students composed at the city's African Free School, Hamilton opened with a lofty Homeric address to liberty, proclaiming that the principles of the Declaration of Independence had finally gone into effect in New York. He then praised the white men who had worked for abolition—first the Society of Friends, then the Manumission Society. Hamilton opined that children should learn the names of the men who founded the society before they learned those of Washington and Jefferson. Hamilton then critiqued the enemies of liberty. Hamilton marveled at "heterogeneous minds" who could assert that all men are created equal yet keep slaves. In soaring rhetoric, he emphasized right conduct and proper reason in philosophy, revealing the efforts of a man who had taken great pains to seek education.[36]

Hamilton closed with exhortations to young and female blacks in a stronger, more forceful tone. He lamented the "frivolity and lethargy" of black youths, whose behavior seemed to confirm white attacks on black intellect and moral character. Rising to passion, he exclaimed, "Oh! That I could enflame you with proper ambition." In keeping with the twin themes of morality and knowledge, Hamilton asked the youths to follow first a "path of virtue," and then the study of the sciences. He lamented that "properly speaking, there is none learned among us." He suggested that literary societies would allow blacks to advance beyond the circumstances that had limited their efforts thus far.[37]

Hamilton closed with an exhortation to women, noting, "It is for you to form the manners of men." He praised women who pursued "female modesty" in speech and manners, in contrast to women who spoke with "loud or vulgar accents." He then asked black women to associate only with men who took pains to improve their minds. Hamilton finished by asking women to improve their own minds and confidently asserted, "you are more than a match for white females in all proper female education."[38]

Hamilton's exhortations fit squarely within the language of uplift that other black leaders promoted. They contained within them both revolutionary and conservative impulses. Emphasizing that blacks were the intellectual equals of whites, Hamilton struck directly at whites' stated reasons for promoting colonization or race-specific laws. But the objects of study—literary studies for men and modest feminine behavior for women—had little practical value for many blacks. Hamilton's program closed the door of educational opportunity to poorer blacks, as it promoted standards of behavior that even among whites only reached the middle classes. With most of their labors devoted to earning subsistence, few blacks could reach such goals.[39]

African Methodists joined with black Episcopalians in supporting acculturated literary societies. Whereas the first decades of the century witnessed the creation of benevolent societies designed to keep the emerging middle classes out of poverty, in the 1830s black leaders promoted literary societies and higher levels of education. In 1833, Mother Zion's Bishop Christopher Rush helped found the Phoenix Society, a group "devoted to the overall improvement of colored people." The society explicitly supported immediate emancipation, but also encouraged blacks "to improve their minds and to abstain from any vicious and demoralizing practice." It required good moral character in the students it promoted, the mechanics it praised, and the workers it placed.[40]

Hamilton called for domesticity in the black church by an emphasis on proper female modesty and male morality. Black Methodist women agreed with Hamilton's calls for female modesty and support for their men. During the 1830s, they participated in several female-run societies. The Female Mite Society, which raised funds to support ministers, held its meetings at Zion Church, as did the Juvenile Daughters of Ruth, which promoted social and philanthropic events.[41]

As a young man, Peter Williams had been a lone black Episcopalian while participating in black shows of solidarity among men of his father's Methodist faith. By the 1830s, a number of prominent black Episcopalians joined Williams in efforts like the Phoenix Society and the American Anti-Slavery Society. By contrast, William Hamilton, who had around him a company of black Methodist men in his youth, grew to be a lonely example of Mother Zion's public prominence. Apart from Hamilton and Christopher Rush, the number of Mother Zion's congregants taking part in the reform communities dwindled.

Perhaps this silence reflected a greater ambivalence among black lay Methodists toward the reform vision. Mother Zion's older leaders such as William Hamilton squarely supported the uplift ideology. In general, all blacks who entered the public sphere with essays or speeches assumed the value of moral elevation and education. Those who did not support the ideals demanding upright character also apparently disagreed with the means of writing essays and delivering speeches, as few opposing messages survive.

One exception came from Peter Paul Simons, a New York City coal porter who delivered a series of withering remarks to the African Clark-son Association in 1839. Simons praised the efforts by the black churches' previous generation to promote moral uplift and intellectual development. But surveying the contemporary situation, Simons complained that black virtue and morality had created habits of submission toward whites. He thundered, "this moral elevation of our people is but a mere song, it is nothing but a conspicuous scarecrow designed expressly, I may safely say, to hinder our people from acting collectively for themselves." Similarly, Simons lamented that the black emphasis on literary education had created a false hope unfilled by the realities of the market. Instead, Simons judged, white colonizationists attempted to persuade educated blacks that the best use of their education, and real opportunity, lay in Africa. And Simons agreed, insofar as he observed that laboring blacks generally outpaced their educated brothers in earnings and opportunity. He closed calling for uplift in physical strength and political participation: such areas, as yet untried, required black cooperation and action to succeed.[42]

Simons made the same pleas for group action that Hamilton did. But he invoked differing means, ones that separated him from the dominant black voices in the public sphere. As a laborer, he saw little benefit in the moral and intellectual aims of the aspiring professionals above him. Always a church of artisan leadership, perhaps many of Mother Zion's laboring voices from below did not assent to the claims from Rush and Hamilton at the head of the church. Certainly most church members remained silent, whether they agreed or not. Such silence might have reflected a working-class ambivalence toward the dominant means employed in abolitionist and reform communities.[43]

Gentrification and Family Organization at John Street

Like black Episcopalians, John Street's white Methodists grew wealthier in the 1820s. When Methodists built their first chapel on John Street in the 1760s, costs dictated a location north of the city center, beyond the colonial port's important civic and residential addresses. By the 1820s, however, John Street was thoroughly downtown. As the city expanded northward, tenements and slums also moved up Manhattan Island, away from the city center. The oldest Methodist building in New York, John Street Church was also the southernmost Methodist house of worship, near the homes of New York's wealthiest.[44]

From its inception, John Street attracted wealthier Methodists. During the 1790s, John Street Chapel contained a disproportionate share of merchants and retailers, compared to New York Methodism as a whole. Even so, workingmen dominated church leadership: in 1796, only one class leader was a merchant; the rest were artisans.[45] In the ensuing decades, the downtown chapel's composition changed. By 1825, retailers and merchants comprised nearly half the male members, outnumbering artisans by 30 percent. About 10 percent of the members worked in the professions or for the government, well above city averages. Unskilled laborers and poor or transient individuals also declined, as unlisted members dropped from one-third the total of the 1790s to just over one-quarter in 1825. By 1825, John Street Church looked remarkably similar to Trinity Episcopal Church in 1790.[46]

Artisans still comprised over one-third of John Street's male members. By the 1820s, however, many of these artisans held secure positions as high-end laborers who worked lucrative economic niches. John Street's artisans included jewelers, copperplate printers, cabinetmakers, ship joiners, and smiths of copper, tin, and silver. Others held positions that inexpensive immigrant labor had not challenged, such as carpenters, masons, and printers. A few had made the transition from artisan producer to marketer and seller of artisan-made goods. Although several tailors and shoemakers occupied the lists, merchant clothiers and proprietors of shoe stores also attended John Street classes.[47]

The merchants, shopkeepers, and grocers who numerically dominated the downtown chapel clung to an older vision of unity. In no class did any occupational category number more than half of the class's membership. Nor did leaders divert unskilled members into a separate class—the numbers of unlisted members ranged between a quarter and a third in all classes. Artisans and merchants joined professionals in varying numbers, with no classes revealing a preponderance of any occupational type. Thus Methodist religious classes avoided divisions by social classes.[48]

In the 1790s, Methodists took such unity for granted. By the middle of the nineteenth century, the idea of unity required a champion, for social cohesion demanded greater effort. When John Street member James Harper ran for mayor in 1844, he embodied the older vision of a common cause between master and journeyman, merchant and

Figure 7.1. James Harper, as a titan of business and
Methodist patriarch, later in life after his political ambitions
(and penchant for practical jokes) had subsided (see also
chapter 8). (From J. Henry Harper, *House of Harper*, [1912].)

artisan. Harper's printing trade remained comparatively untouched
by inflows of inexpensive immigrant labor. Although head of a giant
publishing house, Harper considered himself a mechanic. Stressing
reform in government, Harper's candidacy blurred the lines between
labor and capital, and attempted to mitigate the differences between
occupations by appealing to a common Protestant nativism. Harper's membership at John Street influenced his political stance, as his
everyday experience of worship provided a model that he promoted
in the public sphere.[49]

While John Street's laity like James Harper preserved old forms of
social order, clerical leaders transformed the churches' bureaucratic
organization. The Stilwellites failed to win local and lay control over
the city churches, but in the aftermath of the controversy Methodists

increased local church authority for the sake of efficiency. Presiding elders found it difficult to administer the city society as a whole, since New York's Methodists now numbered in the thousands, in over a half-dozen congregations. Before 1820, New York preachers listed all classes or members together in indistinguishable groups. Each class attained a label as male or female, white or black, but lacked geographic specificity. Shortly after the Stilwellite secession, city ministers recorded classes by church location, linking each class to a specific congregation.

Methodism's national growth encouraged other administrative changes. At the 1820 Methodist General Conference, the denomination's leaders resolved to establish an American Methodist Missionary Society. As scholar Gregory Schneider notes, early Methodism was in itself a mission, carried out in the worship services, love feasts, class meetings, and quarterly conferences. In experiencing God's saving grace and methodically working toward holiness in small groups, Methodists witnessed to others. But the General Conference recognized that the task of conversion was no longer possible on an ad hoc, individual basis. Leaders now attempted to organize the process of reaching lost souls.[50]

Methodist minister Nathan Bangs typified this rationalizing impulse. Historians of American Methodism often present Bangs as embodying the decline of democratized Methodism. In their accounts, Bangs stifled early American Methodists' popular emotionalism and rough equality.[51]

This interpretation is not wrong, but it overstates early Methodist equality and later Methodist hierarchy. Bangs's insistence on order and discipline paralleled the commands of John Wesley's first lieutenants in America. The means by which Bangs promoted discipline, order, and obedience, however, changed. Bangs supported an increasing professionalism among the denomination's ministers, and a greater bureaucratization of the church's structures. Ministers and laity increasingly had to work through proper channels and labyrinthine organizations to rise in the church hierarchy. Thus while early Methodists supported bishops' unchecked authoritarianism, the ostensibly antidemocratic Bangs promoted procedural reforms that limited individual bishops' authority. This managerial consciousness and stress on order led to a focus on respectability and education for both preachers and laity. But the laity viewed clerical compartmentalization as a sign to privatize their own religious experiences. Family life no longer competed with the Methodist mission but complemented it. In this, Bangs was a participant as much as a promoter of such changes.

Nathan Bangs's father was an Episcopalian who exemplified late colonial social deference. Although a blacksmith, the elder Bangs refused to hear Methodist preachers because he considered them uneducated. Bangs remembered his father's prejudices, as he consistently emphasized the importance of education to the Methodist ministry. He spent the bulk of his career building the Methodist Book Concern into the largest publishing house in America, interrupting this calling only briefly to serve as president of Wesleyan College in Connecticut.[52]

Bangs married Mary Bolton in Canada in 1806, before he turned thirty. Through 1800, many Methodist ministers remained bachelors their entire clerical careers, and married only near retirement. Older preachers disparaged Bangs's action. Acting as a buffer between the generations, Francis Asbury soothed ruffled feathers by making light of Bangs's decision at the Annual Conference. Asbury personally approved Bangs's choice to marry early to keep "young maidens" away from the handsome young minister.[53]

These two priorities for education and family life shaped Bangs's career with the church. At the 1816 General Conference, Bangs sponsored two changes that angered the Stilwellites yet standardized church practices. His committee raised the itinerant minister's family allowance from eighty dollars to one hundred dollars. That committee also ruled that local conferences should maintain preachers' family expenses. Bangs also authored a rule mandating a course of study for all future candidates for the ministry.[54]

Unlike Asbury, who never married and traveled tirelessly, Bangs preferred to remain close to his family, usually in the heart of New York City. As his family grew, Bangs lamented itinerants' low salaries. Bangs attributed his election and reelection as head of the Methodist Book Concern to divine providence, for it allowed him to remain near his wife, who was perennially in poor health. In 1832, Bangs's colleagues pressed him to stand for candidacy as bishop, but he refused, again citing his desire to remain close to home. Bangs also cited his work as editor and steward at the Methodist Book Concern, which connected with evangelization efforts in the tract, Bible, and Sunday School societies. He found such work to be "an equally honorable, and a much more useful sphere of labor" than pastoral duties as a traveling bishop.[55]

As elite residences gradually surrounded John Street, the church's wealthier Methodists entered benevolent and reform organizations that Methodists had typically avoided a generation before. The

Figure 7.2. Nathan Bangs, here as a young and ambitious director of the Methodist Book Concern. (Reproduced with permission from the Methodist Collections at Drew University.)

Manhattan-based Methodist Juvenile Missionary Society formed at John Street. Some of John Street's leading members, such as George Suckley and Gabriel Disosway, joined the American Bible Society as officers. They followed Nathan Bangs, who served as the society's secretary for domestic correspondence. The previous generation emphasized the process of making members holy, which stressed introspection and individual transformation. The new generation of New York City's Methodists demanded outward-directed activity. Formerly, evangelization took place on a small scale and personal basis; now it involved managerial skills and institutional involvement.[56]

Between the 1790s and the 1830s, New York Methodism transformed from a society to a denomination, and from an organic new family to a business organization. Corporately, Methodist leaders created auxiliary and institutional surrogates that supplanted the original Methodist command to evangelize individual souls. Personally, Methodist leaders stressed the importance of the nuclear family to the church. They took these steps slowly. Through the early 1830s, New York Methodists attended church separated by sex. Men and women entered the sanctuary at separate doors and sat on opposite sides. In the early 1830s, the city churches adopted a modified system from a New Jersey congregation. The new system continued to restrict specific rows to men and women, but it alternated them, so that women sat in the center-right and far-left aisles, and men in the center-left and far-right aisles. All Methodists, male and female, could enter at any door.[57]

This complex arrangement had a short life. Within a few years, the western circuit, led by John Street, adopted open seating, with men and women sitting where they pleased. Western circuit churches now sat families together. Closer to fine neighborhoods, the western circuit consisted of wealthy, well-established congregations. These churches had more families, and fewer unattached members. Members no longer sat as spiritual brothers or sisters in gendered blocs, but rather with biological ties of kinship in common.[58]

Churches in poorer regions had fewer nuclear families, and more unattached members. The implications of this change seemed ominous to them. Opponents of this transition, mostly laity, criticized the "promiscuous" seating arrangements, a label suggesting sexual immorality. At the quarterly conference, a lone preacher objected to the unregulated seating. Ministers debated the issue, tabled the objection, and did not visit it again. Church historian Samuel Seaman noted that the eastern circuit resisted the new seating and held out until an unspecified later date, clinging to the old ways, or at least the complex adaptation of them that the New Jersey plan suggested.[59]

Paralleling the steps taken toward family seating were organizational changes leaders imposed upon the city society. Around the time the New Jersey seating arrangement took hold, Methodist ministers split the New York City society into east and west circuits. Like the alternating male-female seating arrangement, the bisected circuit structure did not last long. In 1838, city circuits yielded to a truly congregational model, in which each church incorporated itself separately. Instead of rotating each Sunday to a different chapel within one's circuit, city ministers took charge of a single congregation for a one- or two-year period.[60]

This new arrangement bolstered the new family-centered vision of Methodism. City ministers no longer took on the mantle of a wandering prophet seeking the lost, but as shepherds of an established fold, tending those already in the pen. With a settled pastorate, the increasingly trained and professional ministry gained greater influence in each congregation, at the expense of lay ministers and class leaders who had exerted more influence in the absence of a regular pastor. Without class leader oversight, the home came to be the locus of Methodist spirituality.[61]

Trinity's Chapels as Proto-Suburban Retreats

Methodists came to grips with the new economic and managerial order because their ranks contained members of the new elite. By contrast, Episcopalians at Trinity had to adjust to new realities, because the mercantile families of the Revolution—old wealth—filled their pews. Such families lost relative status over time, as new elites in manufacturing and real estate speculation entered their circle. The loss was only relative, however, for new wealth often allied with old wealth to gain social respectability. Cultural adjustments did not alter the general composition of those in charge of the church.

Trinity's chapel pew lists reveal that Trinity parish remained an upper-middle class haven. Compared to the 1790s, the number of merchants decreased slightly, and the number of artisans increased slightly. But the professional and government category actually increased substantially in Trinity's Episcopal chapels: professionals and public officials generally equaled the number of artisans holding pews. Although this composition reflected a slight relative decline in wealth, Trinity parish still lacked unskilled workers.[62]

The professionalization of the church transformed the worldview of old mercantile families. In the Revolutionary era, such elites favored restrictions on the economy or commerce. Demands of the moral economy such as living wages and just prices allowed them to fix prices and regularize profits, and their personal connections with other elite families across the Atlantic gave them advantages in securing contracts and working outside the free market. Such elites favored traditional, paternalist social relations.[63]

The city's expansion challenged these elites' former dominance. The numbers of beggars, thieves, and prostitutes exploded, which almshouse officials and police struggled in vain to manage. Everywhere they walked, the wealthy encountered swarms of nuisances from these lower orders. The expansion of the economy also eroded the gains old mercantile families earned in a regulated market. Auctioneers, whose state-granted licenses gave them near-monopoly power at the ports and wholesale establishments, lost market share to direct shippers and smaller firms. Even domestic servants grew more insolent with the coming of political freedom, and wealthy New Yorkers lamented the difficulties of acquiring dependable help.[64]

Leading men adapted to the social changes by retreating into domestic solace. They increasingly managed their affairs from a distance, their homes moved from the busiest streets and places of business. Stephen Nissenbaum colorfully illustrated this transformation in his description of the life of Clement Clarke Moore. The son of Trinity rector and New York bishop Benjamin Moore, Clement inherited large tracts of land from his mother's family. His associates like John Pintard were also Trinity pewholders, gentlemen of the old school, suspicious of untrammeled urban development and economic expansion.[65]

Like Trinity parish, Moore owned lands north of the city and witnessed the relentless push northward of developers and squatters alike. Seeking to control the development, Moore granted a plot of land to the General Convention of the Episcopal Church, which proceeded to erect an Episcopalian seminary on the site. He held other plots as commercial investments. Gentlemen like Moore adapted to the new situation, largely by moving uptown or out of town. Their new estates with gates and watchmen privatized their living arrangements in a way previously unseen.[66]

Moore's associate John Pintard experienced downward mobility. In the early nineteenth century, Pintard's fortunes had fallen, and although he secured favorable employment with a bank, he was beholden to his wife's social connections and his employer's beneficence. Employer-supplied housing left Pintard and his family near his place of business on Wall Street and far from new, fashionable neighborhoods. The family struggled to find dependable domestic help and complained that even former slaves commanded bargaining power in the free labor market. Without the amenities or privacy of a newly constructed home, Pintard lamented his family's fate. Like Moore, Pintard idealized the concept of a wholly private household. An earlier generation symbolized its importance by living in prominent busy locations; now the wealthy prized seclusion, typified by physical distance from the busiest streets.[67]

In the chapels, Trinity's members found an environment more congenial to their semi-suburban tastes. Originally built as chapels of ease in overlooked locations, St. Paul's and St. John's became home to social networks that rivaled the flagship church. St. Paul's Chapel had originally lain north of the city, near the ramshackle homes of laborers and poor artisans. As the city expanded northward, St. Paul's parishioners noted with horror that houses of prostitution dominated the area. St. Paul's was also the only Episcopalian chapel to reserve pews for free blacks, a practice that instantly challenged its social credit.[68]

The city's northward growth soon passed St. Paul's location on Broadway. The chapel then housed large numbers of professionals, and its occupational composition paralleled that of Trinity, its mother church. The race problem also faded with greater segregation in worship. When black Episcopalians created St. Philip's in 1819, many free blacks left St. Paul's. As free black Episcopalians moved to their segregated parish, St. Paul's complexion again whitened.[69]

On the west side, St. John's neighborhood dramatically transformed from sleepy pastureland to become a center of Manhattan high society. At the turn of the century, Trinity's vestry created Hudson's Square northwest of the city, enclosing the pasture around Varick, Beach, Hudson, and Laight Streets. They hired the noted architect John McComb to erect the neoclassical chapel of St. John's. When McComb completed the square and chapel in 1807, observers deemed it "the most elegant building spot . . . in the whole city." City elites, however, avoided residency there for twenty years. Through the 1810s, wealthy individuals preferred to live closer to the town's center, the lower Manhattan stretch of Broadway from the Battery to the Park. The vestry's insistence that the residences around the square be leased for ninety-nine years also met with cold indifference from upper-class speculators, who watched the value of plots throughout the city accelerate. Ambitious city residents demanded outright ownership of their homes.[70]

Frustrated that its custom-built chapel overlooked an empty pasture, in 1827 Trinity's vestry ended the lease requirement and offered the lots for sale. Lot buyers would gain a portion of square ownership. Soon leading families like the Schuylers and Tappans took up residency. Conservative in politics and patrician in outlook, the new owners placed an iron fence around the square and planted swaths of trees to heighten privacy. On this northwest corner of the city, elites could afford exclusivity and privacy. The chapel's pewholder composition revealed large numbers

Figure 7.3. St. John's Episcopal Chapel, new symbol of elite elegance. (From Morgan Dix, *History of Trinity Church*, vol. 3 [1905].)

of managerial and professional elites, similar in status to those at the mother church of Trinity.[71]

Conclusion

During the economic expansion of the 1820s, each church developed a distinctive identity in response to the increasing gentrification of its parishioners. St. Philip's attempted the greatest change, as its formerly impoverished congregants grew to include the city's wealthiest blacks. But such wealth came with continued signs of deference to white Anglican benefactors. Mother Zion's institutional independence allowed its congregation to celebrate the end of slavery in the city on its own terms. Those terms included an emphasis on moral conduct, cultural attainment, and traditional sex roles. If any members disagreed, they did not do so publicly. John Street's members embraced a new professionalized clergy, as the congregation embodied a new class of professional and merchandizing Methodists. Downtown Methodists further accepted bureaucratic mission societies and worship services centered on the life of the nuclear family. Trinity also professionalized, as old elites underwent the transformation to new elites. Uptown chapels began to hold greater attraction for the church's old wealth.

As churches grew wealthier and more homogeneous, hierarchy came to be found among and between, rather than within, church congregations. Poorer individuals still attended churches, but typically in their own neighborhoods. Trinity, John Street, and Mother Zion all brokered their genteel status into leadership within their respective denominations, as their congregants represented well-off and powerful individuals in the nation's premier city. But churches that relied upon preeminent neighborhoods for status also found that their reputations could suffer when those locations grew less desirable. Economic downturns also shaped religious prestige.

In the following decade, social dislocations upset the churches' push toward gentrification. Immigration, racial conflict, and poverty shook the city. Racial fissures widened. Economic recessions clobbered religious institutions. The resulting adjustments and compromises are the subject of the next chapter, in which immigration, nativism, and riots forced most individuals in these four congregations toward a wholly privatized religious experience.

8 / Reaping the Whirlwind: Immigration and Riot, 1830–1850

In 1827, the New York state legislature completed its slow path to abolition and freed all of New York's remaining slaves. Starting that Fourth of July, and continuing for the next seven years, New York blacks celebrated their freedom with parades, speeches, and demonstrations. The eighth year, their neighborhoods burned. Enraged by the bold political actions of immediate abolitionists and rumors of interracial sex, angry mobs destroyed black businesses and homes and completely dismantled St. Philip's Episcopal Church. William Hamilton's sons remembered their father, a sixty-year-old man, unbowed in his resistance. Grabbing armfuls of iron "missiles," Hamilton ran toward his house, proclaiming his willingness to die in defense of his home.[1]

Hamilton did not die there, in the riots; two years later, however, his death from natural causes marked a transition in the black churches. Hamilton was the last of the original Zion founders and one of a few dwindling members of Mother Zion to remain in the public eye as a leader in reform movements. His passing symbolized a general decline in his church's prestige.

Americans faced generally diminished expectations during the 1830s and 1840s. During the later 1830s, the American economy took a turn for the worse. Andrew Jackson's promise of a democratic revolution had ended in disappointment, as his fiscal policies provoked a massive recession. Even as the economy faltered, the population grew unabated, and immigrants poured into the northern seaport cities in greater numbers.

In New York, radical workingmen's parties appeared. The cause of immediate abolitionism spurred working-class whites' anxieties, and anti-abolitionist, antiblack riots such as New York's rocked northern cities throughout the 1830s.

A half century earlier, John Wesley cautioned that while his followers' industriousness created profit, that profit would lead to spiritual decline.[2] Worldliness strained the organic conception of society that Methodists and Episcopalians both claimed in an earlier era. By the 1830s, the results were clear. The end of slavery heightened racial awareness, and the churches drew strict lines separating blacks and whites. White church leaders championed colonization schemes to send blacks to Africa, a move their colored coreligionists generally opposed. Wealthier members removed themselves from Lower Manhattan congregations, finding spiritual havens outside the city. The holistic colonial ideal was no more, but neither did churchgoers experience a united community within their own congregations. Instead, congregants created personal worlds of meaning within smaller frames of reference. They heightened denominational and congregational identity and guarded attacks on the boundaries of both. They retreated into family life to preserve religious faith against a hostile outside world.

Three major events in the 1830s and 1840s frame city religious experience. First, anti-abolitionist and antiblack rioting polarized attitudes in the churches, black and white. Black leaders discovered that the end of slavery increased whites' hostility toward them, as they now appeared more dangerous without the status limitations. Black churches reiterated their denominational boundaries as a defensive action against a hostile larger society. For black Episcopalians, this required a particularly adroit balancing act, since they remained under the oversight of white church leadership. Second, nativist politics and colonization efforts appealed to many white Protestants as a way to reestablish the organic society lost after the Revolution. Many hoped nativism might dissolve social conflict in a religious unity. Third, because the churches tied their fortunes to the market, they also experienced sharp declines in fortune during economic slowdowns. The city's northward expansion ended the lower wards' social prominence. Congregants resorted to appeals of historical memory and nostalgia to remain relevant. In all cases, the churches reflected diminished expectations, as religious life within the city became a form of cultural expression of public respectability but not of transformation.

The Destruction of St. Philip's and the Difficulties of Uplift

Dozens of anti-abolition riots engulfed American cities in the mid-1830s. In the hot July of 1834, New York City suffered through ten days of intense rioting. Rioters first targeted pro-reform whites, as mobs disrupted abolitionist gatherings organized to commemorate the end of slavery in the British Empire. The crowds then turned their rage on the African American community. Rioters beat individual blacks in the streets, looted African American homes and black-owned businesses, and dismantled the area's chief symbol of black public life, St. Philip's Episcopal Church.[3]

It might appear that African Methodists, not black Episcopalians, would have given the rioters a more obvious target. An older and larger church, Mother Zion had housed the first freedom celebrations, and issued the first black-run benevolence societies. Its ministers and lay leaders loudly and publicly criticized American slavery and racism. The church building hosted public events for abolitionist causes. By contrast, St. Philip's held an ambiguous relationship to the black community. Dependent upon the white church for financial survival, its vestry clung to its relationship with Trinity parish. Its minister supported black-run attempts at colonization to Africa, Haiti, and Canada, when significant numbers of blacks rejected colonizationist ventures. And its congregants were not militant artisans, but service workers whose very livelihood depended upon deference to their patrons.[4]

Nonetheless, far more than Mother Zion, St. Philip's existence threatened anti-abolitionists' beliefs. The black artisans who founded Mother Zion held marginal places in the economy. The most successful remained small producers with modest incomes. In contrast, many of St. Philip's parishioners worked in service industries rather than in artisan crafts. Service workers typically occupied the lower rungs in the mercantile economy's hierarchy, yet in proto-industrializing New York, St. Philip's service workers prospered. Despite their lesser rank, St. Philip's parishioners like Thomas Downing had achieved great standing and wealth. In an environment where many working-class whites languished, black displays of affluence greatly irritated common white men who cherished their racial supremacy.[5]

Further, St. Philip's parishioners chose forms of worship that revealed high aspirations (and for whites, pretension). Compared to the Episcopalians, Mother Zion's Methodists favored an enthusiastic style of worship similar to the practices of many plebeian whites. St. Philip's attendees, however, rejected low Wesleyanism for high Episcopalianism. A bulwark of traditionalism, the Episcopal Church attracted individuals suspicious of social change. Yet black Episcopalians challenged assumptions of rank and order by claiming membership within a church that recognized such rank and order. Within the Episcopal framework, St. Philip's blacks allied with the High Church, a position that claimed special status as the one true church, a distinction that riled other Protestants. Further, High Church theology demanded liturgical precision and order. St. Philip's very order of worship challenged racist assumptions about black unruliness.[6]

New York's anti-abolitionists thus found an obvious target in the African Episcopal Church. Anglican elites like the white Lorillard family rejected racial solidarity to serve as patrons for St. Philip's parishioners. In a capricious economy, black Episcopalians prospered. Blacks dared choose a religious denomination that, to its white adherents, reflected aspirations in rank and quality that they did not deserve. St. Philip's defied the racial order. A monstrosity, its existence caused outrage.[7]

During the riots, many journalists reported rumors of interracial sex among the abolitionists. A false story circulated that St. Philip's rector, Peter Williams, had married an interracial couple, leading rioters to target the church. St. Philip's unique status in the black community aggravated the fear of race mixing. Because the congregation mimicked upper-class white norms, it blurred boundaries between black and white. The church, in essence, appeared to be a collectively passing community, down to the report that its minister joined blacks and whites in sacramental union. The possibility that blacks could and did act like whites apparently drove white anxieties more than issues of black servility or crime. Historian Tyler Anbinder noted that white mobs attacked not the poorest black tenements or run-down businesses, but those that evidenced institutional strength and prosperity.[8]

Most black leaders accepted Euro-American standards of cultural attainment. Black Episcopalians especially pursued European ideals, as their order of worship committed them to following the high-toned English and rich liturgical order of the Book of Common Prayer. Leading laity, such as Boston Crummell, Thomas Jennings, and Peter Vogelsang, joined Peter Williams on the board of the Phoenix Society, which promoted literature and the arts as well as upright and moral behavior.[9]

Blacks who acquired Euro-American culture blurred racial lines, challenging boundaries that whites jealously guarded. St. Philip's rector

Figure 8.1. Peter Williams Jr., learned orator, rector of St.
Philip's, and, like his father, an attempted uniter of black
groups. His passport listed his complexion as "yellow,"
showing the complexities in how Americans saw race.
(Courtesy of Moorland-Springarn Research Center, Howard
University.)

was an accomplished orator. John Jay II judged Peter Williams Jr. "a gentleman both in his character and deportment." In the 1830s, Williams
acquired an American passport to travel to abolitionist meetings in England. The passport recorded his complexion as yellow. The grandson of
Africans, Williams had dark skin, as his portrait reveals. Even so, Williams's professional attire, upright bearing, and polished diction allowed
the issuer of the passport to perceive a mulatto. If the dark-skinned

Williams could become light, then lighter blacks could perhaps pass for white. To most whites, that simply should not happen.[10]

St. Philip's parishioners with light skin and high culture did not attempt to pass racially as whites. Instead, their accomplishments highlighted the inequality of the racial line. Of East Indian and German heritage, Isaiah De Grasse might have passed for white, but he associated with the black Anglican community. Thus when De Grasse petitioned Bishop Benjamin Onderdonk for admission into the Episcopal seminary, Onderdonk refused, citing white resistance to black classmates. James McCune Smith, son of a South Carolina slave, was three-quarters white. He knew of at least six schoolmates who were living as whites. Yet Smith chose to remain in the black community, where he served St. Philip's parish as vestryman, and became the first African American in the United States to earn a medical degree.[11]

Anglican blacks' willingness to combine cultural assimilation and political resistance confused and dismayed their white opponents. Although Thomas Downing's oyster house deferred to white customers and excluded blacks, his business success granted him freedom to resist utter servility. After the mid-1830s, Downing expanded his restaurant and gained the loyalty of New York's finest gourmands. His support for immediate abolitionist organizations subsequently grew public and unyielding. He once forced a driver to let him ride a segregated trolley, and boldly aided abolitionist speakers like Frederick Douglass who passed through the city. His ability to take such positions reflected his wealth, which afforded some insurance against white retaliation. Downing's combination of business deference with political tenacity enraged many whites. It reflected a seeming duplicity no less dangerous than race mixing or race passing.[12]

The aftermath of the riot exposed the fault lines among Episcopal churchmen regarding race. New York's bishop and Trinity's rector, Benjamin Onderdonk, had blocked both Alexander Crummell and Isaiah De Grasse from attending the city's Episcopal seminary. Although he offered cold and formal condolences at the destruction of St. Philip's, Onderdonk also blamed black reformers for the violence directed at the church. The bishop directed Williams to resign his office with the American Anti-Slavery Society (AA-SS), where Williams served as secretary.[13]

Peter Williams resigned his executive position with the AA-SS per Onderdonk's directions, although he pointedly praised the society's principles in a letter to the bishop. The letter reveals a mixture of appeals and motives, perhaps reflecting Williams's own conflicted emotions on

Figure 8.2. James McCune Smith, the first black medical doctor in the United States and a St. Philip's vestryman. He reported classmates passing as white but himself identified as a black Episcopalian. (From Daniel Payne, *Recollections of Seventy Years* [1888].)

the issue. Williams stressed his (and his father's) patriotism, even as High Churchmen typically invoked a scrupulous neutrality in regard to politics. He also affirmed his support for the abolitionist society, again undercutting the High Church's position of silence on public issues.[14] But Williams's letter ultimately affirmed the bishop's authority, and offered only subtle protests. The honey-sweet tone with which Williams addressed the bishop, which resonated in American Victorian oratory, sounds cloying and deferential to the modern ear. And in church matters Williams shied from the public sphere. Williams did not intend that his mild protest to Onderdonk be made public—Onderdonk, not Williams, had their exchange published. Williams complained privately that Onderdonk had edited out his most forceful antislavery stances. But had Onderdonk not published the letter, the public would only have known that Williams resigned as AA-SS secretary after a race riot, with no explanation whatsoever.[15]

Williams's submission to church hierarchy affirmed a uniquely Episcopalian position on race, one that kept blacks subservient. As church historian Craig Townsend has suggested, Williams broke with abolitionists in newer evangelical denominations that promoted various forms of "ultraism." Williams specifically noted that within the AA-SS he attempted to exert a "restraining influence upon measures calculated to advance our people faster than they were prepared to be advanced, and the public feeling would bear." This gradualism affirmed an identity within a traditional denomination at odds with abolitionist evangelicals. The choice to remain Episcopalian entailed submission, despite any subtle protests inserted in the process.[16]

After Williams's death in 1840, St. Philip's parish continued to seek a third way between abolitionism and quietism, but that path ultimately led to a greater acquiescence. Prominent parishioners such as Thomas Downing remained active politically, but as a corporate body, the church retreated from militancy. Thus when Low Churchmen suspended Bishop Onderdonk for moral impropriety, St. Philip's vestry, with the exception of Downing, offered a resolution supporting the bishop, urging him not to resign.[17] This support came despite Onderdonk's continued opposition to blacks attending the New York seminary, and his tepid show of support to the parish after its near-destruction. The vestry also distanced itself from the efforts of Low Churchmen such as John Jay II to have the congregation be represented at the diocesan convention. Vestrymen feared that Jay's strident tones and moral one-upsmanship hurt their chances at winning support from other churchmen.[18]

The vestry hired no rector for thirty-two years after Peter Williams's death. Instead, they appointed white priests as officiating ministers or worship assistants. The Episcopal Church offered few black candidates for the ministry, but St. Philip's also refused to call blacks who had gained proper credentials. The vestry often internally divided on the position of individual candidates, but generally the congregation's decision to cleave to High Church principles and support the church power structure kept black ministers from being hired. In one instance, the vestry rejected Alexander Crummell, despite his impeccable education and high-bred culture, because they feared the strident priest disrespected the church hierarchy. In another case, the church passed over a black candidate as worship assistant, except on a temporary basis, because he lacked the talent to properly lead the liturgy. The result of such decisions was that white assistant ministers who were invariably allied with the High Church hierarchy influenced all congregational decisions.[19] The insistence on institutional unity for St. Philip's meant exclusion of those individuals rejecting the High Church position.

Bolstering Orthodoxy in the Black Church: Retreat from Ultraism

Mother Zion shared with St. Philip's a devotion to orthodoxy, even for those churchmen who, like Peter Williams, voiced the radical strains of abolitionism. As William Lloyd Garrison and his allies pushed the aims of the American Anti-Slavery Society to more extreme reforms, black clergy and laity remained orthodox in matters of religion, theology, and gender norms. In 1839, when Garrison's radicals pushed to include women in the roll call of the American Anti-Slavery Society convention, the New York delegation voted against the measure. This included Episcopal laymen Thomas Jennings, James McCune Smith, and Thomas Downing, who joined with their rector, Peter Williams, in opposing the measure. Joining the Episcopalians was Zion Methodist bishop Christopher Rush. New York was outvoted, and the AA-SS appeared to move in a new direction, supporting women's rights.

Lewis Tappan, a silk merchant who spearheaded New York's antislavery efforts, led an attempt to roll back women's involvement in the society. Tappan argued that including women was not only inexpedient, but failed to reflect the views of abolitionists nationally. His veiled language implied New England's dominance over the society was "local and sectarian" and "of recent origin." After the original measure passed, many abolitionists acquiesced to the Garrisonian vision; Tappan's counterattack received fewer votes. Nonetheless, many churchmen, including most black men, remained with Tappan. In this effort, Episcopal laymen Thomas Downing and Thomas Jennings joined fellow churchman John Jay II, who was theologically an adversary as a Low Church Episcopalian, but similarly inclined to oppose the issue of women's rights. Outvoted, these men joined other black ministers, alongside white reformers like Tappan, and left the American Anti-Slavery Society. In 1840, they formed the American and Foreign Anti-Slavery Society (AFASS).[20]

The AFASS drew support from orthodox Protestants and reformers outside New England. Its leaders rejected Garrison's principle of moral suasion in favor of promoting abolitionist political parties. They further held that the AA-SS's recognition of women's rights and tolerance of members with heterodox religious beliefs harmed the abolitionist cause. AFASS reformers argued that support for such measures painted the movement as an extreme sect to most Americans. The AFASS offered black clerics two options that the first abolitionist group ignored. First, it rejected moral suasion as ineffective and utopian, and promised greater future change by advocating political involvement. Second, it affirmed orthodox Protestant doctrine and cultural norms, which attracted clergy invested in protecting their churches from heresies and nontraditional beliefs. From their inceptions, St. Philip's and Mother Zion housed men who valued order and who went through the proper channels. The AFASS's unwillingness to associate with heretics attracted many black churchmen. Most black Christians apparently agreed, for after 1840 few blacks joined the AA-SS in leadership roles.[21]

Denominational Infighting and Outfighting at Mother Zion

Mother Zion escaped major damage in the 1834 riots. Lacking prominent congregants like Thomas Downing or public leaders like Peter Williams, anti-abolitionist mobs apparently overlooked it. While the congregation's individual leaders—clergy like Christopher Rush and laity such as William Hamilton—were involved in benevolence, reform, and abolitionist movements, the church occupied a separate social space not entirely part of the reform community. The church's increasing focus on ecclesiastical matters led inward, not outward, to emphases on institution building and theological orthodoxy.

While Bishop Christopher Rush retained a public presence in reform organizations, he took a less prominent role in the national conversation. The author of the Zionite Methodist denomination's first history, Rush focused on internal church development and bureaucratic forms over external networking. William Hamilton, of Varick's generation, had taken the lead in creating cross-congregational and interdenominational connections in the city. Hamilton's sons judged Rush as "meek"; they intended the characterization to compliment his piety, but the label also suggests Zion's underwhelming public presence after the 1830s.[22]

Continued rivalries between black Methodist groups also contributed to Zion's public retreat. Issues of prestige and social status, so central to initial black efforts at church independence, and a crucial ideological aspect of reforms stressing uplift, drove divisions that kept Mother Zion off the public stage. Richard Allen proposed a national convention for all African Americans to be held in his home city of Philadelphia. Allen's success in attracting the convention apparently suppressed New York's black Methodists from participating. Black Episcopalians, not Methodists, tended to represent New York, supplemented by Presbyterians. Thomas Jennings, Thomas Downing, Boston Crummell, and Peter Vogelsang appeared as provisional committee members or convention delegates. Methodist preacher William Miller attended, but at that time he associated with Allen's Bethel group, not the Zionites. Henry Sipkins and William Hamilton remained the only prominent names from Zion's African Methodists. With Hamilton's passing a few years later, Zion's early connections to reform strained further. A new type of reform would emerge with fewer institutional church connections, as symbolized by laity like Sojourner Truth and David Ruggles.[23]

Zion's emphasis on order and orthodoxy helps explain why members shied away from connections with some abolitionists and fellow black Methodists. Such a stance did contain benefits. The black church's penchant for order is striking in contrast with the democratically minded white Stilwellites, whose church did not last. The Stilwellites retreated into congregational utopianism and failed to create broader denominational connections. Stilwellites reabsorbed into the main body of Methodists in one generation. By contrast, black Methodists explicitly created connections to grow the denomination. The difference lay in the type of fellowship extended to others: although the Stilwellites promoted a primitive Christianity that stressed common bonds between groups as different as Quakers and Methodists, they regarded institutional structures as evidence of clerical corruption. The Zionites, however, took a much narrower view of their religious practices, embracing an orthodox, Methodist position on matters of doctrine and church order. But such orthodoxy allowed for the creation of institutional connections. Consequently, the black church expanded throughout the Northeast.[24]

Mother Zion's denomination made impressive gains on its black Methodist rival. Richard Allen's Philadelphia-based Bethel connection remained larger, as it benefited from an earlier start and a proximity to large black populations in the Upper South. The Zionites, however, made national gains, expanding into New England and Upstate New York. And within New York City the once-hot rivalry between the two groups abated as the Allenites suffered losses. Formerly a congregation of 350 souls, New York's Bethel church dwindled to about 40 by 1850. Mother Zion, in contrast, housed 2,000, not counting the members of its daughter chapel Asbury. Even as black Baptists and Presbyterians built their own churches in New York, Mother Zion remained the largest black-run church in the city.[25]

By the 1840s, Mother Zion's status as home church to a growing denomination was secure. In 1843, the Zion connection could boast of forty-five congregations in nine states, including two in the Allenites' home city of Philadelphia. It reached southward into slave territory, planting churches in the District of Columbia and Maryland. Although two-thirds of the denomination's congregations were in the states of New York and Pennsylvania, Bishops Varick and Rush had laid the foundation for massive growth after the Civil War, when the Zion connection would aggressively expand into the states of the defeated Confederacy.[26]

The growth of the African Methodist Episcopal Zion (AMEZ) denomination came at a cost. For twenty years after 1840, political infighting wracked the AMEZ church. Conferences debated the rights of competing bishops to govern, and elected different slates of assistant bishops in varying numbers, even though the discipline did not make provision for such an office. Church leaders valued the right to titles and authority within the denomination over issues of evangelization.[27] The impulse toward respectability that initially created the church, and led to calls for reform, could also tear the church apart when carried to extreme conclusions.

Lay and Female Opposition to Black Church Leadership

At the congregational level, it appears that Mother Zion remained somewhat more working-class, and thus less pro-reform or pro–moral uplift, than other elite black churches. This allowed the church to be spared some of the harshest criticisms that reform-minded blacks sometimes levied. Abolitionist orator Frederick Douglass shared black ministers' goal of promoting acculturated education for African Americans. He painstakingly acquired literacy and eloquence acceptable to highly cultured whites. But as Douglass promoted immediate abolitionism as

a moral imperative, he broke with the ministers on the proper defini-
tion of religious responsibilities. Over time Douglass criticized limitations in the Protestant churches generally, and in many black churches
specifically.

A Methodist convert, Douglass's encounters with Methodist slaveholders in his native Maryland left a lasting impression on him. Noting
that the most revered religious men in the local Methodist society were
also often the cruelest drivers and owners, Douglass grew impatient with
the church's promises of equality before God. Douglass's later messages
presented God's activity in the world as largely limited to setting moral
laws, the prohibition of owning slaves chief among them. Douglass
asserted that after setting up the laws of the universe, God required his
people to act on their own. His early encounter with religious hypocrisy
left Douglass with little interest in doctrinal orthodoxy. Consequently,
he remained with the Garrisonians in 1840.[28]

During the 1840s, Douglass criticized black churches for accepting society's racial caste system. Racially segregated churches removed
blacks from the minds of white congregants. Douglass also condemned
ministers interested in their own aggrandizement over their congregants' needs. He also disparaged preachers who did not emphasize abolitionism first and foremost. Certainly Peter Williams fit the description
when he resigned his position in the AA-SS at his bishop's command.
Christopher Rush also rejected Douglass's Garrisonians for the orthodox
AFASS, and tended to focus on denomination building over reform. By
the 1840s, then, a professional black abolitionist community embraced
the ministers' call for benevolence and moral activity, but exceeded the
ministers' bounds of theological orthodoxy. Increasingly, though, such
abolitionists found themselves without a home; the Garrisonian AA-SS
grew increasingly white in composition, especially among its leadership,
while black leaders tended to join the forces of religious orthodoxy in
groups like the Tappan brothers' AFASS.[29]

Many common churchgoers also objected to black ministers' pursuits
of cultural attainments, a charge Mother Zion also managed to sidestep
given its greater artisanal composition. Unlike abolitionists, these commoners opposed uplift for cultural rather than ideological reasons. As a
young minister in Baltimore, AME Bishop Daniel Payne banned what
he deemed "cornfield ditties," the slave call-and-response songs that
had migrated into African Methodist meetinghouses. His opposition
offended many of his congregants, who disliked his intentions to promote a high-toned worship. Members accused the minister of putting

on airs and refusing to join them for tea, and criticized his carpet as "too fine." Such opponents damned ministers for ignoring the primitive gospel that required retrenchment and limited consumption from its preachers.[30]

The biggest lay opposition to Mother Zion, albeit a largely silent and implied opposition, lay in those who stayed away from the church, or attended different churches. For example, some black Methodists never left John Street Chapel. Almost all women, this group consistently numbered between thirty and fifty members through the 1820s and 1830s. By 1840, they had dwindled to twenty souls. In 1840, the six elderly black women in one class had spent nearly a half century in the same church. They continued to find solace in their small white-led class meetings, and during services at John Street worshiped from the balcony.[31]

Sojourner Truth represents a more direct example of opposition to the black Methodist men who ran the church. Her experience of popular Christianity linked her with many common black men and women in the churches, even as her commitments to reform arose, not from professional development or uplift, but from a deep-seated desire for personal holiness. Sojourner Truth was born Isabella, a slave to a Dutch family in New York State, just before the beginning of the nineteenth century. Upon gaining freedom in 1827, Isabella took the surname Van Wagenen from a former master's family.[32]

Van Wagenen differed from the men who ran Mother Zion on many fronts. She was raised upstate, in the heavily Dutch (and enslaved) Hudson River Valley, neither from the city (like Peter Williams or James Varick), nor the South (like George White or Thomas Downing). She grew up speaking Dutch, not English; she worked on farms, not in artisan trades; she was very dark-skinned, not light. Her two most recent biographers have stressed differing aspects of her childhood and young adult years that nonetheless separated her from black church leaders: Nell Irvin Painter has highlighted the abuse and suffering that slaves, especially women, faced, whereas Margaret Washington noted Isabella's African heritage, not as a badge of public identity as acculturated black men embraced, but in real connections with spiritual power and women's leadership.[33]

In 1828, Isabella experienced a sudden conversion, in which she felt the overwhelming presence of God. This experience occurred outside the bounds of the church, and thereafter she took little interest in conforming her experiences to the formal demands of theology or institutional affiliation: Van Wagenen considered joining the Society of Friends

Figure 8.3. Sojourner Truth, a prophetic voice who
defied easy categorization, rejected black ministers'
emphasis on cultural uplift. (From *Narrative of Sojourner
Truth* [1878].)

but ultimately chose the Methodists for their extensive hymnody. But
she preferred quiet religious responses over enthusiastic expressions. Isabella condemned prayer meetings that degenerated into "the most noisy,
shouting, ranting, and boisterous of gatherings."[34]

Van Wagenen moved to New York City around 1830. She first attended
John Street Methodist, although she did not stay there long, for her name
does not appear in the class lists. Van Wagenen transferred from John
Street to Mother Zion, hoping to find a larger audience than the approximately fifty blacks, mostly women, at John Street. She lamented that the

black congregation was "more inclined to hear great people," and generally preferred educated male ministers to unlettered female exhorters. Van Wagenen approached one woman, offering to pray with her, but left weeping when the woman insisted that she had several black male ministers who could better care for her spiritual needs.[35]

Isabella Van Wagenen's religious intensity led her through a number of differing religious expressions. She ministered to prostitutes in the Five Points neighborhood near Mother Zion preaching conversion, followed the sect leader Matthias to a communal and patriarchal religious community, then eventually left New York City to join abolitionist and reform communities, where she took upon herself a new name, Sojourner Truth.[36]

Isabella's religious experience rejected the ideology of intellectual uplift that black churchmen advocated. She repeatedly refused friends' attempts to teach her to read and write. Caring little for education, she mocked Frederick Douglass's efforts at learning proper diction and literacy. In her later public speeches, she regularly interspersed songs, some improvised on the spot, others adapted to well-known tunes. Her rambling, extemporaneous style incorporated stories and jokes, and she rarely if ever repeated herself.[37]

Like Frederick Douglass, Sojourner Truth critiqued the black church for its inattentiveness to rights and reform. But while Douglass focused on political rights at the expense of religious orthodoxy, Sojourner Truth closely linked personal righteousness, even individual perfection, with her conceptions of reform. Focusing on the simplicity and power of the gospel message, Truth was alarmed that Douglass could countenance slave rebellion or war to pursue abolitionism; for her, the will of God did not depart from the imperatives of pacifism.[38]

This searing message of righteousness transferred from slavery to women, a major focus for Truth in later years. Her dissatisfaction with the male leadership in the city's black churches grew over time. Her words to black men were strident: "You have been having our right so long, that you think, like a slaveholder, that you own us."[39] Increasingly after 1840, abolitionists whose causes challenged the status quo would have to find resources outside the churches, apart from the black male ministers who had led them.

Yet Sojourner Truth's vision differed from the protests of many abolitionists, whose acculturated, masculine calls for uplift connected at least in part with the ministers. Associates who heard her on the abolitionist lecture circuit recognized that Sojourner Truth's power came from what many deemed a strange delivery. Truth's presentation diverged from the learned, polished deliveries that black men gave at public celebrations. This forceful presence appealed to activist abolitionists in the 1850s.[40] In the 1830s and 1840s, however, New York's black Methodists had little use for Truth's ministry. The masculine church leadership minimized the female and slave-dominated experiences within black religion.

Urban Decline and Nativist Responses at John Street

In the early Republic, the churches reflected, rather than challenged, the surrounding commercial order. As the city grew in the boom years of the 1820s, downtown churches like Trinity and John Street prospered, for they lay in neighborhoods where their parishioners were among the city's wealthier inhabitants. But that willingness to capitalize on the fat years led to a corresponding trouble in the lean years. When New York's economy suffered a major recession during the late 1830s, churches led by merchant elites struggled to remain viable.

The recession hit John Street especially hard. At first glance, many wealthy members remained in John Street's classes. The percentages of professionals, merchants/retailers, and artisans remained roughly equal between 1825 and 1840. But by 1840, the church's overall membership had halved. The 128 male members in the boom year of 1825 had shriveled to 62 in 1840. The number of poorer members had increased; four of every ten male members were unlisted in the city directories, an increase half again as large. Some of the most prominent wealthy members had moved away. Some, like Francis Hall and George Suckley, had gone to west side congregations. Others, like the Harper brothers, traveled farther uptown.[41]

Facing such hardships, some Methodists turned to nativist politics, which heightened their identity as Protestants. Ethnicity in conjunction with religion proved to be a potent force for political organization. Immigrants poured into seaport cities in greater numbers each year. They brought with them the religion of their lands of origin, increasingly a Roman Catholicism from Ireland or Germany. As early as the 1830s, American nativists saw the ethnic and religious foreignness of immigrants as the major problem facing the Republic. Third parties gained traction in the 1840s, accusing one major party (the Whigs) of ignoring the immigrant problem and the other (Democrats) of courting the unwashed masses. In antebellum politics, nativism took on an explicitly Protestant ethos. Nativists condemned Catholicism as a false religion, as political tyranny, and as sexual predation. They promoted answers in temperance, enforcement of a Sunday Sabbath, and stricter limits on immigration. For nativists, the questions posed and solutions posited often took on religious forms, if not religious content.[42]

For a short time, a member of John Street, James Harper, became the native Protestants' champion in New York. When controversy and scandal weakened the two major parties, Harper won election as mayor of New York on the American Republican ticket in 1844. A third-party candidate, Harper only served a single one-year term, but his candidacy illustrates the Methodists' attraction to nativist politics in these transitional years.[43]

James Harper self-identified as an artisan, despite managing the largest publishing house in America with his three brothers. This connection to Protestant labor ran strong in the nativist movement, allowing Harper to paper over class divisions. Nativist parties were often workingmen's parties that, because of their anti-Catholicism, adopted a Protestant ethos. The more famous American Party, which achieved national prominence in the 1850s as the Know-Nothings, exhibited this combination of Protestantism and labor. In Massachusetts, the American Party platform included opposition to gambling, prostitution, alcohol, and slavery. The party also regulated industrial welfare and workplace safety, and made Christmas, Washington's Birthday, and July 4 state holidays, thereby discouraging industrialists from compelling their employees to work on those days.[44] This working-class Protestant ethos attracted James Harper, even as his personal fortune placed him securely in the upper classes.

As former artisans who became managers and owners of a large-scale enterprise, the Harper brothers exemplified a new class, the new artisans. Entrepreneurs who no longer fit artisan status, their Methodist identity allowed them to claim a working-class identity for decades.[45] James's story illustrates the transformation of city Methodism.

The Harpers came from a well-established Methodist family based in Long Island. In his travels, Francis Asbury stayed with the Harpers on several occasions. The Harper family regularly intermarried with other leading Methodist families, the well-established kinship groups resembling an aristocratic family tree. Joseph Harper was the father of the four Harper brothers of publishing fame, including James, the eldest. Joseph's youngest half brother was Samuel B. Harper. Thus when the daughters of John Street trustee Philip Arcularius married James and Samuel Harper, they married uncle and nephew! The close marriages and family

connections betray preferences for clan and community. Early Methodism was close-knit, but aristocratic as much as democratic.[46]

But Methodism placed much weight on actions, and proper behavior
was essential to righteous standing within the community. When Joseph
Harper's sons entered the publishing world, the Wesleyan command to
be holy transformed into secular maxims for doing business. Speaking
much later on the subject, James piously noted, "Yes, sir, the basis on
which we commenced was *character*, and not *capital*."[47] James had begun
work as an apprentice in the shop of leading Methodist Abraham Paul,
but shortly moved to Jonathan Seymour's shop, just a few houses over
from the Methodist church on John Street.

Religious topics swirl within the Harpers' remembrances of their
early employment, often in contradictory memories. James suggested
that he risked being fired as an apprentice for refusing to work on Sunday. This would have been unlikely at Abraham Paul's, as his master was
an ardent Methodist. It could have happened at his next master's, yet
Jonathan Seymour's shop was next to the John Street Chapel, where the
printer would have to face the disdain of his neighbors. Further, James
Harper's early fellow apprentice, Thurlow Weed, remarked that he and
James regularly did half a day's work before breakfast, while the grateful
proprietor Seymour slept.[48]

Protestant piety prevailed throughout the printing industry, which
was little affected by subsequent waves of immigration in the 1830s and
1840s. As an apprentice, James printed a variety of religious literature,
including family Bibles. When the brothers set off on their own, many of
their early jobs consisted of religious works, which reached willing audiences throughout the United States. Among their first job as independent
printers, James and Joseph printed a catechism for Methodist youth and
an Episcopalian prayer book. As the two younger siblings John and Wesley joined their brothers, the firm grew. It specialized in high-volume,
inexpensive editions of English literature, but religious texts continued
to comprise a large portion of their catalogue.[49]

Methodist itinerants hoped at least one Harper boy would enter the
ministry, but all four joined the family business. When he first set off
to Manhattan to work, James Harper's mother intoned, "Don't forget
your home or your religious duties, James, and always remember that
you have good blood in you." As the Harpers progressed in the business world, their identity as Methodists became a sort of public badge, a
stamp of identity. It guided their work ethic and became a useful promotion for business associates seeking to partner with coreligionists. Each

brother played a role in the family firm, the better to appeal to various customers. From these roles, brothers John and Wesley projected great earnestness and religious sincerity. Of the firm's religiosity, their fellow publisher Evert Duyckinck noted that "some people requir[ed] more of this article or what passes for it than others."[50]

But earnest behavior did not apply as much to brothers James or Fletcher. An affable politician, James loved to provoke laughs. The seriousness of early Methodist revivals, in which earnest itinerants demanded moral rectitude, had given way to a lightheartedness and playful joking that extended to all matters, even religious ones. A local businessman recommended that Harper publish a Greek New Testament with English notes, because most Methodist ministers' limited education rendered the standard testaments, with Latin commentary, incomprehensible. James replied, "Don't, they're nice people, they are—but they all think the New Testament was written in English, and it would only unsettle their minds and throw them into horrid perplexities to be undeceived; they do very well as they are—let 'em alone."[51] This playfulness grew more pronounced with the following generation, to whom itinerants existed only as stories from their older relatives. In the 1840s, two Harper cousins happened upon a drunken, stumbling Edgar Allen Poe, and announced their names to be Tay and Toe, thus making a Potato of the three. Despite their uncle's public political support of temperance, the younger Harpers viewed heavy drinkers with merriment, not scorn.[52] Given their uncle's penchant for practical jokes, he may not have disapproved too much.

The Methodist society reconfigured worship space to reflect a greater importance of families to the community. Class meetings also adapted to new emphases within Methodism. Increasingly, Methodist classes included couples, and integrated the sexes. Formerly the New York society only offered integrated classes in outlying regions, when class leaders were scarce. Thus the group at Two-Mile Stone in the 1790s, as yet without a chapel or meetinghouse, held integrated classes. The first black classes in the 1780s were unisex, reflecting an early ambiguity in how to classify black members. Neither necessity nor ambiguity forced this new change. Instead the classes no longer practiced the intense melting worship that was kept sex-segregated to avoid mixing of passions. Class leaders increasingly reported spotty attendance and long, boring meetings with little emotional movement. In fact, the class meetings may have served to funnel activity not toward deeper spirituality, but to family life: the 1840 class lists record that Mary McCuttien and Stephen F. Ralph, both in John Dunn's class, apparently courted and married while attending classes together. A single notation by McCuttien's name, "married brother Ralph and removed," and by Ralph's simply reading "removed," records the event matter-of-factly.[53] Even so, the 1830s and 1840s represented a transition between strict sex separation and full integration. Only two white classes and one black class at John Street mixed male and female members, with the rest comprised of all men or women.

The entrance of pewed churches into the New York Methodist society in the 1830s marked a great departure from early American Methodist practice. The city society's debt had grown to nearly ten thousand dollars per congregation, making the erection of new churches prohibitive. Nathan Bangs's brother, the Reverend Heman Bangs, proposed to the trustees the erection of a chapel funded by subscribers, who would then receive pews. The trustees appointed a committee that rejected Bangs's proposal as "neither lawful nor expedient." Methodist leaders continued to reject the concept of pews as unchristian; after all, the mere hint of pews had fueled the Stilwellite schism less than two decades earlier. But in a striking display of independence, leading men moved forward with the plan. Led by John Street members Francis Hall and George Suckley, the First Wesleyan Chapel laid its cornerstone on Vestry Street in 1833, and opened at Christmas that year. West of Broadway, its neighborhood was among Lower Manhattan's most exclusive real estate.[54]

In the creation of the pewed chapel, Methodist unity ultimately broke down. One of the lay leaders in the new church, Francis Hall, had formerly typified the early Methodist trustees who acted as patriarchs of a new Methodist family. Mostly foreign-born, their commitment lay with a new church community rather than to a political nation. Often old Tory or Federalist in outlook, they supported the church with their wealth and remained committed to its organic structure. The English-born Hall fit this bill: as editor of the *Commercial Advertiser*, he steered the publication to support the Whigs under his tenure. And Hall accepted the old Federalist position on blacks as participating, albeit less-than-equal, members in the church—for years he led one of the two black classes remaining at John Street. But as ministers like the Bangs brothers promoted a greater professionalization of mission duties to the clergy, laity like Hall let go of their older commitments. Hall left the old John Street Chapel for the new Wesleyan one, safe in its position on the elite west side of town with its pews committed to the chapel's wealthiest benefactors.[55]

This retreat from engagement also cut the last ties to the black church. Methodist minister Freeborn Garrettson might have married into money when he wed Catherine Livingston, but he consistently opposed slavery and racism in the church. By the 1830s, after Garrettson's death, the situation had changed. White Methodist churchmen and reformers could take on the mantle of respectable moderates when they, having been gradualists, moved to a position supporting colonization. Such was the case of Nathan Bangs, who, in his efforts to build denominational organizations, supported colonization as a way to minimize disputes that might tear apart the church body. Bangs offered too little, too late, as the ACS had become largely a dead letter in influencing the slavery debate by the time he backed the group. But the stance, coming from northern and ostensibly antislavery churchmen, demonstrated that city life had removed Methodist society members from much contact with black coreligionists.[56]

Like other American Methodists, John Street's members entered reform movements in increasing numbers in the 1820s and 1830s. A defensive action, their participation in reform represented a desperate attempt to wrest control from an unruly environment. Although the downtown church's historic position granted it prominence in the minds of many American Methodists, few congregants wished to remain in the area. Streets remained mired in muck, and pigs roamed freely. Leading congregants like the Harpers—both the merchant (Samuel) and artisan (James) wings of the family—moved to houses uptown, and stayed on the church's board of trustees at a distance. When the city government demanded that the church be rebuilt a third time in the early 1840s, the circuit leaders considered abandoning the location. Although he rarely attended there, trustee board president James Harper led the fight to keep the church in its downtown location.[57] Symbolically, the city code mandated a smaller building, to make room for wider streets. Less than thirty years earlier, the enlarged second chapel on the site drew criticism for its ostentatious design. Now the smaller John Street Church had become a virtual museum of early Methodism, supported by the leading families who no longer attended there.

The Decline of Downtown Prestige at Trinity

In the short story "The Two Temples," Herman Melville attacked the combination of religious and social elitism in midcentury America. Melville's narrator tries to worship at an elite New York Episcopal church, but the sexton bars him from entering because of his shabby dress. Upon inquiry, the church official sniffs with disdain that there is no gallery in the church (and thus no place for the poor). Sneaking into the belfry, the narrator observes the service from on high, marveling that the parishioners' high social status renders them little more than cold-hearted Pharisees. In the second half of the story, the narrator attends a play in London, where he again perches in the rafters, this time in the cheap seats at a playhouse where he watches a drama. Despite his poverty, working-class Londoners hand him a ticket and then buy him a mug of ale. Melville paralleled the forms of the play with the liturgical ritual of the High Church service, contrasting the playgoers' bonhomie with the snobbery of the churchgoers.[58]

When Melville wrote the story, the rebuilt and newly Gothic Trinity was the tallest building in the city, and contained pews for old and wealthy families who had attended for generations. But surprisingly, Trinity Church was not Melville's chief target as a model of snobbery. The narrator complained that he walked three miles up Manhattan Island from his residence in the Battery to attend church. Too far for Trinity or St. Paul's, the stroll probably reached Grace Episcopal on Tenth Street, much closer to the uptown homes of the wealthiest and most prestigious members of New York high society.[59]

The continuing development of Manhattan Island rearranged the mental maps of many of its inhabitants. No longer were the lower wards and financial centers the only, or even chief, centers of amassed wealth. Astute observers like Melville lifted their eyes to the stately homes erected to the north. In an exhaustive analysis of New York's wealthiest citizens, Edward Pessen notes that between the 1820s and 1840s a marked shift occurred: although many wealthy individuals still lived in the lower wards, newer developments uptown had eclipsed them. Whereas in 1828 half of the city's wealthiest citizens lived in the geographically small lower three wards, by 1848 only one-quarter remained in Lower Manhattan.[60]

Trinity still controlled vast tracts of land and claimed the prestige of age as well as wealth. But Grace's new prominence indicated that most wealth had migrated uptown. Much of it remained old wealth, simply consisting of individuals who, like Clement Clarke Moore, had moved their estates north. But the volume of wealth in the new northern wards had created a buzz of impressions that upstaged the prestige of age at Trinity. When Alexis de Tocqueville toured America in 1831, he marveled at the mansions in Upper Manhattan, complete with classical columns and imposing facades. And when social critic Nathan Parker Willis listed the requisite characteristics of New York's highest society—what he deemed the "upper ten thousand"—he zeroed in on geographic location that specifically noted distance from the city center. These elites, wrote Willis, "keep carriages, live above [north of] Bleecker, are subscribers to the opera, go to Grace Church, have a town house and country house, give balls and parties." Willis identified the Episcopal Church with high society, but the specific congregation emblematic of that society had moved.[61]

Consequently, in the years after 1840 Trinity lost some of its social cachet. Many churchgoers displayed greater levels of transience and inconsistent attendance, as revealed in the parish's later communicant lists. After 1845, the vestry allowed nonpewholders to vote in parish elections if they had been attending communicants at Trinity for at least one year. The men in the post-1845 communicant lists appear to have been less well-off than those in Benjamin Moore's 1801 list, nearly a half century earlier. Between 1845 and 1855, more than two hundred men gained status as voting communicants—a number greater than the number of rented pews in the church. Over two-thirds of these left the parish before 1868, when the record ends. Of those who left, the average stay was just under five years. A significant number of individuals did not even last that long: nearly one-third of all communicants, or almost half of all those who left the parish, stayed three years or less. This greater mobility suggests a decline in social status.[62]

Indirect evidence bolsters the statistics from the communicant lists, suggesting that the numbers of Trinity's poor increased as the church lost prestige. In church one Sunday in October 1837, George Templeton Strong found that nonpewholders had crowded him out of his usual seat. The displacement suggests that more fluid arrangements had supplanted the rigid social hierarchy of the colonial church. Strong also complained that many parishioners were increasingly stingy in their almsgiving. As a vestryman, he wryly commented that he could have used a teaspoon to collect the offering on the north side of the church, for the offering plate seldom held anything larger than a five-cent piece. Strong's description of his "beggarly beat" suggests that the city's most affluent parishioners who attended church to see and be seen were not at Trinity on Sundays.[63]

Trinity was a church of diminished social prestige. The parish's younger members accepted this fact, and turned to internal religious experience as consolation. Older members cursed the darkness in the world that had passed them by. The diaries of two prominent parishioners reveal this, in their reports on the rise of Methodist nativist James Harper to mayor in 1844. Former mayor Philip Hone, an older man who truly believed that the wealthy and well-born should govern, viewed

Harper's rise with suspicion. He noted in his diary that "nobody knows where he stands or who are his associates."[64] George Templeton Strong did not share Hone's reflexive support for the Whigs, and viewed Harper's win with ironic detachment. Removed from partisan boosterism, Strong praised the "natives" as striking a blow against "the Hibernian race." Such praise was not partisan—Strong later mocked Harper for thinking he had a chance to gain reelection—but did reflect that Strong's cultural sensibilities moved him to cheer the anti-Irish sentiment that briefly won out in city politics.[65]

Hone's religious life appears cold and formal, similar to the Revolutionary generation's penchant for rational discourse from the pulpit. But he kept a sense of greater connection with other friends of order, and other coreligionists. Strong's own church life was internally rich, but not full of large social connections and grand plans. We know his private life largely through his diary, which he never intended for public reading. Strong adhered to an extreme High Church position that verged on an Anglo-Catholic sensibility. An admirer of the Tractarians, Strong embraced a heavily sacramental view of worship in the church.[66]

The differences come out in the two men's position on race and the church. After the summer 1834 riots, Hone forcefully condemned the "diabolical spirit" of the mobs who destroyed the African Episcopal church and Peter Williams's house. By contrast, although Strong adhered to a High Church position, he had little good to say about the black Episcopalians who shared his religiosity. Rejecting any assumption of organic connection in Christ that former bishop John Henry Hobart had promoted, Strong repeatedly dismissed John Jay's "penchant for niggers" in his attempt to gain St. Philip's diocesan representation.[67] Thus although Strong's midcentury romanticism led him toward a rich, full religious life, it avoided the organic social connections of a previous generation of Trinity vestrymen.

Low Churchmen thwarted the High Church party's attempt to claim moral superiority within a unified church. When Bishop Hobart criticized Anglican involvement in the American Bible Society, evangelical Episcopalians formed Low Church institutions in opposition to the High Church program. Formerly Trinity's oldest chapel, St. George left the mother church and became the city's leading evangelical Episcopal parish. Other elites attended ostensibly High Church parishes, yet marginalized their own ministers by joining evangelical benevolent institutions. The expansive church that High Churchmen envisioned had dwindled so that even prochurch parishes contained individual dissenters.[68]

Just as at John Street Methodist, Trinity Church turned to managerially control its world. In the 1840s, Trinity's vestry began to manage the church properties with an eye toward the future. Previously the parish had sold parcels of its land whenever it approved a request for funds. By the mid-nineteenth century, such actions threatened remaining income. Uptown Episcopal churches overshadowed Trinity's dwindling status, and the vestry knew it could not count on the benevolence of its parishioners indefinitely. Although the church's location in the heart of the financial district limited its attractiveness to wealthy individuals living uptown, that location was a key asset in property valuations. In the 1840s, the parish increasingly held properties for rent, gaining indefinite income streams in contrast to earlier lump sums.

Conclusion

Economic downturn treated city churches hard. Increased white hostility pushed black congregations in different directions: black Episcopalians remained politically active and committed to cultural and economic uplift, but retreated from full resistance in matters dealing with the church hierarchy. Black Methodists appear to have retreated even further from attempts at persuasion in the public sphere. In the white churches, their once-prestigious downtown locations were now hindrances to social prominence. Trinity came off better because of its landholdings, but the city did not treat the churches well.

After 1840, New York City's population and its commercial influence, despite previous expansion, would magnify exponentially. The previous half century of growth had already set the patterns of religious life for the city's inhabitants. Social stratification and racial division reflected the typical experiences of New Yorkers. Each church congregation attempted new ways to reach out to other groups, and create new forms of unity. The efforts reflected a narrower religious vision than the expansive, universal dreams of the late colonial era.

Conclusion. Elusive Unity: City Churches in a Romantic Age, after 1840

Developments after 1840 in church and American history promised to revive some form of the colonial-era promise of organic unity. The holistic vision never completely died among religious leaders, who retained dreams of universal conversion or affiliation. Each of these churches participated, on some level, with attempts to create new and larger associations, but in so doing broke with older ties and connections.

Evangelical unity promised to connect churches in greater communion. Fierce sectarian infighting characterized the early years of the Second Great Awakening for most Protestants. Denominations that supported revivalism nonetheless drew distinct lines apart from each other to secure their membership. As the revivals waned at midcentury, some churchmen stressed the differences between their denominations as cosmetic, and emphasized the common theological ends that united them. Evangelicals united around a streamlined message of forgiveness of sins in Christ, and joined together in movements like the American Sunday-School Union as evidence of a greater cooperation and unity. This ideal particularly touched the Methodists, whose early years were marked with denominational conflict: breaking from the Anglican fold, vigorously opposing Calvinist theology with outspoken Arminianism, and defending support for infant baptism against resurgent Baptists.[1] While not retreating from theological purity, Methodist ministers now acknowledged the common goals that united evangelicals.

City evangelicals found a pressing need to minister to those brave souls wounded in the dog-eat-dog world of finance. The New York economy served as the center of the national economy, linking finance and trade in a single setting; as New York went, so went the nation. Fueled by a national economic contraction, in October 1857 the stock market crashed, pushing many businesses into ruin. Spreading to the larger economy, thirty thousand individuals found themselves out of work.[2] While politicians pointed fingers of blame, businessmen prayed. Surrounded by the drama of ruined businesses and shattered homes, a religious revival originated in downtown New York.

The revival began in the Dutch Reformed Church on Fulton Street, but moved around the corner to John Street Methodist. For months under-worked and out-of-work businessmen attended the downtown chapel's daily noontime prayer meetings. By April 1858, twenty similar meetings had sprung up throughout the city. Despite John Street's participation, this revival was multidenominational, not Methodist. Further, the tradi-tional Methodist rituals of heated, even loud, outbursts of emotion did not accompany it. Desperate businessmen ducked into John Street to pray for deliverance. Anyone was welcome to participate, provided that they avoided controversial theological and political topics and hewed to a five-minute limit. Leaders rang a bell to call the meeting to order, mim-icking the patterns of the nearby stock exchange.[3]

Nathan Bangs, who had condemned too-fervent Methodist revivals a half century before, looked upon these sedate meetings in his old age with approval. Although as a young Methodist minister he had written several tracts attacking Calvinist doctrines, Bangs saw these revivals as the works of God, uniting those with whom he had previously disagreed. He gladly watched "sectarian prejudices" torn down as the denomina-tions joined together in the pious transformation of individual souls. Laying aside theology, Bangs championed all who would support the "experimental and practical" outpourings that occurred in the down-town churches.[4] In revivalism, Bangs saw a communal spirit in the city re-created.

In contrast to John Street, Trinity Church rejected any unity through the revival, choosing to remain aloof from the excitement. After wan-dering into an 1858 prayer meeting at John Street, George Templeton Strong grumbled, "what I heard seemed to me . . . the profane and mis-chievous babblings of blind, foolish, shallow, vulgar Pharisaism. . . . The great object of the meeting seems to be to drug men up to a certain point of nervous excitement and keep them there."[5] Yet having rejected evangelical unity, Episcopalians began to consider other forms of con-nection. High Church Episcopalians eschewed connections with revival

Protestants, but looked more closely at Roman Catholicism. In New York, many in the High Church party found intellectual solace in the Tractarian or Oxford Movement in England, where John Henry Newman and his allies penned a series of tracts defending the heritage and institutional authority of the church. Tensions peaked with the publication of Newman's Tract XC (90), which argued that the Anglican Church's Thirty-Nine Articles, properly understood, were compatible with Roman Catholicism. Newman's conversion to Catholicism in 1845 abruptly ended Anglican Tractarianism. But the Oxford Movement's stress on liturgy and sacrament (especially the Eucharist) resonated with High Churchmen, who continued to oppose evangelicals in their midst.[6]

The High Church movement promoted the idea of an undivided, true church, combining the truth of apostolic succession with pious faith in order. Agnostic on social and political matters, High Churchmen valued ecclesiastical unity enough to tolerate theological variations in their midst. Alone among the major Protestant denominations, the Episcopal Church did not split into northern and southern factions with the coming of the Civil War. After the war, the emphasis on tolerance and church unity came to be expressed as the Broad Church movement, dissolving the heat of the tensions between Low Church evangelicals and High Church ritualists.[7]

Black churchgoers would have considered white calls for unity with suspicion, for they saw firsthand that unity among whites generally excluded them. Further, black churches had to deal with larger social problems, as their members lived in the midst of the poor and vicious. Mother Zion stood next to a brothel, and St. Philip's lay in the path of working-class whites who eviscerated it. Even well-off blacks rarely took summer retreats up the Hudson or lounged in the confines of uptown parks. But despite this clarity about their situation, blacks faced a great challenge in how best to respond to white opposition.

Of all these churches, Mother Zion receded from the public record the most after 1840. As a denomination, the African Methodist Zionites were known for their uncompromising stance toward abolitionism and equal rights. The denomination's center of gravity lay farther north than Richard Allen's Bethel, and as such it contained congregations farther away from the centers of slavery and also less accommodating or compromising. Consequently, well-known reformers such as Frederick Douglass, Harriet Tubman, and Jehiel Beman all belonged to congregations within the Zion denomination.[8] But references to Mother Zion as a congregation in New York grew scarce.

William Hamilton died in the 1830s, and Christopher Rush turned to history and institution building. Apart from the white church, few of Zion's records survived, and much of the church's remaining record exists through oral histories and repeated institutional memories. This silence might have been, ironically, the congregation's strength. Zion remained a working-class church: the middling artisan status of earlier leaders like Varick and Hamilton had not translated into great accumulated wealth. As such, the church departed from notions of uplift that black protest writers advanced, but remained quietly connected to reform. David Ruggles emerged as the most prominent member of the congregation during this time. Ruggles was known for his support of the Underground Railroad, which passed through New York. Against opposition from some elite abolitionists who advocated nonviolence in all circumstances, Ruggles promoted the right of individuals to forcibly resist kidnapping and attack, to physically fight back against their assailants. Zion's silence allowed it lower-profile but effective action against slavery. The cost was, however, a smaller public profile. Political tenacity entailed social and cultural silence, or retreat.[9]

St. Philip's congregation faced an especially difficult situation, for the church's Episcopalian status required assumptions of hierarchy and expectations of deference. Thus the language of religious unity that Trinity's High Churchmen voiced, and St. Philip's congregation largely accepted, came at a cost. The vestry's rejection of native son Alexander Crummell to serve as St. Philip's rector in 1847 holds much symbolic weight. When Crummell applied to the position of St. Philip's rector, white leadership balked, deeming Crummell too strident. The vestry divided over his application, but ultimately rejected Crummell for his divisiveness, siding with their Episcopalian superiors in the name of religious unity. The decision highlighted that unity was no longer, truly, a possibility. In the name of church unity Crummell was excluded, and broke racial connections long established. Crummell advocated uplift, but was also an unyielding abolitionist and supported colonizationist ventures on blacks' own terms. His departure limited St. Philip's future activities. The vestry's embrace of uplift, shorn of its political or colonizationist strategies, cut off an avenue of identity separate from their white leaders.[10]

In 1853, St. Philip's congregation won a hard-earned battle to be represented in the diocesan convention. Such victories came with a cost; by accepting the High Church submission to spiritual hierarchy and unity in Episcopalianism, the members of St. Philip's accommodated to white preferences for quietism that reverberated into the twentieth century. St. Philip's parishioners tried to straddle the line between black and white in maintaining their religious commitments, and found themselves, for a long time, not quite accepted by either.[11]

Each of the four churches participated in larger forms of union: evangelical revivalism, High Church and later Broad Church communion, abolitionist activism, and a cultural embrace of black uplift and cultural achievement. Each connected the congregations with some groups, but none had within their congregations the class and racial breadth of the colonial-era churches. Each congregation represented a slice of the city, not the full sweep of the city streets.

The Importance of Place: Church Survival and Church Mobility in the City

This study highlights the significance of place in considering religious life. All four churches occupied space in Lower Manhattan, a site of increased commercialism and waning residence even at the turn of the nineteenth century. All four churches have survived as entities, in part because of their historic origins, a characteristic not true of many New York houses of worship. However, not all have remained in the same place, highlighting the challenges of urban worship even for the most resourceful and energetic congregations.

Trinity Church's status remained the most secure, despite George Templeton Strong's grumblings of financial decline. The church occupied a prominent location on Broadway, at the foot of Wall Street, and still held large tracts of land. For many years after the Revolution, the church had generously parceled off land grants to fellow churches and causes, including non-Episcopalian ones, in a show of fraternal unity. As the city relentlessly grew and accelerated its commercialization, Trinity's landholdings magnified in value. Trinity returned to its colonial-era practice of renting its real estate, thus allowing the church to preserve its privileged status indefinitely.[12]

In the mid-nineteenth century, Trinity's vestry also erected new chapels to reassert its organic vision. Trinity rector Morgan Dix organized some chapels in newer neighborhoods without pew rents, dedicating them as missionary outposts to the unchurched. As the city grew, Trinity also erected chapels in elite neighborhoods to woo respectable citizens seeking Episcopalian forms of worship. Trinity Church's namesake, Trinity Chapel on Twenty-Fifth Street, rivaled its mother church in its members' social prominence.[13] Trinity's chapel structure therefore

Figure C.1. Gothic Trinity. The third church built on the site, this building would tower as the city's highest building for a half century, even as its public status had declined from earlier decades. (From Morgan Dix, *History of Trinity Church*, vol. 4 [1906].)

preserved two sides of the organic vision: it represented outreach to the lost outside the church walls, and it also continued to reach like-minded social elites in new neighborhoods. In 1850, Trinity's spire towered over all other New York buildings, a distinction it would hold for nearly a half century. While Episcopalians no longer held de facto social prominence as they had in the colonial and Revolutionary eras, Trinity remained a symbol of the hierarchical past.

In contrast to Trinity's fixed, prominent location, the black churches were forced into mobility. Mother Zion began near the Five Points in its Cross Street Chapel, so its first move to Church and Leonard in 1800 reflected a move up, even as it stood in a marginal location in the city. St. Philip's occupied the black school before it built its Centre Street church in 1819, which parishioners bravely rebuilt after its destruction in the 1834 riots. In 1856, St. Philip's moved to a formerly Methodist church on Mulberry Street, across from police offices and presumably with greater police protection. After the Civil War, the moves continued: Mother Zion moved to Bleecker Street in 1864 and to Eighty-Ninth Street in 1903, at each stop its financial straits requiring it to occupy a church building of another denomination on the site. St. Philip's abandoned Lower Manhattan for a Twenty-Fifth Street location in 1886.[14]

In the early twentieth century, the black churches' circumstances finally matched their proclamations of uplift. St. Philip's moved to its current Harlem location on 134th Street in 1911, erecting an impressive neo-Gothic building on the site. Mother Zion moved to Harlem in 1914, occupying another church's building until the congregation built upon its current 137th Street location in 1925, also an imposing neo-Gothic edifice. Both churches' new, opulent buildings matched the aspirations of the black middle class, heightened by opportunities embedded in the cultural flowering of the Harlem Renaissance. Ironically, the churches' physical mobility over the years, forced by racism and economic marginality, allowed for an eventual gentrification. Once fixed to a location, however, challenges remained; in the twenty-first century, Harlem's historic black churches face declining populations as members seek economic opportunities elsewhere.[15]

Of the four churches, John Street struggled the most to remain viable in its urban location. Unlike Trinity, John Street Methodist held no additional property, nor did it lie alongside a prominent thoroughfare. Unlike the black churches that had little outside support, John Street's legacy led the larger Methodist denomination to treasure it. The church's location, however, proved to be as much a prison as a source of pride. The Panic of 1837 and following recession bled the church of its wealthier members, who retreated uptown. Commercial buildings towered over the church in its narrow Dutch-era street. In the mid-1840s, city officials planned to widen the narrowest colonial streets in Lower Manhattan, and demanded that Methodists rebuild John Street Church in a smaller fashion. Only thirty years earlier, John Street's large new neoclassical building promised downtown expansion. Now, politicians and bureaucrats demanded it downsize; the urban environment dictated to the church, and not the reverse. Methodist leaders nearly abandoned the church then, as its attendance lagged compared to larger uptown churches. Prominent Methodists who had once worshiped there, like James Harper, saved it by judicious appeals to church leaders.[16]

Only a decade later, John Street's membership again waned. Methodist elders once again considered closing the doors on the nation's oldest Methodist house of worship. The 1857–58 revivals represented a final hurrah for John Street, reviving interest in the old congregation and in the possibility of renewed urban religious presence. Soon thereafter Methodist leaders organized a fund that would keep the church in Lower Manhattan in perpetuity. As a historical monument, the church's basement houses a museum to early American Methodism, embalming it in time. John Street's status as a centrally managed denominational icon typified the bureaucratic standardization that city Methodism ultimately encouraged. By surviving, however, the church remained a viable option for city religious expression, and to this day remains a place of worship.[17]

These churches' transformations highlight the anomalous place of religion in the American city. Religion in the city never completely went away, was never fully destroyed. However, churches were shaped and formed, sometimes buffeted and battered, by the social forces surrounding them. Historians who study religious experience in the city can neither announce its ultimate demise, nor proclaim its ultimate triumph, but rather note that religion, as such, is connected to the people who practice it, and thus also to the environments in which those people live and worship.

Comparisons: New York's Similarities and Differences

The history of these four New York churches provides some suggestions toward larger comparisons about American religious life. These New York congregations were significant because they were, in many matters, the first to experience social pressures that all American churches eventually faced. The major themes of American religious history—disestablishment and democratization, segregation and black independence, gentrification and domestication, benevolence and transformation—occurred early in New York City. The urban environment meant greater population densities of laborers and blacks, who might gain faster connections with others like them. The city also boasted increased networks of global trade, capitalist wealth, and political elites.

Social factors informed church life as well as theological ones, and the pressures of demography, race and ethnicity, markets, and prosperity and poverty all figured into the history of these religious groups.

In New York, Methodism experienced growing pains early, with congregations separating over occupational and class differences that historians have typically attributed to Methodists at later dates elsewhere. Similarly, Episcopalians in New York faced clashes between High Churchmen and evangelicals that prefigured later divisions nationally. Black segregation in church attendance, followed by separate black congregations, occurred as fast as other large cities, and faster than in rural or small town settings. Larger black numbers and population densities in New York also allowed for interdenominational freedom celebrations and attempts to gain a black presence in the public sphere. At the same time, New York's merchant connections to Britain and its status as a commercial and publishing center fostered the growth of reform movements, religious institutions, and benevolent organizations that was faster and farther-reaching than elsewhere. Finally, even as New Yorkers remained close together, the separation of race and class difference in the churches, and the movement toward domesticity as a religious ideal, accelerated in the urban environment.

Such comparisons emphasize similarities. In other matters, though, New York churches were not first, but simply different, given the city's unique history. More than any other colony, New York's clergy embraced a pro-establishment, High Church theology, and after a revolutionary interlude such churchmen took the lead in the early Republic. The pro-establishment clergy particularly influenced the creation of a sense of universal, holistic community: Revolutionary laymen who opposed their priests and nonetheless embraced the ideals of organic unity in their affiliations with the New York Manumission Society and the Federalist Party. Methodists in New York shared close ties to Anglicanism and appear to have valued forms of unity even after Methodist denominational independence. New York's centrality as host of institutions such as the American Bible Society may have betrayed such a line of connection with the colonial past.

New York's uniqueness shows up, too, in black church development, also spurred in part by colonial-era churchmen's attempts at evangelization. New York City's large northern black population had long exposure to church life. But British occupation during the Revolution complicated racial relationships. Slavery in New York remained entrenched longer than elsewhere in the North. Black leaders took longer to develop a voice in the public sphere, and black churches remained more narrowly denominationally affiliated in New York than in Philadelphia. This difference did not hold for all New York history, but the differing origins gives reason to pause in too quickly making comparisons between the black communities in American cities.

Religion in America often serves as a lightning rod for controversy. Political controversies, culture wars, charges of hypocrisy or fanaticism: none are new to the American religious scene. The story of these four congregations reveals something a bit more mundane. American churchmen and churchwomen carried their social identities with them into the pews. As the society outside the churches changed, so did the people inside. The two worlds of society and religion were not disconnected, hermetically sealed, or in opposition, but in a relationship, and we do well to examine the changes in that relationship, for it reveals more about the world we inhabit today.

Notes

Notes to the Introduction

1. The preceding examples are designed to be evocative, not exhaustive, but for examples of histories that examine the above, see David D. Hall, *Worlds of Wonder, Days of Judgment*; Nathan O. Hatch, *The Democratization of American Christianity*; Johnny E. Williams, *African American Religion and the Civil Rights Movement in Arkansas*; and Anne C. Loveland and Otis B. Wheeler, *From Meetinghouse to Megachurch*.

2. Graham's revival is analyzed in Jon Butler, "Religion in New York City." Butler notes that religion had never disappeared from New York, exposing the ambiguities of, and irony in, Graham's position.

3. Francis Asbury, *Journal*, 3:143.

4. See, for example, Raymond Mohl, *Poverty in New York, 1783–1825*; Paul Gilje, *The Road to Mobocracy*; Elizabeth Blackmar, *Manhattan for Rent, 1785–1850*; and Timothy J. Gilfoyle, *City of Eros*. A masterful synthesis encompassing many of these occurs in Edwin G. Burrows and Michael Wallace, *Gotham*.

5. For examples of works on the Dutch Reformed, see Gerald Francis De Jong, "The Dutch Reformed Church and Negro Slavery in Colonial America"; and Randall Balmer, *A Perfect Babel of Confusion*. Classic formulations on Quakers and slavery include Herbert Aptheker, "The Quakers and Negro Slavery"; and David Brion Davis, *Problem of Slavery in the Age of Revolution*; more recent efforts are Jean R. Soderlund, *Quakers & Slavery;* and Ryan P. Jordan, *Slavery and the Meetinghouse*. For Moravians, see Jon F. Sensbach, *A Separate Canaan*; and Sensbach, *Rebecca's Revival*. On Presbyterians, see David E. Swift, *Black Prophets of Justice*; and Leo P. Hirrel, *Children of Wrath*.

6. Arminianism refers to a theological position concerning salvation that, in general, stresses the ability of humans to exercise free will; it is popularly opposed to Calvinism, which emphasizes the sovereignty of God. The rise and dominance of

Arminian theology in American religion is interwoven throughout Hatch, *Democratization*, esp. 40–43,170–79, and his appendix of anti-Calvinist verse, 227–43. Evangelicalism is a movement within Protestantism that stresses the importance of individual conversion and experiential faith centered on the person of Jesus Christ; it places more authority in the Bible than in historical creeds and confessions. In most historical settings, as also today, evangelical groups varied widely in doctrinal specifics and social makeup. At its most basic level, in early America "evangelical" denotes "pro-revival."

7. This social and theological range is particularly important because the objects of study—congregations—are necessarily narrowly focused. New York City contained dozens of churches, expanding to hundreds by this study's end. But these four churches contained both a range of differences to make their histories broad and applicable, as well as a common core of similarities to make the comparisons intelligible.

8. James P. Wind and James W. Lewis, *American Congregations*, vol. 2.

9. This is well told in Craig D. Townsend, *Faith in Their Own Color*; see the latter half of this work, esp. 108–93.

10. On New York's relative population, and contemporary observers' impressions, see Bayrd Still, *Mirror for Gotham*, 54, 69.

11. Billy Graham was not the only individual to assume New York was a place where religion suffered. Scholars who have made similar points about New York, pointing to its material striving or its religious indifference, include Carol V. R. George, *Segregated Sabbaths*, 142; and Russell Shorto, *The Island at the Center of the World*.

12. I would add names of individuals well-known to historians of New York, such as Philip Hone, George Templeton Strong, Peter Williams (both Senior and Junior), and Thomas Downing.

13. Relevant early church histories include William Berrian, *A Historical Sketch of Trinity Church, New York*; Morgan Dix, *A History of the Parish of Trinity Church in the City of New York*; Christopher Rush, *A Short Account of the Rise and Progress of the African Methodist Episcopal Church in America*; B. F. De Costa, *Three Score and Ten*; and Samuel A. Seaman, *Annals of New York Methodism*. More recent works of value include, among others, James Elliott Lindsley, *This Planted Vine*; William J. Walls, *The African Methodist Episcopal Zion Church*; and John H. Hewitt Jr., *Protest and Progress*.

14. Clifford S. Griffin, "Religious Benevolence as Social Control, 1850–1860"; Paul E. Johnson, *A Shopkeeper's Millennium*; Sean Wilentz, *Chants Democratic*.

15. Christine Stansell, *City of Women*, esp. 63–75; see also Mary P. Ryan, *Cradle of the Middle Class*; and Nancy F. Cott, "Young Women in the Second Great Awakening in New England." Ryan's work is particularly important, as her findings upend many of Paul Johnson's assertions on Upstate New York religion.

16. See, for example, Eugene D. Genovese, *Roll Jordan Roll*; John W. Blassingame, *The Slave Community*; Clarence E. Walker, *Rock in a Weary Land*; Lawrence S. Little, *Disciples of Liberty*; and Clarence Taylor, *Black Religious Intellectuals*. Scholars of New York City have made this connection throughout their works (see Craig Steven Wilder, *In the Company of Black Men*; Leslie Harris, *In the Shadow of Slavery*; Townsend, *Faith in Their Own Color*; and Graham Russell Hodges, *Root and Branch*).

17. The foundational study in anthropology is Clifford Geertz, *The Interpretation of Cultures*.

18. Examples of such occur in D. Hall, *Worlds of Wonder, Days of Judgment*; D. Hall, "From 'Religion and Society' to Practices: The New Religious History," in St.

George, ed., *Possible Pasts*; Robert Orsi, "Everyday Miracles: The Study of Lived Religion," in D. Hall, ed., *Lived Religion in America*.

19. For the former, see Hatch, *Democratization*; and John Wigger, *Taking Heaven by Storm*. Wigger's stance contains less caution or declension than other recent scholars of Methodism; see particularly his conclusions, 190–95, in which Wigger minimizes the complaints of old Methodist itinerants like Peter Cartwright, suggesting Methodism's transformation as necessary changes in a movement joined so closely to the surrounding culture. For the latter, see Christine Leigh Heyrman, *Southern Cross*. One notable exception, a fine, richly detailed social history that keeps an eye on both theology and lived religious experience, can be found in Dee Andrews, *Methodists in Revolutionary America*.

20. For the former regarding the High Church, see Robert Bruce Mullin, *Episcopal Vision/American Reality*; for those of the Low Church camp, see Diana Hochstedt Butler, *Standing against the Whirlwind*. For the latter regarding race and gender in the South, see Richard Rankin, *Ambivalent Churchmen and Evangelical Churchwomen*; for New York black Episcopalians, see Townsend, *Faith in their Own Color*. Hodges, *Root and Branch*, considers both religious and social factors, although his consideration of religion tends to place most blacks under the Anglican umbrella, especially in the colonial years.

21. David W. Wills discusses a "persistent and seemingly intractable gap" between black and white religious experience in "The Central Themes of American Religious History: Pluralism, Puritanism, and the Encounter of Black and White," in Fulop, ed., *African American Religion*, 15. See also Will B. Gravely, "The Dialectic of Double-Consciousness in Black American Freedom Celebrations, 1808–1863"; and Thelma Wills Foote, *Black and White Manhattan*. Foote labels studies that examine black or white social and political developments in isolation as "apartheid narratives" (13). Recent works exploring such interracial contact include Dickson D. Bruce Jr., *The Origins of African American Literature, 1680–1865*; Timothy Patrick McCarthy and John Stauffer, eds. *Prophets of Protest*; and Patrick Rael, *Black Identity & Black Protest in the Antebellum North*.

22. Johnson, *Shopkeeper's Millennium*, 140–41; Hatch, *Democratization*, 3–5; Hodges, *Root and Branch*, 3–5.

23. Regarding this book's title, Kyle Roberts helpfully pointed out that only Trinity Church had a steeple during the eras analyzed; the other congregations worshiped in buildings without steeples, and intentionally built their churches without them. I have retained the concept of "four steeples" as symbolic, not literal: colonial prints of New York often present church steeples dominating the skyline. That visual image complemented Trinity's original vision of church ("steeple") influencing its surroundings. The following narrative, however, reveals that such visions proved to be elusive, as the realities of city life ("the streets") forced religious experience in other directions.

Notes to Chapter 1

1. *New-York Mercury*, November 3, 1766.

2. Ibid.; the quoted portion of the verse is from Exodus 3:5, KJV.

3. Ibid.

4. Frederick V. Mills, *Bishops by Ballot*, viii; Peter M. Doll, *Revolution, Religion, and National Identity*, 15–18.

5. Rhode Island remained an exception in New England, given the insistence of its founder, Roger Williams, on religious liberty. On the concept of establishment, see Mills, *Bishops by Ballot*; Doll, *Revolution, Religion, and National Identity*, esp. 11–34; and Alan Taylor, *American Colonies*, 140–41. A colonial synthesis that pays close attention to matters of establishment can be found in Daniel K. Richter, *Before the Revolution*, esp. 241–64. For the post–Glorious Revolution compromise, see Andrews, *Methodists in Revolutionary America*, 13–14.

6. This stance frustrated Dutch ministers and leaders in New Netherland, chief among them the orthodox Calvinist governor Pieter Stuyvesant (see Jay Gitlin, "Empires of Trade, Hinterlands of Settlement," in Milner, O'Connor, and Sandweiss, eds., *The Oxford History of the American West*, esp. 101–2; and Richter, *Before the Revolution*, 217).

7. On New Netherland and the English transfer of power, see A. Taylor, *American Colonies*, 248–61.

8. Dongan quoted in Robert E. Cray Jr., *Paupers and Poor Relief in New York City and Its Rural Environs, 1700–1830*, 22; see also Gabriel P. Disosway, *The Earliest Churches of New York*, 45.

9. Patricia U. Bonomi, *Under the Cope of Heaven*, 51–52; Jon Butler, *Awash in a Sea of Faith*, 102.

10. Bonomi, *Under the Cope of Heaven*, 51–52. Butler, *Awash in a Sea of Faith*, 103, notes that Anglicans won votes from Dutch and Huguenot congregations by aiding them legally and financially.

11. Bonomi, *Under the Cope of Heaven*, 51–52; Henry F. May, *The Enlightenment in America*, 76 77; Foote, *Black and White Manhattan*, 112–13.

12. Bonomi, *Under the Cope of Heaven,* 51–52; Butler, *Awash in a Sea of Faith*, 107, 111.

13. Mills, *Bishops by Ballot*, 6. Peter Doll notes that more recent scholarship has emphasized the theological rigor of eighteenth-century Anglican churchmen (see Doll, *Revolution, Religion, and National Identity*, 18, 267–68n30). The following chapter should show that many Episcopalian laymen retained more latitudinarian conceptions of belief and behavior.

14. May, *Enlightenment in America*, 75; Doll, *Revolution, Religion, and National Identity*, 160–62; Jeremy Gregory, "Refashioning Puritan New England: The Church of England in British North America, c. 1680–1770," *Transactions of the Royal Historical Society*, 6th series, vol. 20: 85–112. Frederick Mills notes that in the 1750s and 1760s the Anglican Church grew fastest in formerly arch-Puritan Connecticut (Mills, *Bishops by Ballot*, 11–12). Bonomi, *Under the Cope of Heaven,* 93; Foote, *Black and White Manhattan*, 114–16.

15. Nan A. Rothschild, *New York City Neighborhoods*, 56; Butler, *Awash in a Sea of Faith*, 114.

16. Bonomi, *Under the Cope of Heaven*, 90; Mills, *Bishops by Ballot*, 3.

17. Burrows and Wallace, *Gotham*, 187.

18. May, *Enlightenment in America*, 75. See also Doll, *Revolution, Religion, and National Identity*, 157–58, for a discussion of how the Anglican liturgy helped unite conceptions of religious and civic community.

19. Andrews, *Methodists in Revolutionary America*, 22–23. See also David Hempton, *Methodism: Empire of the Spirit*, 19.

20. Andrews, *Methodists in Revolutionary America*, 19–22.

21. On the standard early Republic vision of Methodist primitivism, see Hatch, *Democratization*, 82–83, 167–70. On the Anglican concept of primitivism, see Doll, *Revolution, Religion, and National Identity*, 14; see also Andrews, *Methodists in Revolutionary America*, 5–6, 14.

22. Andrews, *Methodists in Revolutionary America*, 24–29.

23. Ibid., 34–37. Boardman's comment is found in a November 4, 1769, letter to John Wesley, cited in *The Letters of the Reverend John Wesley, A.M.*, 5:231. Even if inflated, the numbers are significant for a town of twenty thousand inhabitants.

24. J. B. Wakeley, *Lost Chapters*, 55, 71–72, 94–96.

25. Asbury, *Journal*, 1:52–53; Trinity Church General Register of Baptisms, Trinity Church Archives. Classes were small prayer meetings where individuals worked toward greater holiness; class leaders were often lay members known for their spiritual authority.

26. Richard W. Pointer, *Protestant Pluralism*, 44.

27. Lindsley, *This Planted Vine*, 53; Pointer, *Protestant Pluralism*, 66.

28. Rev. Samuel Auchmuty to Rev. Dr. Burton, May 1, 1767, Records of the Society for the Propagation of the Gospel, Letters Series B, 1701–1786, vol. II, item 23 (p. 89).

29. Asbury, *Journal*, 1:375. For examples of clergy movement, see Abel Stevens, *Life and Times of Nathan Bangs, D.D.*, 196; and Wakeley, *Lost Chapters*, 216–17.

30. Winthrop D. Jordan, *White over Black*, 103; Cray, *Paupers and Poor Relief*, 190; Graham Russell Hodges, "Black Revolt in New York City and the Neutral Zone: 1775–83," in Gilje and Pencak, eds., *New York in the Age of the Constitution 1775–1800*, 20–47.

31. Ira Berlin, *Many Thousands Gone*, esp. 47–63, 95–108. See also Hodges, *Root and Branch*, 36, 68. The literature on the rise of racism in America is enormous; important foundational works in the larger debate include Edmund Morgan, *American Slavery, American Freedom*; and W. Jordan, *White over Black*.

32. Frank Klingberg, *Anglican Humanitarianism in Colonial New York*.

33. Hodges, *Root and Branch*, 54–58.

34. Wilder, *In the Company of Black Men*, 17–19.

35. Ibid., 18–21; Hodges, *Root and Branch*, 60–61.

36. Hodges, *Root and Branch*, 61; Neau to Mr. Chamberlayne, October 3, 1705, Item 138–39, Papers of the Society for the Propagation of the Gospel in Foreign Parts, Vol. XIII; Manross, ed., *The Fulham Papers in the Lambeth Palace Library*, 181–82; Henry Newman to the Bishop of London, March 31, 1726, Catalog of the Records of the Christian Faith Society, 1691–1792, Lambeth Palace Library, London.

37. Recent overviews of the 1741 conspiracy include Peter Hoffer, *The Great New York Conspiracy of 1741*; and Jill Lepore, *New York Burning*.

38. W. Jordan, *White over Black*, 115–16, 118–20. Foote, *Black and White Manhattan*, 159–86, argues that the governmental scapegoating was intentional; Jordan suggests it was subconscious. In *New York Burning*, Jill Lepore rejects government conspiracy; she suggests that the lessons of 1741 lie more in white prejudice than in blacks' actions.

39. Hodges, *Root and Branch*, 69–100. Thomas J. Davis first suggested real conspiracy in *Rumor of Revolt*. Proletarian union is found in Marcus Rediker and Peter Linebaugh, *Many-Headed Hydra*, 174–210; African survivals are emphasized in Wilder, *In*

the Company of Black Men, 22–26. See also Hoffer, Great New York Conspiracy, who argues that by eighteenth-century legal standards, the defendants were guilty of the charge of conspiracy.

40. Hoffer, Great New York Conspiracy, 63, 73.

41. Samuel Auchmuty letters, September 19, 1761, June 29, 1762, March 30, 1763, September 29, 1763, March 29, 1764, Papers of the Society for the Propagation of the Gospel, Lambeth Palace Library MS 1124, I: 19a, 69a, 163a, 205, 260; Samuel Auchmuty to Rev. Dr. Burton, January 30, 1770, and August 16, 1770, Records of the Society for the Propagation of the Gospel, Letters Series B, 1701–1786, II: 35, 37.

42. Slave imports into colonial New York are available in Betty Wood, Slavery in Colonial America, 1619–1776, Appendix: table 2, p. 88. On the Negro burying ground, see Foote, Black and White Manhattan, 141–42.

43. For the classic account of the Great Awakening, see Alan Heimert, Religion and the American Mind from the Great Awakening to the Revolution; useful overviews include Bonomi, Under the Cope of Heaven, 131–60; and A. Taylor, American Colonies, 344–62. A brief overview that stresses the revivals' social radicalism is Gary Nash, Red, White, and Black, 221–25. On the Baptist example in Virginia, see Rhys Isaac, "Evangelical Revolt," expanded in his work The Transformation of Virginia.

44. Wakeley, Lost Chapters, 439; Asbury, Journal, 1:10, 41.

45. Donald G. Mathews describes early Methodist opposition to slavery in Slavery and Methodism, 8–9.

Notes to Chapter 2

1. Hugh Hastings, ed., Ecclesiastical Records, State of New York, 6:4291–300; Maya Jasanoff, Liberty's Exiles, 29–30.

2. Bonomi, Under the Cope of Heaven, 195, 198; Donald F. M. Gerardi, "King's College Controversy, 150, 163, 165; May, Enlightenment in America," 79.

3. Gerardi, "King's College Controversy," 166–67; Bonomi, Under the Cope of Heaven, 195–97.

4. Gerardi, "King's College Controversy," 169–71; Doll, Revolution, Religion, and National Identity, 188.

5. Gerardi, "King's College Controversy," 188–89, 193; May, Enlightenment in America, 79; Mills, Bishops by Ballot, 20.

6. Gerardi, "King's College Controversy," 171.

7. Ibid., 190–91, 195.

8. Bonomi, Under the Cope of Heaven, 199.

9. Ibid., 199, 205.

10. Doll, Revolution, Religion, and National Identity, 188; Bonomi, Under the Cope of Heaven, 199.

11. Hamilton's response foreshadowed the post-Revolutionary world, for with the departure of loyal clergy, lay patriots refashioned the clerical vision of unity to be social rather than political. The Seabury-Hamilton exchange is described in Allan McLane Hamilton, The Intimate Life of Alexander Hamilton, 64, 441; Hamilton's pamphlets are reprinted in Alexander Hamilton, The Papers of Alexander Hamilton, ed. Syrett and Cooke, 1:45–78, 81–165; Seabury's pamphlets can be found in C. H. Vance, ed., Letters of a Westchester Farmer, 1774–1775.

12. The one patriot clergy exception was Samuel Provoost, then in retirement (Hastings, ed., *New York Ecclesiastical Records*, 4291–300).

13. The wartime privileges granted to Episcopalian and Methodist churches can be found in Seaman, *Annals of New York Methodism*. On examples of anti-Anglican resentment, see Bonomi, *Under the Cope of Heaven*, 199–209; and Burrows and Wallace, *Gotham*, 252. Loyalist lives are recounted in Jasanoff, *Liberty's Exiles*; for a closer look at New York City, see Ruma Chopra, *Unnatural Rebellion*.

14. Hodges, "Black Revolt," in Gilje and Pencak, eds., *New York in the Age of the Constitution*, 20–47; Burrows and Wallace, *Gotham*, 249.

15. Foote, *Black Manhattan*, 213–15; Douglas R. Egerton, *Death or Liberty*, 65–92; Silvia R. Frey, *Water from the Rock*.

16. Foote, *Black Manhattan*, 212; Burrows and Wallace, *Gotham*, 248–49.

17. Foote, *Black Manhattan*, 216; Hodges, "Black Revolt"; Burrows and Wallace, *Gotham*, 249.

18. Foote, *Black Manhattan*, 213; Burrows and Wallace, *Gotham*, 249. The above paragraphs minimize the antislavery impulse many patriots voiced, including strong words from the Anglican and Trinity parishioner John Jay. The patriots' need for unity against the British tended to minimize or isolate antislavery sentiment through most of the war, however. On antislavery currents among the patriots, see David N. Gellman, *Emancipating New York*, esp. 27–34.

19. Mills, *Bishops by Ballot*, 178; Pointer, *Protestant Pluralism*, 104; Hastings, ed., *Ecclesiastical Records*, 4327. Jasanoff's *Liberty's Exiles* provides a moving portrait of loyalist experiences throughout the British Empire.

20. Andrews, *Methodists in Revolutionary America*, 49–50.

21. Pointer, *Protestant Pluralism*, 94; Andrews, *Methodists in Revolutionary America*, 53–55.

22. Pointer, *Protestant Pluralism*, 107, makes explicit that the vestry tapped Provoost explicitly for his political views, citing their "utmost confidence in his political principles" in addition to his "learning, Virtue, and Piety." See also Mills, *Bishops by Ballot*, x.

23. Burrows and Wallace, *Gotham*, 269, 274, 279–81.

24. Rufus King, *Life and Correspondence of Rufus King*, vol. 1, *1755–1794*, 95; Doll, *Revolution, Religion, and National Identity*, 226; Pointer, *Protestant Pluralism*, 107; Mills, *Bishops by Ballot*, x.

25. Lindsley, *This Planted Vine*, 60–61. Average terms of service come from Berrian, *Historical Sketch of Trinity Church*, 358–65; and Philip Ranlet, *The New York Loyalists*, esp. 191–92.

26. William H. Nelson, *The American Tory*, 133.

27. Joseph S. Tiedemann, *Reluctant Revolutionaries*, 206–7.

28. Conservative Whig Alexander Hamilton was a leading proponent of this unity of the propertied (see Burrows and Wallace, *Gotham*, 274, 279–80). For examples of how this applied in Greater New York, see John L. Brooke, *Columbia Rising*, 41–42, 56–57, 90–94.

29. Berrian, *Historical Sketch*, 359; Ranlet, *New York Loyalists*, 191–92; *The New-York Directory, and Register, for 1790*. Sherbrooke is unlisted in the 1786 directory, New York's first, but reappears in the 1787 directory (David Franks, *The New-York Directory* [1786], and Franks, *The New-York Directory* [1787]). Lindsley, *This Planted*

Vine, 62. On Livingston, see Clare Brandt, *An American Aristocracy*, 95, 195. Livingston also first appears in the 1787 directory, but his term in the vestry began in 1785, according to Berrian's *Historical Sketch*, 359.

30. Lindsley, *This Planted Vine*, 72. Anglican historians, who often emphasize the High Church theology of the majority of their clergy, tend to minimize Provoost's significance. I find Provoost's social status, and his connections to the laity, extremely important in explaining the path Trinity took as a congregation for the next two decades; for examples, see esp. chaps. 3 and 6.

31. Andrews, *Methodists in Revolutionary America,* 62; Seaman, *Annals of New York Methodism*.

32. Pointer, *Protestant Pluralism*, 104.

33. Ibid., 94, 116–19.

34. Hodges, "Black Revolt," 45–47.

35. Sidney I. Pomerantz, *New York, an American City 1783–1803*, 221–22; Gellman, *Emancipating New York*, esp. 56–77. Scholars have often noted the elite and professional bent of the NYMS, without finding any significance in the fact that such elites were almost exclusively Anglican (see D. Davis, *Problem of Slavery in the Age of Revolution*, 239–40). One prominent exception is found in passing in Robert J. Swan, "Prelude and Aftermath of the Doctors' Riot of 1788," 432–34.

36. Gellman, *Emancipating New York*, 65–68.

37. This topic occupies the bulk of Gellman's *Emancipating New York*. See also L. Harris, *In the Shadow of Slavery*, 56–71.

38. Gellman, *Emancipating New York*, 72–73; L. Harris, *In the Shadow of Slavery*, 49, 64–65; Shane White, *Somewhat More Independent,* 84.

39. John Jay uttered an oft-quoted line that "prayers to Heaven for Liberty will be impious" if coming from slaveholders (see L. Harris, *In the Shadow of Slavery*, 53; and S. White, *Somewhat More Independent*, 82). Here I emphasize harmony in the NYMS membership, which reflects the Anglican impulse in the mid-1780s to connect to majority trends in the new American nation. In the next chapter, I discuss NYMS members' hypocrisy on slavery, which grew more pronounced as abolition became a more viable option.

40. De Costa, *Three Score and Ten*, 14; Hewitt, *Protest and Progress*, 18.

41. James Walker Hood, *Sketch of the Early History of the African Methodist Episcopal Zion Church, with Jubilee Souvenir and Appendix*, 16.

42. Methodist society classes for the years 1785 to 1787 are found in vol. 233, Methodist Episcopal Church Records, New York Public Library (hereafter NYPL).

43. Wakeley, *Lost Chapters*, 438–79; the story of the Methodist minister and British officer appears on 456–58.

44. Williams's portrait hangs in the New-York Historical Society, postcard copies of which are available in the gift shop. His story is prominently featured in white Methodist oral history, and in city history generally.

45. Wakeley, *Lost Chapters*, 454–56, 458–60.

46. Frey, *Water from the Rock*; Hodges, *Root and Branch*. The passage of manumission acts in northern states challenged, but did not eradicate, the assumption of white rule. I examine the implications of manumission throughout the next chapters. The story of manumission in New York is well told in Gellman, *Emancipating New York*; for an opposing interpretation see S. White, *Somewhat More Independent*.

47. Discussion of the rise of the black church follows in the next several chapters; on blacks' acceptance of American identity in the early Republic, see Rita Roberts, *Evangelicalism and the Politics of Reform in Northern Black Thought, 1776–1863*.

48. Here I use the term "Trinity" in its corporate sense, as the burned-out church remained a husk in the 1780s. Trinity's parishioners worshiped at St. Paul's or St. Mark's chapels while artisans rebuilt the mother church.

Notes to Chapter 3

1. On New York's economic advantages, see Robert Greenhalgh Albion, *The Rise of New York Port, 1815–1860*, 16–37; and Gellman, *Emancipating New York*, 173. On the city's population growth, see Campbell Gibson and Kay Jung, *Historical Census Statistics on Population Totals by Race, 1790 to 1990, and by Hispanic Origin, 1970 to 1990, for the United States, Regions, Divisions, and States*.

2. Pointer, *Protestant Pluralism*, 129.

3. Seaman, *Annals of New York Methodism*, 85.

4. Lindsley, *This Planted Vine*, 60–61. See also chapter 2 of this work.

5. On Federalist culture, see, among others, Linda K. Kerber, *Federalists in Dissent*; Dixon Ryan Fox, *The Decline of Aristocracy in the Politics of New York, 1801–1840*, 25–29, 137–38; and David Hackett Fischer, *The Revolution of American Conservatism*. A recent collection that revises yet expands upon these classic works can be found in Doron Ben-Atar and Barbara B. Oberg, eds., *Federalists Reconsidered*.

6. William Maclay, *Journal of William Maclay*, 3. On Washington's pew, see Trinity Vestry Minutes, Vol. I, p. 525, Trinity Church Archives. The Federalist affinity for religion was not generally based on personal piety. Washington promoted the outward forms of Christianity to instill moral conduct among the masses, and he regularly attended Anglican Church services where he resided. But Washington apparently did not believe in a Trinitarian God or an atoning death of Christ; he pointedly left services before communion was served, and in one of his letters he referred to God as "it," along the lines of the Deistical watchmaker (see Thomas Fleming, *Duel*, 4). The literature on the Founders' religiosity is vast and often highly charged; a good documentary starting point is Matthew Harris and Thomas Kidd, eds., *The Founding Fathers and the Debate over Religion in Revolutionary America*.

7. Maclay, *Journal*, 4, 9.

8. When the city directory contained multiple listings for a name that revealed conflicting occupation categories—for example, a name having both artisan and retail/merchant categories represented—I tabulated the figures twice: once including all occupations in the listings, and once excluding the conflicting numbers. This reveals a range of probability for each occupational group.

9. I based overall city averages from Jacob M. Price, "Economic Function and the Growth of American Port Towns in the Eighteenth Century." Price derived them from an analysis of 1795 yellow fever death lists, presumably cross-listed with city directories. Price's categories were concerned with economic structures and functions, as he broke them down into service, industrial, and commercial categories. I have reorganized them largely based upon Dee Andrews's pattern, with government-professional, merchant-retail, artisan, service-transport-marine, and unskilled the five major categories.

10. "Trinity Church Pew Rents before 1828," in record 17905, Trinity Church Archives, New York City; *The New-York Directory, and Register, for the Year 1790*; *The*

New-York Directory, and Register, for the Year 1795. Trinity Church Archives pew diagrams date from the 1840s, with the third Trinity building, so it is not clear exactly where Jay's and Livingston's pews were. Judging from their pew numbers and rent levels, I believe they sat in gallery boxes, at the church's rear but in a prominent location above the main level.

11. Ibid.

12. Again, Price's figure of 40 percent is derived from yellow fever death lists and (presumably) corroborated by directories; Howard B. Rock estimates the artisan population at 50 to 60 percent in *Artisans of the New Republic*, 12.

13. Rock, *Artisans of the New Republic*, 12; "Trinity Church Pew Rents before 1828." Hugh Gaine, in fact, was a printer along the lines of Benjamin Franklin—much more an entrepreneur than mechanic. He printed New York's *Mercury* and *Gazette* in the 1760s and 1770s, and in his newspaper placed advertisements for his shop, which sold not only books but medicines and stationery.

14. "Trinity Church Pew Rents before 1828"; *1790 New-York Directory*; *1795 New-York Directory.*

15. L. Harris, *In the Shadow of Slavery*, 56–71.

16. S. White, *Somewhat More Independent*, 33, 34–35, 46; Gellman, *Emancipating New York*, 130–39.

17. For the abolitionist perspective, see Gellman, *Emancipating New York*, quote on 60; see also Paul J. Polgar, "To Raise Them to an Equal Participation." Older studies supporting the abolitionist interpretation include Edgar J. McManus, *A History of Negro Slavery in New York*; Broadus Mitchell, *Alexander Hamilton*; and Forrest McDonald, *Alexander Hamilton*. For the charge of hypocrisy, see S. White, *Somewhat More Independent*, statistics on 81, 86; a similar charge is contained in L. Harris, *In the Shadow of Slavery*, which follows the NYMS through its falling out with the black community and subsequent demise in the 1830s. White notes the average city slaveholder owned two slaves in 1790; for NYMS members, the average was 2.9.

18. Rob N. Weston, "Alexander Hamilton and the Abolition of Slavery in New York"; Gellman, *Emancipating New York*, 58–59; S. White, *Somewhat More Independent*, 82. See also Hodges, *Root and Branch*, 166–67.

19. Andrews, *Methodists in Revolutionary America*, 62; Seaman, *Annals of New York Methodism.*

20. Asbury, *Journal*, 1:237.

21. Ibid., 2:136.

22. Ibid., 2:226–27. Immediately after this quote, Asbury noted having read Uzal Ogden's response to Thomas Paine's Deist treatises, suggesting perhaps a link between too much politics and false religion.

23. Ibid., 1:355.

24. Ibid., 2:14.

25. See, for example, his 1793 visit, where the quote occurs (ibid. 2:174).

26. Ibid., 2:260, 293–94.

27. Ibid., 2: 226–27.

28. Ibid., 2: 259; 1:48; 3:143.

29. Ibid., 1:81; 2:260.

30. Andrews, *Methodists in Revolutionary America*, 239, 155. Among all the scholars of Methodism, Andrews acknowledges the greatest social (and racial and

gendered) heterogeneity in the movement, including the presence and influence of wealthier believers in the movement's early years.

31. The concept of declension figures strongly in Methodist historiography, and a vast literature describes declines from early classless purity or racial equality. For recent examples from scholars who interpret the Methodists very differently, see Hatch, *Democratization*, 201–6; and Heyrman, *Southern Cross*, 206–7.

32. For much of this section, I attempt to use terms such as "occupation" and "wealth" instead of the socioeconomic term "class," in part because working-class formation in the 1790s is premature, and also to avoid confusion with Methodist "classes" as small groups.

33. I determined average figures for all occupational categories from Jacob Price's study, "Economic Function and the Growth of American Port Towns," 123–86. I follow, for the most part, Dee Andrews's reformulation of Price's list, with a couple of exceptions: I combined the professional and government categories, and I include cartmen and marine as separate categories from other service industries. Cartmen were in the carrying trade, often as individual proprietors. The city government limited their numbers and set barriers to entry through licensing, and the government similarly set the rates for services rendered. Cartmen's knowledge of the streets and ability to navigate them made them semi-skilled rather than unskilled workers, and this plus the barriers to entry and the cartmen's own sense of solidarity lead me to consider it a distinct occupation within the service industry. On cartmen, see Graham Russell Hodges, *New York City Cartmen, 1667–1850*.

34. "Methodist society class records, 1796," vol. 241, Methodist Episcopal Church Records, NYPL; David Longworth, *The American Almanack, New-York Register, and City Directory, for the Twenty-First Year of American Independence* (1796). The Methodist record keepers numbered the city classes consecutively; thus in the records each class has a distinct number assigned to it. Classes identified as strongly Bowery: 7, 11, 17, and 27; likely Bowery: 20; strongly John: 23 and 28; likely John: 25 and 30; 14 and 19 were unidentified. According to Samuel Seaman's account, class 14 was comprised of individuals who would form the Seventh Street, or Two-Mile, church on the outskirts of the city, and class number 19 met at John Street in 1793.

35. "1796 Class Records."

36. In contrast, no Bowery class had more than three retailers or fewer than seven artisans in it.

37. "1796 Class Records."

38. Wilentz, *Chants Democratic*.

39. Rock, *Artisans of the New Republic*, 65.

40. Two of every three blacks in 1790 New York City were slaves (Walls, *Reality of the Black Church*, 41; Andrews, *Methodists in Revolutionary America*, 135; Gibson and Jung, *Historical Census Statistics*).

41. For a general analysis of the historical expansion of the franchise, see Alexander Keyssar, *The Right to Vote*. On the parties' different stances on voting, citizenship, and equality, see Kerber, *Federalists in Dissent*; David Waldstreicher, *In the Midst of Perpetual Fetes*, esp. 242–45; Paul Finkelman, "The Problem of Slavery in the Age of Federalism," in Ben-Atar and Oberg, eds., *Federalists Reconsidered*, 135–56. Finkelman's argument that the Federalist movement promoted a consistently antislavery stance is overstated, but his evidence suggests that Federalists were in general more

favorable to abolition than their rivals. Waldstreicher, by contrast, asserts that both parties used blacks merely to slander their political rivals (230–31).

42. Shane White, *Stories of Freedom in Black New York*, 12–13; see White, *Somewhat More Independent*. Gibson and Jung, *Historical Census Statistics*.

43. "1801 Communicant List," Trinity Church Archives. Bishop Moore recorded blacks in the communicant lists by placing the letter "n" after the name. I included Thomas Bartow among the eleven men. The notation "n/w" following his name perhaps suggests mulatto status, but his directory-listed profession of merchant implies that the notation does not represent his race.

44. One duplicated name—Joseph Brown—listed an occupation as a physician, which I excluded as no blacks received professional training at this time. Other duplicate occupations for John King were merchant and mason, as well as a John King on 37 Liberty Street with no occupation listed. William Martin's name was duplicated as "blockmaker and grocer" and merchant. The eighth name, John Nixon, is listed at 49 Cedar Street, with no occupation.

45. Jacob Jacobs, however, was a mason, a trade with lucrative possibilities given the dramatic expansion of the city northward on Manhattan Island.

46. "Methodist Society Class Records, 1795," vol. 241, Methodist Episcopal Church Records, NYPL; Longworth, *New-York City Directory, 1796*.

47. St. Paul's pew rent list, from a book marked "Second Trinity Church Building," record 17905, Trinity Church Archives. This geographic location did not keep prominent whites from attending Saint Paul's; men such as Robert Troup held pews at the chapel. It is significant, however, that with the rise of a free black population, the place for African Americans clearly moved to a secondary institution, outside the most visible and prominent branch of the church.

48. On Methodist classes, see chapter 2 of this work; see also Philip F. Hardt, *The Soul of Methodism*.

49. Methodist society classes for the years 1785 to 1787 are found in vol. 233, Methodist Episcopal Church Records, NYPL.

50. In certain cases, white Methodists mixed men and women in classes. In the outlying Two-Mile Stone group, for example, distance briefly necessitated gender-integrated groupings. As time passed, Methodism lost its early militancy and gender segregation was less heavily enforced; in the 1830s, New York's white Methodist churches allowed families to sit together, and many classes were mixed-gender.

51. Black men numbered three in 1785, and forty in 1795.

52. This continued into the 1790s, where black women's classes continued to have women without surnames, while the black male classes of 1796 reveal only one man without the last name ("1796 Class Records"; Federal Censuses for the Years 1800, 1810, 1820, and 1830).

53. Wilder, *In the Company of Black Men*, 36. Wilder draws his conclusions about New York's African Society from the similarly named but better-documented Free African Society in Philadelphia. Walls, *Reality of the Black Church*, 1–50 passim; George McMurray and Ndugu G. B. T'ofori-Atta, *Mother Zion African Methodist Episcopal Zion Church*. One exception to these misinterpretations can be found in Swan, "Doctors' Riot of 1788," 443, 456.

54. Richard S. Newman, *Freedom's Prophet*, esp. 120–26.

55. "Petition of the African Society on the Subject of two Lots purchased for burial ground," Petitions May–August 1795, Box 15, Folder 465, Common Council Papers, New York Municipal Archives.

56. Saint Philip's Church Petition to the Corporation of Trinity Church, November 8, 1826, Trinity Church Archives. Trinity vestry affirmed Williams's claims.

57. Names taken from "Petition of the African Society," Common Council Papers, New York Municipal Archives; affiliations found in marriage and baptismal records, Trinity Church Archives. In most, but not all, cases, blacks in the marriage and baptismal records are recorded as Negro, thus making positive identification more likely.

58. Jupiter Hammon, *An Address to the Negroes in the State of New-York*. Page iii reads "To the Members of the African Society, in the County of New-York."

59. Ibid., quote on 17–18. See also Bruce, *Origins of African American Literature*, 50–52.

60. "Petition of the African Society," Common Council Papers, New York Municipal Archives.

61. Hood, *Sketch of the Early History*, 16; Rush, *Short Account*, 9–10. Why did Asbury change his mind? An opponent of slavery, perhaps he was saddened by the inability of blacks to gain greater equality in Methodist fellowship in the previous fifteen years and hoped this would allow them the ability to practice their gifts. Perhaps the growth of the free black community convinced him of the feasibility of their request by 1796. Or the decision may simply have intended to open more space in the crowded Methodist chapels.

62. Hood, *One Hundred Years of the African Methodist Episcopal Zion Church*, quoted in Angela H. Dunlap, *Voices of the Freedom Church*, 9; see also Walls, *Reality of the Black Church*, 44–45.

63. B. F. Wheeler, *The Varick Family*, 16.

64. Rush, *Short Account*, 9–10.

65. Methodist society class records, 1795 and 1796; Rush, *Short Account*, 9. On the turmoil of the early years of Mother Zion, and Varick's position, see Rush, *Short Account*, 9–41 passim. For an example of Hamilton's rhetoric, see William Hamilton, "An Oration Delivered in the African Zion Church, on the Fourth of July, 1827, in Commemoration of the Abolition of Domestic Slavery in this State, 1827," reprinted in Porter, ed., *Early Negro Writing 1760–1837*, 98–102.

66. Methodist society class records, 1795 and 1796.

67. Ibid.

68. The first free black in New York to purchase and free his wife and son, John Fortune, shared a surname with Isaac Fortune of the African Society. The Fortune family, at least, had dealt with slavery for a long time (see Sherrill D. Wilson, *New York City's African Slaveholders*, 30).

69. Carol George's study of Richard Allen assumes that the black church in New York developed in roughly the same way; George, *Segregated Sabbaths*, 100–102, although she does suggest that New York's smaller black Methodist population might be attributable to the city's more worldy and materialistic reputation, 142. Wilder, *In the Company of Black Men*, similarly assumes that Philadelphia's Free African Society can be transposed to New York; see above for a discussion of New York's African Society.

70. Richard Allen and Absalom Jones, *A Narrative of the Proceedings of the Black People, during the Late Awful Calamity in Philadelphia, in the Year 1793*. Newman, *Freedom's Prophet*, esp. 120–26; Richard S. Newman, "'A Chosen Generation': Black Founders and Early America," in McCarthy and Stauffer, eds., *Prophets of Protest*, 59–79. On Philadelphia blacks, see also Gary Nash, *Forging Freedom*.

71. David Gellman asserts that white representations of black voices in New York's public sphere in the 1780s and 1790s advanced the cause of antislavery by creating a discourse that made it possible to consider an interracial society. Gellman acknowledges that with the exceptions of sentimental literature (especially poetry), newspaper re-creations of black dialogue and racial satire, not blacks' own words, usually harmed public images of blacks. Further, in Gellman's analysis, only Jupiter Hammon's poetry and William Hamilton's letter appear as New York blacks' own voices. Transatlantic black voices, and fictional black voices, that appeared in New York newspapers and literature may have created a discourse about citizenship, but New York's black men had not yet fully advanced their own cause (Gellman, *Emancipating New York*, 102–29). Richard Newman has found an interesting exception, one "Africanus," who mocked white stereotypes in his response to racist taunts (Newman, "Chosen Generation," 68).

72. William Hamilton to John Jay, March 8, 1796 (ID 7312), John Jay Papers, Rare Book and Manuscript Division, Butler Library, Columbia University; conveniently reprinted in J. Jay, "Anti-Slavery Papers of John Jay." The school opened in 1788, and educated students between five and fourteen years of age; it is possible, then, that Hamilton attended the school for a year. It is unlikely, however, as only twelve students attended the first year (see Robert J. Swan, "John Teasman," 334).

73. J. Jay, "Anti-Slavery Papers of John Jay," 492.

Notes to Chapter 4

1. "A Householder," *Republican Watch Tower*, October 26, 1805, quoted in I. N. Phelps Stokes, *The Iconography of Manhattan Island*, 5:1439.

2. The vivid quote is from Stansell, *City of Women*, 9.

3. Rock, *Artisans of the New Republic*, 31–36.

4. Pintard, *Census of the Electors*. Howard Rock estimated that the figure of retreat for the lower wards was 70 to 90 percent, compared to 10 to 20 percent in uptown working-class wards (Rock, *Artisans*, 3).

5. Stansell, *City of Women*. On women's population in the city, see Pintard, *Census of the Electors*. On women's roles generally, see Rosemary O'Day, *Women's Agency in Early Modern Britain and the American Colonies*.

6. Representative examples of such church histories include Dix, *History of the Parish of Trinity Church*; Seaman, *Annals of New York Methodism*; Walls, *Reality of the Black Church*; de Costa, *Three Score and Ten*; and Rush, *Short Account*. All provide valuable historical narratives of the congregations but focus on ministerial profiles at the expense of the social identities and lived experience of the church's members.

7. See, for example, Linda K. Kerber, *No Constitutional Right to Be Ladies*; and Mary Beth Norton, *Separated by Their Sex*. But see also Norton, *Liberty's Daughters*, for Revolutionary alterations to some gender roles.

8. Anna M. Lawrence, *One Family under God*, esp. 44–71; see also A. Gregory Schneider, *The Way of the Cross Leads Home*.

9. Conversely, 17 percent of male communicants also rented pews. Beginning in 1845, Trinity communicant lists recorded individuals who did not rent pews but who wished to vote in vestry elections; that year nonpewholders could vote provided they had regularly attended Trinity for a year. Those later lists were therefore not a complete record of all participating communicants in the church. The fact that 17 percent of this 1801 list consisted of pew renters suggests it was a working list of regular communicants, rather than simply a record of nonpewholding communicants.

10. "1801 Communicant List," Trinity Church Archives; *Longworth's American Almanac, New-York Register, and City-Directory, for the Twenty-Sixth Year of American Independence* (1801); *Longworth's American Almanac, New-York Register, and City-Directory, for the Twenty-Seventh Year of American Independence* (1802). Compare with "Trinity Church Pew Rents before 1828"; *1790 New-York Directory*; *1795 New-York Directory*; all analyzed in chapter 3.

11. "1801 Communicant List" and "Trinity Church Pew Rents before 1828."

12. Ibid.

13. The parallel on the other side is also striking—only 19 percent of communicant men shared a name with a female. This is especially significant compared to black women; see chapter 5 of this work.

14. "1801 Communicant List." Only 12 percent of male communicants—half the percentage of women—shared a surname with a pewholder. Male piety, tied to the outward forms of display, apparently discouraged participation without the public involvement. Women suffered no such stigma.

15. Because women rarely appeared in the city directories, and the city Methodist records before 1820 did not list the congregational affiliation of individual classes, it is difficult to determine which women's classes attended John Street for worship (Andrews, *Methodists in Revolutionary America*, 112; John Pintard, *Enumeration of the Inhabitants*).

16. On Methodist challenges to the traditional family, see Lawrence, *One Family under God*, 44–71, esp. 48–50, 58–59.

17. Andrews, *Methodists in Revolutionary America*, 112–14. Thus this consideration of women in the church notes the differences between younger, unmarried, and poorer women, on the one hand, and older, married or widowed, and wealthier women, on the other. I discuss black women's religious identity in conjunction with that of black men in chapter 5.

18. For the classic exposition of how republican motherhood allowed women a limited role in the new Republic, see Linda K. Kerber, "The Republican Mother."

19. In the 1790s, Methodists also followed more traditional patterns of relief; see Andrews, *Methodists in Revolutionary America*, 117.

20. Papers of the Society for the Relief of Poor Widows with Small Children (hereafter Widows' Society Papers), vol. I, New-York Historical Society; Divie Bethune, *The Power of Faith*, 39–40.

21. Widows' Society Papers, vol. I.

22. Ibid.; Bethune, *Power of Faith*, 50; "1801 Communicant List."

23. Widows' Society Papers, vol. I; Bethune, *Power of Faith*, 50.

24. Bethune, *Power of Faith*, 30, 45, 47. On the upper-class nature of the organization, see Anne M. Boylan, "Women in Groups"; and Boylan, "Timid Girls, Venerable Widows and Dignified Matrons."

25. Elizabeth Hamilton's involvement in benevolent societies may have stemmed from a desire to protect her husband Alexander's political reputation after his death, preserving her family's public image as benevolent givers. Her actions thus connect the worlds of benevolence and politics to a larger world of elite reputation.

26. Boylan, "Women in Groups"; Boylan, "Timid Girls, Venerable Widows and Dignified Matrons."

27. Elizabeth Mason North, *Consecrated Talents*, 59–61.

28. Yet Morgan also stood as a normative example for young single women, for she actively embraced the ministries of older married Methodist matrons, and eventually became one such matron herself.

29. North, *Consecrated Talents*, 68–69.

30. Ibid., 69–75.

31. Ibid., 75–76.

32. Edward Pessen, *Riches, Class, and Power before the Civil War*, 205–20.

33. Geraldine Brooks, *Dames and Daughters of the Young Republic*, 43–83; Martha J. Lamb, *History of the City of New York*, 2:301–2; 3:402–3.

34. Sarah Livingston to Catharine and Susan Livingston, March 4, 1780, in S. Livingston, *Selected Letters of John Jay and Sarah Livingston Jay*, 74.

35. Catherine Allgor, *Parlor Politics*.

36. Kelly and Melville, introduction to *Elizabeth Seton: Selected Writings*, 15–72.

37. Tuberculosis is not genetically determined, but spread environmentally.

38. A published account of her diary is available in the New-York Historical Society: [Elizabeth Seton], *Memoirs of Mrs. S*****.

39. Ibid., 31, 34, 49, 78.

40. Ibid., 78.

41. Ibid., 40–42, 60, 78.

42. Ibid., 14, 17, 41–42, 54, 62.

43. On High Church theology, see Mullin, *Episcopal Vision/American Reality*; see also Mullin, ed., *Moneygripe's Apprentice*.

44. Joseph I. Dirvin, *Mrs. Seton*, 92; see also Kathleen Flanagan, "The Influence of John Henry Hobart on the Life of Elizabeth Ann Seton."

45. Shin Ja Lee, "The Practice of Spiritual Direction in the Life and Writings of St. Elizabeth Ann Seton," 105; Kelley and Melville, eds., *Selected Writings*, 67. Elizabeth's grandson, the Catholic priest Robert Seton, condescendingly labeled his grandmother's relationship with Hobart a romantic infatuation in Seton, *Memoir, Letters and Journal of Elizabeth Seton*, 1:83.

46. E. Seton, *Selected Writings*, 79.

47. Hobart to Seton, New York, November 23, 1803, in Lee, "Practice of Spiritual Direction," 110.

48. Lawrence, *One Family under God*, 44–45, 162–63.

49. Abel Stevens, *The Women of Methodism*, 45–46; George White, *A Brief Account of the Life, Experience, Travels, and Gospel Labours of George White, an African*, reprinted in Hodges, ed., *Black Itinerants of the Gospel*, 58–59.

50. On Lady Huntingdon, see Stevens, *Women of Methodism*, 145–73.

51. Diane Lobody, "Lost in the Ocean of Love," 34, 44.

52. Ibid., 45–46, 48–51, 53.

53. Robert Drew Simpson, ed. *American Methodist Pioneer*, 10.

54. Lobody, "Lost in the Ocean of Love," 52, 55–56, 62.

55. Ibid., 58, 62, 64; Simpson, *American Methodist Pioneer*, 10, 14; Lawrence, *One Family under God*, 64–69.

56. Lobody, "Lost in the Ocean of Love"; Simpson, *American Methodist Pioneer*, 15, 31.

57. Lobody, "Lost in the Ocean of Love," 67; Simpson, *American Methodist Pioneer*, 15–16, 20–21.

58. Lobody, "Lost in the Ocean of Love," 66–67; Simpson, *American Methodist Pioneer*, 11, 14, 29–30.

59. Schneider, *Way of the Cross*, 149–68; Lawrence, *One Family under God*, 163.

60. Lobody, "Lost in the Ocean of Love," 68; Simpson, *Pioneer*, 18, 23, 24, 27.

61. The changes Methodism wrought in families and marriages are compellingly described in Lawrence, *One Family under God*, 218–23.

62. North, *Consecrated Talents*, 11, 14–15, 23.

63. Ibid., 69–75. On the social dynamics of church battles, including gendered components, see chapter 6 of this work. For an excellent study that examines the issue of gender in relation to conflicts within early Republic Catholicism, see Rodney Hessinger, "A Base and Unmanly Conspiracy."

64. Bonomi, *Under the Cope of Heaven*, 112–15; Curtis D. Johnson, *Islands of Holiness*, 168–69, 173–74. Similarly, Walls, *Reality of the Black Church*, 40, asserted that many black men were attracted to Methodism, but stayed away from the church because of its racism.

Notes to Chapter 5

1. For the account from white Methodists, see Wakeley, *Lost Chapters*, 438–79; for the son's account, see Woodson, ed., *The Mind of the Negro as Reflected in Letters Written during the Crisis*, 630–31.

2. On portraits as historical sources, see Carrie Rebora Barratt, "Faces of a New Nation: American Portraits of the 18th and Early 19th Centuries." On Methodist simplicity in dress, see Leigh Eric Schmidt, "A Church-Going People Are a Dress-Loving People," esp. 40, 48.

3. On Williams's wig, see Wakeley, *Lost Chapters*, 446.

4. Shane White, "A Question of Style"; Shane White and Graham White, *Stylin'*. For examples of other black portraits, see Gwendolyn DuBois Shaw, *Portraits of a People*,

5. L. Harris, Shadow of Slavery, 73–74; Swan, "John Teasman," 341.

6. Still, *Mirror for Gotham*, 73; L. Harris, *In the Shadow of Slavery*, 72, 77–78, 82–83.

7. In discussing the public sphere, I rely upon the clear examples of Newman, *Freedom's Prophet*; and Brooke, *Columbia Rising*.

8. Rush, *Short Account*, 11–22.

9. Historians who repeat the idea that Williams led blacks out of John Street to Mother Zion include Gellman, *Emancipating New York*, 158; Hodges, *Root and Branch*, 183; Walls, *Reality of the Black Church*, 58, 88; David Henry Bradley Sr., *A History of the A.M E. Zion Church, Part I, 1796–1872*, 44–45; Margaret Washington, *Sojourner Truth's America*, 89. The most complete portrait of Williams, stressing his devotion, patriotism, and industriousness, is filtered through the perception of white Methodist clergy, in Wakeley, *Lost Chapters*, 438–79. As a businessman, Williams did well; tax records list his house and shop on Liberty Street as among the highest-valued

properties in the biracial neighborhood. See the "Assessed Valuation of Real Estate Collection" for any year in the 1810s, New York City Municipal Archives. Walls, *Reality of the Black Church*, 62–64, blames Williams for betraying Zion to white church leaders in the incorporation arrangement; I find this unlikely, given Williams's continuing relationship with Zion's leaders.

10. The account first appeared in the *New York Minerva, & Mercantile Evening Advertiser*, December 16, 1796, vol. 3, issue 1024, p. 3. It was reprinted in the December 27 edition of *Argus Greenleaf's New Daily Advertiser* and the December 28 editions of the Newark *Centinel of Freedom* and *New York Herald*. It reached New England the following week, appearing in January 3, 1797, issues of the *Massachusetts Mercury* and *Newport Mercury,* and the *Political Gazette* (Newburyport, Mass.) and the *New Hampshire Gazette* (Portsmouth) a few days later.

11. On fires and the 1741 rebellion, see chapter 1 of this work; L. Harris, *In the Shadow of Slavery*, 69, contextualizes the fears of white New Yorkers in 1796.

12. Methodist society class records, 1795 and 1796. Church histories of Mother Zion and the AMEZ denomination have placed much emphasis on the fraternal bonds of class 31. Many also repeat the received wisdom that Peter Williams was central in leading blacks to the new church, even though Williams appears to have been outside such bonds.

13. Wakeley, *Lost Chapters*, 445–46, 456.

14. Class lists for the 1780s and 1790s are in Methodist Episcopal Church Records, vols. 233, 241, NYPL. Burrows and Wallace, *Gotham*, 398–99; *New-York Evening Post*, May 1, 1821.

15. Histories that assert that Williams remained with John Street include George, *Segregated Sabbaths*, 141–42; Walls, *Reality of the Black Church*, 62–63; and Burrows and Wallace, *Gotham*, 398–99. On Sojourner Truth, see Washington, *Sojourner Truth's America*, 84, 88.

16. "Pre-1820 Class Lists," and "1818 Class Lists," vols. 79–80, Methodist Episcopal Church Records, NYPL. Nathan Bangs, *The Substance of a Sermon Preached on Opening the Methodist Church in John-Street, in the City of New-York, on the Morning of the 4th of January, 1818*, 17.

17. "Pre-1820 Class Lists" and "1818 Class Lists."

18. "Blacks received on trial," 1802–1804, vol. 237, Methodist Episcopal Church Records, NYPL; Asbury, *Journal*, 3:138; Wakeley, *Lost Chapters*, 446; De Costa, *Three-score and Ten*, 31–33; Townsend, *Faith in Their Own Color*, 14.

19. Swan, "John Teasman," 342–43, 348–49; Townsend, *Faith in Their Own Color*, 27.

20. De Costa, *Threescore and Ten*, 31–33; Townsend, *Faith in Their Own Color*, 27–32. For more on St. Philip's connections to white leadership, see chapter 6 of this work.

21. George, *Segregated Sabbaths*, 143–44; Townsend, *Faith in Their Own Color*, 13–14, 18–24.

22. On African connections, see Wilder, *In the Company of Black Men*; on education, see Swan, "John Teasman." I do not dispute Wilder's colonial-era findings on African cultural survivals, but argue that the black church and mutual relief societies reflected the efforts of literate, skilled black males to assert their authority over and against older remaining cultural patterns. As such, the black community that emerged post-1800 was a different creature from Africanized groups of the colonial era.

23. The motivations of some of those politicians can be found in Steven Deyle, "The Irony of Liberty."

24. Swan, "John Teasman," 344; Walls, *Reality of the Black Church*, 52, 58, 62–63; Rush, *Short Account*, 29; Baptism, Marriage, and Death parish registers, Trinity Church Archives. William Hamilton, Thomas Miller, Thomas Sipkins, and William Brown were all Methodist clergy or trustees, and Daniel Berry was an associate of James Varick. Nicholas Smith, Daniel Berry, and William Green participated in sacraments at Trinity Church, Isaac Fortune had been an African Society Member, and Peter Williams, of course, had recently become Episcopalian.

25. Peter Williams Jr., "An Oration on the Abolition of the Slave Trade, Delivered in the African Church, in the City of New York, January 1, 1808," reprinted in Porter, ed., *Early Negro Writing 1760–1837*, 344–45.

26. Henry Sipkins, "The Introductory Address," in Peter Williams Jr., "An Oration on the Abolition," in Porter, ed., *Early Negro Writing*, 344.

27. Williams, "Oration on the Abolition," 345–53, quotes on 345, 346, 348, 352–53.

28. Ibid., 353–54.

29. L. Harris, *In the Shadow of Slavery*, 89–90.

30. Joseph Sidney, "An Oration Commemorative of the Abolition of the Slave Trade: Delivered before the Wilberforce Philanthropic Association, in the City of New York, on the Second of January, 1809," in Porter, ed., *Early Negro Writing*, 355–64.

31. Committee names found in Sidney, "Oration," 364; Trinity Church baptism and marriage registers, Trinity Church Archives.

32. Henry Sipkins, "An Oration on the Abolition of the Slave Trade; Delivered in the African Church, in the City of New York, January 2, 1809. With an Introductory Address by Henry Johnson," in Porter, ed., *Early Negro Writing*, 365–73; William Hamilton, "An Address to the New York African Society, for Mutual Relief, Delivered in the Universalist Church, January 2, 1809," in Porter, ed., *Early Negro Writing*, 33–41.

33. Hamilton, "Address to the New York African Society," 36–37. It is interesting that Hamilton praised two young black men compared to an older black woman; this paralleled almost exactly the contrast between the (then) young and male-led black church with the older and female-dominated blacks in biracial Methodist settings.

34. Daniel Perlman, "Organizations of the Free Negro in New York City, 1800–1860," 182–83; Swan, "John Teasman," 346.

35. L. Harris, *In the Shadow of Slavery*, 87; Swan, "John Teasman," 346–47; Hamilton, "Address to the New York African Society," 40.

36. "Constitution of the African Marine Fund, for the Relief of the Distressed Orphans, and Poor Members of This Fund," in Porter, ed., *Early Negro Writing*, 42–44.

37. Rita Roberts argues that evangelicalism provided the rhetorical base for black males in this era. She carefully notes that at this time middle-class ideology had not fully developed, as most men were too close to their slave and artisan roots; see Roberts, *Evangelicalism and the Politics of Reform*, 9–10. I agree with Roberts's further contention, however, that the evangelical inclinations of such men created attitudes that helped cultivate a middle-class identity among them.

38. On Arcularius, see Lathrop Colgate Harper Family Papers, Box 1 (genealogy), New-York Historical Society. See also chapter 3 of this work for his actions as a master tanner.

39. "October 30, 1805, To the Honorable Common Council the Representation of the Superintendent of the Alms House," Common Council Papers, Box 26, Folder 722, Almshouse 1805, New York Municipal Archives.

40. Cray, *Paupers and Poor Relief*, 196–98.

41. As a former immigrant, Arcularius may have overlooked the large numbers of immigrant whites on the poor rolls. Indeed, far more Irish and Germans benefited from public relief than did blacks (Cray, *Paupers and Poor Relief*, 198–99).

42. Shane White's careful analysis of early Republic New York City demonstrates that slavery existed in every quarter of the city. By visually plotting slaveholding households on maps, however, White's study leaves the impression that slavery was equally present throughout the city. Censuses reveal that slaves were far more numerous in the southern wards, living in denser concentrations than to the north (S. White, *Somewhat More Independent*).

43. Ibid., 48–49; Pintard, *Enumeration of the Inhab*itants; Gibson and Jung, *Historical Census Statistics*.

44. Pintard, *Enumeration of the Inhabitants*. Because black women, like white women, generally lived longer than men, even among free blacks women outnumbered men, although the sex ratio among free blacks was closer to equal.

45. John Jay to John Murray, Jr., October 18, 1805, in *Correspondence and Public Papers of John Jay*, 4:304.

46. Carol George noted that while New York had more free blacks than Philadelphia by 1801, it contained fewer black Methodists. She attributed this difference to the stereotypical assumption that New Yorkers were devoted to the accumulation of wealth rather than cultivation of piety (George, *Segregated Sabbaths*, 142). On sweeps, see L. Harris, *In the Shadow of Slavery*, 88, 92.

47. The figures for black communicants may have been depressed by the fact that thousands of loyalist blacks had fled the country in the wake of the British army's defeat. Trinity, as a Tory center during the war, may have attracted more black loyalists than elsewhere, and thus been hit harder with those blacks' flight (see Frey, *Water from the Rock*; and Hodges, "Black Revolt," 20–47). David Gellman notes that in absolute numbers, the number of slaves in New York State dropped by one thousand following British emancipation; given that rural areas in Long Island and the Hudson River Valley remained relatively dense with slaves, the population drop must have largely centered on New York City (see Gellman, *Emancipating New York*, 40).

48. Neau to Chamberlayne, October 3, 1705, SPG Papers, vol. XIII (New York 1700–1706), items/pages 138–39; SPG Papers, vol. XIV (New York 1707–undated), items/pages 137–39. These figures also included Indian catechists—two female and two male in 1705, eight female and four male in 1707.

49. "1801 Communicant List." Some names in common may reflect the fact that, emerging from slavery, many family names were new creations, and not necessarily indicating kinship. For example, there were two individuals surnamed Black and three surnamed Brown on the list, perhaps descriptive names that masters imposed before manumission. Ten of the forty blacks, or one-quarter, shared a surname with a white communicant at Trinity. This could reveal slave status, or former slave status—having been given the name of one's master—but without additional information, no such assumption could be made. In counting surnames, I am indebted to the pathbreaking

work by Dee Andrews, who found new ways to interpret gender using difficult sources (Andrews, *Methodists in Revolutionary America*, 112–14).

50. "Baptisms 1819–1829," St. Philip's Record Books, Schomburg Center for Research in Black Culture, New York City. The baptismal records are not without problems, as I discuss in chapter 7 of this work.

51. "Baptisms 1819–1829," St. Philip's Record Books.

52. See, for example, Walls, *Reality of the Black Church*, 40.

53. Methodist Society class records, 1792, 1795, and 1796, Methodist Episcopal Church Records, vol. 241, NYPL. Because record keepers often recorded names aurally (a comparison of class lists with city directories reveals numerous misspellings), I attempted to be generous in counting identical surnames. For example, I matched David Byes with Sarah Beiyes in 1795 and Sarah Beyrs in 1796—probably the same woman in both lists. This may slightly inflate the percentages of those holding common names, but the ratio of men sharing women's names remains higher than all other gendered comparisons (man-man, woman-man, woman-woman) for all three years, regardless of the method of counting.

54. Pintard, *Enumeration of the Inhabitants*; L. Harris, *In the Shadow of Slavery*, 76, 79, 80–81.

55. White, *Brief Account*, reprinted in Hodges, ed., *Black Itinerants of the Gospel*, 74–75.

56. White Americans, including abolitionists, often depicted slaves with feminine characteristics. On this, see Bruce Dorsey, *Reforming Men and Women*, 186–94. Dorsey's work focuses largely on discourse; my work here supports his argument in providing social context and data to the rhetoric. On the persistence of women as slaves, see L. Harris, *In the Shadow of Slavery*, 79.

57. "Blacks received on trial" 1802–1804, Methodist Episcopal Church Records, NYPL.

58. Ibid. After 1804, the records from Mother Zion grow extremely scarce and must largely be inferred from outside sources.

59. Swan, "John Teasman," 349–50; Sidney, "Oration," 464. On white opposition to black ceremonies, see Waldstreicher, *In the Midst of Perpetual Fetes*, 294–348.

60. Regarding black New York in this era, Nell Painter controversially states, "What we can identify in retrospect is less a black community than a few educated black New Yorker men who enter the historical record through written documents" (Nell Irvin Painter, *Sojourner Truth*, 69). As far as the public sphere, which deals with the written record, Painter is correct; most scholars reject her inference about the lack of a black community. Patrick Rael offers a slightly different emphasis: "The dearth of women's voices in the movement permitted the emergence of a mutually reinforcing process whereby a heavily masculinized style of public protest marginalized women's roles, thereby minimizing the possibilities that African American women might exert greater influence over the gender components of black protest" (Rael, *Black Identity & Black Protest*, 6).

Notes to Chapter 6

1. Asbury, *Journal*, 3:327. On Methodist disputes regarding church polity at this time, see Stevens, *Life and Times of Nathan Bangs*, 196 passim.

2. Hatch, *Democratization*; Joyce Appleby, *Inheriting the Revolution*. A related argument about early Republic liberalism that pays less attention to religious matters can be found in Gordon Wood, *Radicalism of the American Revolution*.

3. Gibson and Jung, *Historical Census Statistics*; Stansell, *City of Women*, 8, 32.

4. A detailed description of the expansion of New York City's economy is found in Robert Greenhalgh Albion, *The Rise of New York Port, 1815–1860*; for a wider view, see Charles Sellers, *The Market Revolution*; and Daniel Walker Howe, *What Hath God Wrought*.

5. Cave Jones, *A Solemn Appeal to the Church*, 3, 6–9, 23–25, 30, 26, 85.

6. Dix, *History of Trinity Church*, 2:216, 222–25; Cave Jones, *Dr. Hobart's System of Intolerance Exemplified*. Jones argued several points, among them being that his dismissal hearings were invalid because they were not impartial.

7. Matthew L. Davis, *Report of the Case between the Reverend Cave Jones and the Rector and Inhabitants of the City of New-York*; Dix, *History of Trinity Church*, 2:225–26.

8. For examples of both anti- and pro-Hobart perspectives, see *The Resolutions Adopted at a Meeting of the Episcopalians at Mechanic Hall* 10–12; An Episcopalian [pseud.], *A Plain Address to Episcopalians on the Proposed Meeting at Mechanic-Hall*; *The Charter of the Rector and Inhabitants of the City of New-York*; *Communion of the Protestant Episcopal Church in the State of New-York*; John Henry Hobart [A Friend to Truth, pseud.], *The Charter of the Corporation of Trinity Church Defended against the Attacks of a Late Pamphlet*; Hieronymous [pseud.], *Serious Thoughts on a Late Administration of Episcopal Orders*; Bowden, *The Essentials of Ordination Stated, in a Letter to a Friend; on the Subject of the Right Reverend Bishop Hobart's Consecration*; Hobart, *A Defence of the Essentials of Ordination in Answer to a Pamphlet Entitled Serious Thoughts on a Late Administration of Episcopal Orders*. These are a few examples; pamphlets flooded the presses between 1811 and 1813.

9. Dix, *History of Trinity Church*, 2:216–26.

10. Mullin, *Episcopal Vision/American Reality*; Mullin, *Moneygripe's Apprentice*.

11. M. Davis, *Report of the Case between the Reverend Cave Jones and the Rector and Inhabitants of the City of New-York*.

12. Ibid.; Peter Augustus Jay to John Jay, January 31, 1812, John Jay Papers, Butler Library, Columbia University; Mullin, *Episcopal Vision/American Reality*.

13. Pessen, *Riches, Class, and Power*, 320–22; Fischer, *Revolution of American Conservatism*, 301. On other studies linking strong clerical presence with depressed male attendance in churches, see Bonomi, *Under the Cope of Heaven*, 112–15; and C. Johnson, *Islands of Holiness*, 168–69.

14. *The Resolutions Adopted at a Meeting of the Episcopalians at Mechanic Hall*, 10–12. Hobart's reply to Jay can be found in Hobart, *Remarks on the Honorable John Jay's Letter, to the Reverend Cave Jones; In a Letter to a Friend*. Hobart mildly rebuked Jay for commenting from afar on matters of which he had little knowledge. Provoost's kinship connections came largely through his grandmother Maria Spratt, who was related to the De Peyster, Van Cortlandt, and Livingston families. Maria's daughter from her second marriage, to James Alexander, also married into the Livingston clan.

15. M. Davis, *Report of the Case between the Reverend Cave Jones and the Rector and Inhabitants of the City of New-York*; Peter Augustus Jay to John Jay, January 31, 1812, John Jay Papers; Dix, *History of Trinity Church*, 2:225–26. King's testimony may

have been legalistic in part because he delivered it in writing, since by the time of the trial he was in Washington serving as a U.S. senator. Jones remained a naval chaplain in Brooklyn until his death in 1829.

16. Peter J. Wosh, *Spreading the Word*, 40. On benevolent societies generally, see Clifford S. Griffin, *Their Brothers' Keepers*; Charles J. Foster, *An Errand of Mercy*; and Ronald G. Walters, *American Reformers, 1815–1860*.

17. *Proceedings of a Meeting of the Citizens of New-York and Others, Convened in the City-Hall*, 9–10.

18. Wosh, *Spreading the Word*, 121; Hobart, *An Address to Episcopalians on the Subject of the American Bible Society*.

19. William Jay [An Episcopalian, pseud.], *An Answer to Bishop Hobart's Pastoral Letter*.

20. For an example of the exchanges, see W. Jay, *A Reply to a Second Letter to the Author*. The High Churchman Morgan Dix declared Hobart the winner in *History of Trinity Church*, 3:5–6; E. Clowes Chorley suggested that Jay was the victor in *Men and Movements in the American Episcopal Church*, 281–82.

21. The historians who have noted the elite status of many benevolent society participants have attributed the efforts at evangelization as attempts to control unruly lower orders. The classic formulations of this social control interpretation are found in Foster, *Errand of Mercy*; and Griffin, *Their Brothers' Keepers*.

22. J. Jay, *Correspondence and Public Papers*, 4:459–61. Due to poor health, John Jay attended few meetings and issued his annual presidential addresses in absentia. A list of active ABS board members is found in Wosh, *Spreading the Word*, 38. Pewholders and vestrymen at Trinity can be found in "Trinity Church Pew Rents before 1828"; and Berrian, *Historical Sketch*, 358–65. I am indebted to Kristen Miller, archivist at the American Bible Society, for compiling a list of early ABS board members, which I used to supplement Wosh's list.

23. M. Davis, *Report of the Case between the Reverend Cave Jones and the Rector and Inhabitants of the City of New-York*, 122.

24. This dichotomy is found in, among others, Andrews, *Methodists in Revolutionary America*, 93–95; and William R. Sutton, *Journeymen for Jesus*, 81.

25. Stevens, *Life and Times of Nathan Bangs*, 183–84.

26. On the downtown location's preponderance of women, see chapter 4 of this work; on its merchant status, see chapter 3. Stevens, *Life and Times of Nathan Bangs*, 183–84.

27. Stevens, *Life and Times of Nathan Bangs*, 185–86.

28. Ibid., 225. The issue of pew rents was an old one among Methodists generally and in New York City in particular, for by 1796 some members feared John Street would implement pews and rents (see Seaman, *Annals of New York Methodism*, 137).

29. Seaman, *Annals of New York Methodism*, 215–31.

30. Ibid.; Samuel Stilwell, *Historical Sketches*. See also Sutton, *Journeymen for Jesus*, 75–78.

31. Stilwell, *Historical Sketches*, 11–12.

32. Several class leaders' names were crossed out in the 1819 class lists. Because most of these names were clearly Stilwellite (since they appeared in Stilwellite publications or on the Methodist Society's new charter), I assumed the x's by all the names indicated the defection.

33. The story of the returning defectors is found in Stevens, *Life and Times of Nathan Bangs*, 234–35. Bangs estimated that seventy members and three class leaders returned to the mother church. I found just over thirty names listed together in the probationer lists, returning with three former Stilwellite class leaders. Although many other names are listed as probationers under the three Stilwellite leaders' names, they are placed singly or in small groups in the lists; each individual's entrance into the Methodist Episcopal Church may therefore not have reflected status as a former Stilwellite but rather as a new probationer. I compiled the list determined to err on the side of caution.

34. Members 1819; Probationers 1822–32; Stewards, Exhorters, Leaders, Local Preachers 1818–35, in Methodist Episcopal Church Records, vols. 75, 76, 79, respectively, New York Public Library; *Longworth's American Almanac, New-York Register, and City Directory, for the Forty-Fourth Year of American Independence* (1819); *Longworth's New York Directory, for the Forty-Seventh Year of American Independence* (1822). Trustees' names are available in *Office of the County Clerk, New York County, Religious Incorporations 1784–1836*, vol. 1, New York Municipal Archives. On church locations and founding dates, see Seaman, *Annals of New York Methodism*, 110, 152, 155, 180–81.

35. William Stilwell, the group's first minister, had attended John Street earlier in the 1810s. Forsyth had also been called the Bowery chapel in its first years. The city's second chapel after John Street, its working-class composition is discussed in chapter 3 of this work.

36. *The Discipline of the Methodist Society, as Adopted in the City of New-York, 16th July, 1821*, 16–17, 25–26.

37. Trials were to be held by three, five, or seven members of the same sex as the disputants (*Discipline of the Methodist Society*, 1, 13).

38. Ibid.; Sutton, *Journeymen for Jesus*, 78. That men and women entered classes together is deduced from the list of the defecting Stilwellites, who reentered the Methodist Episcopal Church in mixed-sex classes.

39. North, *Consecrated Talents*, 69–75. See chapter 4 of this work.

40. Sutton, *Journeymen for Jesus*, 92–93; Stilwell, *Historical Sketches*, 11–12.

41. Seaman, *Annals of New York Methodism*, 215–31; Stilwell, *Historical Sketches*, 9; *Friendly Visitor* vol. 1 (1825); Asbury, *Journal*, 3:265. The *Friendly Visitor* was William Stilwell's attempt to reach a wider audience with nondenominational stories of moral instruction and uplift.

42. Seaman, *Annals of New York Methodism*, 215–31; Stevens, *Life and Times of Nathan Bangs*, 234–35; Sutton, *Journeymen for Jesus*, 94.

43. On these ambiguities, see, among others, Andrews, *Methodists in Revolutionary America*, 93–95; and Sutton, *Journeymen for Jesus*, 81. For accounts that specifically deal with Methodist attempts to grapple with slavery, see Mathews, *Slavery and Methodism*, esp. 8–9, 12, 23–24; and Heyrman, *Southern Cross*, 92–94, 154–60.

44. Rush, *Short Account*, 27–28. The date of the Thompson-Scott defection must have occurred between 1810, when the two represented Mother Zion for the African Marine fund, and 1819, when Rush narrates the conflicts with the Bethelites, during which Thompson weighed in as an active participant. Rush does not record what church Scott ultimately joined.

45. Andrews, *Methodists in Revolutionary America*, 321n144; Longworth, *1796 New-York City Directory*; Rush, *Short Account*, 28.

46. The single name "Abraham," suggesting slave status, appears in both the 1785 and 1786 class lists. In 1785, only three male names appear; the following year, the number increases to nine.

47. On Arcularius, see chapter 5 of this work, Methodist Episcopal Church records, NYPL.

48. Opposition had been planted by Daniel Coker, a minister in Richard Allen's rival Philadelphia-based African Methodist group. White would later join Allen's group (G. White, *Brief Account*, reprinted in *Black Itinerants*, 69–70).

49. G. White, *Brief Account*, reprinted in Hodges, ed., *Black Itinerants of the Gospel*, 63–67; Wheeler, *Varick Family*, 15.

50. Account of the *City Hall Recorder*, March 1817, recounted in Rock, *Artisans of the New Republic*, 170.

51. Rush, *Short Account*, 32–33. On this and the following events, see also George, *Segregated Sabbaths*, 99–103. Sutton, *Journeymen for Jesus*, 75–77, provides a truncated account that identifies the African Methodists almost wholly as a branch of Stilwell's group. The Zionites held considerable autonomy apart from Stilwell's status as a leader of the plebeian church.

52. Rush, *Short Account*, 34–35.

53. Ibid., 35–37.

54. Ibid., 33. Rush notes that the Bethel Church on Mott Street was consecrated on July 23, 1820, the week after Stilwell approached the Zionites. Varick opened the service for Allen "the second or third Sunday night" after the consecration. Facing the threat that whites would confiscate black church property, Zion's early opposition to Allen temporarily faded.

55. Ibid., 39.

56. Ibid. The first black Episcopal Church in America had formed in this manner, when Philadelphia Episcopalians induced the former Methodist Absalom Jones to form a church with them. Thompson's hesitation shared another parallel with Philadelphia, for Allen rejected the Episcopalian overtures and preferred to live and die a Methodist (see Newman, *Freedom's Prophet*, 70–72).

57. Rush, *Short Account*, 45, 78.

58. In *Journeymen for Jesus*, however, Sutton disagrees, arguing for a common identity between the Stilwellites and African Methodists.

59. Rush, *Short Account*, 34, 46.

60. Wilentz, *Chants Democratic*; Stansell, *City of Women*.

61. On Neau, see chapter 1 of this work; for the African Society, see chapter 3; on the Wilberforce Association, chapter 5.

62. Swan, "John Teasman," 342–43, 348–49; Townsend, *Faith in Their Own Color*, 27–28.

63. De Costa, *Threescore and Ten*, 31–33; Townsend, *Faith in Their Own Color*, 27–32. For more on St. Philip's connections to white leadership, see chapter 7 of this work.

64. Wakeley, *Lost Chapters*, 456; Hewitt, *Protest and Progress*, 18–20; De Costa, *Three Score and Ten*, 14–15; Townsend, *Faith in Their Own Color*, 30–31. Hewitt takes

from De Costa, *Three Score and Ten*, 23, that Williams "was a friend of" Lyell, and thus assumes that Williams studied under him.

65. See chapter 5 of this work.

66. Hewitt, *Protest and Progress*, 18–20; De Costa, *Three Score and Ten*, 14–15.

67. Hewitt, *Protest and Progress*, 18; De Costa, *Three Score and Ten*, 14–15, 18–19; Trinity Vestry Minutes, October 10, 1814, and June 8, 1818, Trinity Church Archives.

68. De Costa, *Three Score and Ten*, 20–21, 23; Trinity Vestry Minutes, April 13, 1819, Trinity Church Archives.

69. De Costa, *Three Score and Ten*, 17, 21–22.

Notes to Chapter 7

1. On the national changes the canal made, see George Rogers Taylor's classic, *The Transportation Revolution, 1815–1860*. More recent, and contrasting, interpretations appear in Sellers, *The Market Revolution*; and Howe, *What Hath God Wrought*.

2. I. N. Phelps Stokes, *New York Past and Present*, 77–79. The arithmetic growth of thirty thousand inhabitants per decade from 1790 to 1820 might be attributed to steady expansion through space; while this continued through the century (even to the unification with the other boroughs in 1898), population densities necessarily increased after 1820.

3. Stuart M. Blumin, *The Emergence of the Middle Class*, 86; Pessen, *Riches, Class, and Power*, 169–82; Blackmar, *Manhattan for Rent*, 114–15, 123. On Five Points, see Tyler Anbinder, *Five Points*.

4. On black and slave population changes by decade, see Gibson and Jung, *Historical Census Statistics*. In 1820, even though the state's black population decreased by 983 during the previous decade, free blacks increased by 3,946. On the revisions to manumission, see Gellman, *Emancipating New York*, 205–6.

5. Rael, *Black Identity*, 119–56, 173–80.

6. Many of St. Philip's earliest members remain unknown, as fire consumed the first church building and its records. Fire again destroyed the baptism records after 1829; they resume in 1865. Baptisms may, of course, reflect only tenuous church affiliation. Craig Townsend's work on St. Philip's, for example, uses vestry lists to create a parish blueprint, for vestry members reflect a church's most dedicated and central individuals. I use the larger baptismal lists, however, because they are more inclusive and create a congregational portrait that is less heavily skewed toward well-off members. Further, standards for church membership and receiving the sacraments were higher then, than now, so individuals on such lists were less likely to be uninvolved in church life. Baptisms were more than ceremonial familial events and implied at least a promise of church involvement.

7. On the changing labels such as "African" and "colored" applied to and taken by blacks in the course of American history, see Rael, *Black Identity*, 83–117.

8. *Longworth's American Almanac, New-York Register, and City Directory, for the Forty-Fourth Year of American Independence* (1819); "St. Philip's Baptisms 1819–1829." For the St. Philip's records, I established the following categories: service workers, "service" artisans (such as hairdressers, barbers, and cooks), marine industries, other artisans, retailers, and address only/unskilled. This better shows the range of occupations blacks held in the city beyond the simple retail-artisan distinction that, in general, works well for white groups.

9. *Longworth's 1819 New York Directory*; "St. Philip's Baptisms 1819–1829." Because the Browns appear on the baptismal records in 1820 and the Greys in 1823, it is possible, but unlikely, that the men lived together as bachelors in 1819. *Longworth's American Almanac, New-York Register, and City Directory, for the Fiftieth Year of American Independence* (1825); "St. Philip's Baptisms 1819–1829." As the Polstons and Lawrences presented their children for baptism in 1820 and 1826, respectively, it is almost certain the two families, with children, lived together in the tenement in 1825. Further, the Polstons may have brought the Lawrences into the church, another example of familial and female connections working through religious forms.

10. Craig Townsend argues that the presence of whitewashers, laborers, and bootblacks in St. Philip's vestry proves the church was not wealthy (see *Faith in Their Own Color*, 86–87). By this measure, however, no church, including Trinity, would be labeled wealthy. Given the presence of a number of extremely well-off individuals, and a preponderance of certain occupations that generally had great earning potential, I would argue that St. Philip's was materially a wealthy church, at least compared to any other subset of the black population.

11. Hewitt, *Protest and Progress*, 82, 85. Oystering provided work for many black New Yorkers. Shane White noted that in 1810 a majority of the city's oystermen were free blacks (S. White, *Somewhat More Independent*, 61–62). White's numbers, taken from city directories that did not always note race, reflected only known blacks; the numbers of black oystermen were likely even higher than the 16 of 27 that White found in 1810.

12. George T. Downing, "A Sketch of the Life and Times of Thomas Downing." Henry Highland Garnet called Downing "distinguished son of Virginia" and "playfellow of Hon. Henry A. Wise" (see Garnet, *A Memorial Discourse*, 24).

13. Hewitt, *Protest and Progress*, 84–85. For a typical oyster house environment, see "Admitting Very Disorderly Persons," in Gilje and Rock, eds., *Keepers of the Revolution*, 228–29, which details a complaint of unruliness against the black proprietor William Brooks.

14. Captain John Downing from this family, who may have been the master in question, was a militia officer in 1786.

15. *Genealogies of Virginia Families, from the William and Mary College Quarterly Historical Meeting*, 218–21; Howard Pyle, "Chincoteague: Island of Ponies," and Maude Radford Warren, "The Island of Chincoteague," both reprinted in Miles and Truitt, eds., *Seashore Chronicles*, 58–71, 168–81; Craig M. Simpson, *A Good Southerner*, xi. See also "Thomas Downing Obituary," *New York Times*, April 12, 1866. Downing's conversion to Episcopalianism may also be due to the fact that, early in New York, black Episcopalian William Hutson (a founding trustee of St. Philip's and an older member of the African Society) aided him in gaining employment (see Downing, "Sketch," 405).

16. The term used in the directory was "refectory." This suggests an informal arrangement, as refectory tables are long with heavy legs, set for large numbers to eat in a shared space.

17. Hewitt, *Protest and Progress*, 82–83.

18. Ibid., 79–83. In working-class neighborhoods, rife with violence and alcohol consumption, most oyster houses served a multiracial clientele. But in other neighborhoods, black restaurateurs and barbers could serve either black or white customers,

not both. Black proprietors aspiring to respectable status gained cultural capital with whites by excluding blacks. Englishman Henry Fearon reported a visit to one barbershop where the black owner had instructed his employee to turn away all black customers. The barber noted "the slimmest gentleman in York would not come to his store if coloured men were let in" (see Leon F. Litwack, *North of Slavery*, 180–81; "If He Cut Coloured Men," in Gilje and Rock, eds., *Keepers of the Revolution*, 235–37, quote on 236). I discuss Downing's political activism in the following chapter, as this business deference did not necessarily translate to political quietism.

19. *Longworth's American Almanac, New-York Register, and City Directory, for the Fifty-fifth Year of American Independence* (1830); *Longworth's American Almanac, New-York Register, and City Directory, for the Sixtieth Year of American Independence* (1840); "St. Philip's Baptisms 1819–1829"; Hewitt, *Protest and Progress*, 90; J. H. Harmon Jr., "The Negro as a Local Business Man," 120; Townsend, *Faith in Their Own Color*, 2. Ray had two children baptized, but did not appear in the 1819, 1825, 1830, 1835, or 1840 directories. Scott was not in the baptismal lists. Both appear in Hewitt's work, and in Craig Townsend's analysis of St. Philip's parishioner occupations, which are almost exclusively comprised of vestry members dating from the 1840s and 1850s.

20. *Longworth's 1840 New York Directory*; "St. Philip's Baptisms 1819–1829."

21. *Longworth's 1825 New York Directory*; "St. Philip's Baptisms 1819–1829." The one-in-six figure comes from tabulating all possible occupations, including those names with duplicate positions. The number of mariners ranged from three to eight; other than barbers/hairdressers, who had four certain listings, no other occupation matched three. On white opposition to black economic competition, see Litwack, *North of Slavery*, 154–66. Litwack notes that the term "help" as in "help wanted" originated in the early Republic, in part due to white laborers insistence that as heirs of the Revolution they were servants to none. On black seamen, see Jeffrey Bolster, *Black Jacks*.

22. "St. John's Pewholders before 1828," "St. Paul's Pewholders before 1828," "Trinity Church Pew Rents before 1828," in record 17905, Trinity Church Archives; *1819 New York City Directory*; *1825 New York City Directory*.

23. "Table 2: Occupations and Occupational Categories, St. Philip's Church Members-sorted by category," in Craig Devine Townsend, "An Inexpedient Time," 146–49. The information is available in more convenient book form, but listed alphabetically by last name rather than by occupation, in "Appendix: Parishioners of St. Philip's Church," in Townsend, *Faith in Their Own Color*, 199–202.

24. Crummell, of course, would soon become clergy. *First Annual Report of the American Anti-Slavery Society*, 61; *Sixth Annual Report of the American Anti-Slavery Society with the Speeches Delivered at the Anniversary Meeting, Held in the City of New-York on the 7th of May, 1838*, 32.

25. St. Philip's took collections for the New-York Bible and Common Prayer Book Society; the announcement of the collection suggests the parish had given support on more than one occasion. Organized by then-bishop Hobart, the Prayer Book Society was explicitly High Church in aim. *Freedom's Journal* 1, no. 7 (April 27, 1827): 26.

26. Newman, *Freedom's Prophet*, 183–208; George M. Frederickson, *The Black Image in the White Mind*, 6–27; Goodman, *Of One Blood*, 11–22.

27. On black uses of Africa as a heritage, see Rael, *Black Identity, Black Protest*, 85–91. On the ACS, see Mathews, *Slavery and Methodism*, 89–90; Goodman, *Of One*

Blood, 11–22; Rael, *Black Identity, Black Protest*, 160, 163; Frederickson, *Black Image*, 6–27; Sandra Sandiford Young, "John Brown Russwurm's Dilemma: Citizenship or Emigration?" in McCarthy and Stauffer, eds., *Prophets of Protest*, 90–113.

28. Africa as a cultural heritage is the central focus of Wilder, *In the Company of Black Men*; for a sensitive historical treatment of the rise and fall of Africa as heritage, see James Sidbury, *Becoming African in America*; for an emphasis on names and titles, such as "African" versus the later "colored," see Rael, *Black Identity and Black Protest*, 83–117. Black responses to colonization can be found in Goodman, *Of One Blood*, 23–44; and Young, "Russwurm's Dilemma," 100–102.

29. The strongest of these is Goodman, *Of One Blood*. Richard Newman has noted that Richard Allen's previous biographers have downplayed Allen's periodic support for colonization, which mirrored Williams (Newman, *Freedom's Prophet*, 183, more broadly 183–208).

30. In this, Williams did not deviate greatly from the other black reformers in the city, for the Reverend Samuel E. Cornish, Thomas L. Jennings, and Samuel Ennals all served on the board of managers with Williams. All three had been involved in other reform efforts. Yet later Williams's continued support would cause tension with other reform-minded blacks who rejected colonization.

31. Hewitt, *Protest and Progress*, 24–27; Townsend, *Faith in Their Own Color*, 48–50.

32. Young, "Russwurm's Dilemma"; Wilson Jeremiah Moses, *Alexander Crummell*, 23–25.

33. References to the Methodist Society's early poverty can be found throughout Seaman, *Annals of New York Methodism*.

34. *Minutes of the Common Council of the City of New-York 1784–1831*, 11:440; 12:678; 13:494; 14:83; 16:28, 686–87; Washington, *Sojourner Truth's America*, 92.

35. See, for example, Rael, *Black Identity*, 6–7.

36. William Hamilton, "An Oration Delivered in the African Zion Church, on the Fourth of July 1827, in Commemoration of the Abolition of Domestic Slavery in this State, 1827," reprinted in Porter, ed., *Early Negro Writing*, 96–104. Hereafter listed as "1827 Oration." The first name Hamilton praised on the list of Manumission Society sponsors was John Jay; on Hamilton's previous attempt at correspondence with Jay, see chapter 3 of this work. "Heterogeneous minds," 101–2, undoubtedly referred to Thomas Jefferson.

37. Hamilton, "1827 Oration," 102–3.

38. Ibid., 104.

39. This is the interpretation in R. Lawrence Moore, *Religious Outsiders and the Making of Americans*, 176–80. More recently, the scholars Patrick Rael, Dickson Bruce, and Stephen G. Hall have defended the context of the elite black position (Rael, *Black Identity*; Bruce, *Origins of African American Literature*; Hall, *A Faithful Account of the Race*). In the following chapter, I discuss how these cultural tendencies affected black participation in the reform and abolitionist communities.

40. Wilder, *In the Company of Black Men*, 74; Perlman, "Organizations of the Free Negro," 191. When James Varick died in 1827, Rush succeeded him as bishop.

41. Perlman, "Organizations of the Free Negro," 187.

42. Peter Paul Simons, "An Oration, Delivered 23rd of April, 1839," *Colored American*, June 1, 1839. See Rael, *Black Elevation*, 157–59, for a counter to Simons's criticisms; see also L. Harris, *In the Shadow of Slavery*, chap. 4.

43. Jon Butler warns that the black church should not be equated with the black community (Butler, "Communities and Congregations," 118–34). I might add that the black church, or any church, should not be equated solely with the voices of its leaders.

44. On John Street's prime location, see Burrows and Wallace, *Gotham*, 456–57.

45. See chapter 3 of this work for details.

46. 1825 John Street Class Lists, Vol. 66, Methodist Episcopal Church Records, NYPL; *Longworth's 1825 New York Directory*.

47. "1825 Class Lists"; *Longworth's 1825 New York Directory*.

48. Ibid.

49. Ibid. On Harper's candidacy see Wilentz, *Chants Democratic*, 316–24. I discuss Harper's religious identity in greater detail in chapter 8 of this work.

50. A. Gregory Schneider has described the organization of conferences, bishops, and itinerants as a "salvation machine," in *Way of the Cross*, 196. Schneider explains the changes that the creation of the missionary society brought on 201–3.

51. See, among others, Hatch, *Democratization*, 201–6; Wigger, *Taking Heaven by Storm*, 189–90; and Andrews, *Methodists in Revolutionary America*, 230–31.

52. Stevens, *Life and Times of Nathan Bangs*, 17, 335.

53. Ibid., 156, 167.

54. Ibid., 215. When the New York society shifted funds from local churches to preachers' salaries, it greatly concerned the uptown contingent, who believed it took money out of lay control and placed it directly in ministers' pockets. Because Methodists often heavily depended on lay involvement, members debated this measure for several days before passing it. The Stilwellites stressed, in their schism, that education for ministers was a secondary concern that should not take away from the drive for conversions.

55. Ibid., 255, 271, 280. Bangs's long residence in the city made him appreciate the need for ministers' salaries to be paid in cash, as city life discouraged a barter economy, and forced even preachers to pay for their daily bread.

56. Hardt, *Soul of Methodism*, 199n9; Wosh, *Spreading the Word*, 38; Miller, comp., "A List of Methodist and Episcopalian Bible Society Officers."

57. Seaman, *Annals of New York Methodism*, 268–69.

58. Open seating did not apply to race, however: at churches like John Street where a few blacks remained, blacks were still restricted to the gallery (Seaman, *Annals of New York Methodism*, 275–77).

59. Ibid., 275–77.

60. Hardt, *Soul of Methodism*, 69–70. In so doing, the churches divided the society's debt and claimed local assets as their own. Churches still reported to quarterly and general conferences, but yielded less in day-to-day matters, a shift the Stilwellites would have applauded.

61. This is the general focus of Hardt, *Soul of Methodism*, who places heavy emphasis on the structural changes of the 1830s, and blames large class sizes in leading to declining religious ardor. I would suggest, however, that the structural changes reflected an earlier commitment to professionalism in the clergy, and also followed major changes in the social makeup (and cultural assumptions) of the congregants.

62. "St. John's Pewholders before 1828," "St. Paul's Pewholders before 1828," "Trinity Church Pew Rents before 1828"; *1819 New York City Directory*; *1825 New York City Directory*.

63. This generally describes the Federalist "Gentlemen of the Old School" in Fischer, *Revolution of American Conservatism*.

64. Albion, *Rise of New York Port, 1815–1860*, 279–80; Stephen Nissenbaum, *The Battle for Christmas*, 52–53; Blackmar, *Manhattan for Rent*, 118–19.

65. Nissenbaum, *Battle for Christmas*, 64–67.

66. Ibid., 88–89. The seminary became a forerunner for General Theological Seminary.

67. Blackmar, *Manhattan for Rent*, 116–19; Harris, *Shadow of Slavery*, 81.

68. On St. Paul's earlier undesirable location, see Burrows and Wallace, *Gotham*, 483.

69. Information on the chapels' social structure in relation to the mother church can be found in: "St. John's Pewholders before 1828," "St. Paul's Pewholders before 1828," "Trinity Church Pew Rents before 1828"; *1819 New York City Directory*; *1825 New York City Directory*.

70. Burrows and Wallace, *Gotham*, 373–74; Stokes, *New York Past and Present*, 76.

71. Burrows and Wallace, *Gotham*, 457–58.

Notes to Chapter 8

1. "The First Colored Convention," *Anglo-African Magazine* 1, no. 10 (October 1859): 1–2, reprinted in Bell, ed. *Minutes of the Proceedings of the National Negro Conventions 1830–1864*.

2. Repeated and paraphrased in numerous places, one variation from John Wesley, *Works of the Reverend John Wesley*, 7:317: "For religion must necessarily produce both industry and frugality; and these cannot but produce riches. But as riches increase, so will pride, anger, and love of the world in all its branches." See also Andrews, *Methodists in Revolutionary America*, 156.

3. The riot's first phases were ignited by a black reformer's attempt to attend a white church, and a pro-reform Presbyterian minister's insistence to his congregation that Christ was dark-skinned. But these were hardly spontaneous uprisings. Leonard L. Richards has demonstrated that the anti-abolition riots in New York and elsewhere were well-organized affairs (see Richards, *"Gentlemen of Property and Standing,"* esp. 120–21, 114–15).

4. On this generally, see chapters 6 and 7 of this work.

5. On this, see chapter 7 of this work. Regarding white fears of black advance, see also Rael, *Black Identity, Black Protest*, 165–67.

6. Although all Protestant churches in America made similar claims to unique truth, Episcopalian claims set it apart from evangelical denominations by locating authority in tradition and ecclesiastical office, rather than creeds or charismatic authority. By the twentieth century, many High Church proponents rejected the Protestant label, seeing themselves as negotiating a separate truth between Protestant and Catholic traditions. The best historical treatment of the theology can be found in Mullin, *Episcopal Vision/American Reality*; for a concise version, see Townsend, *Faith in Their Own Color*, 18–24.

7. The fact that St. Philip's received patronage from Trinity, the city's most prestigious Episcopal church, adds another dynamic. Perhaps whites targeted black Episcopalians precisely because of their connection to wealthy whites, linking class resentment of elite whites to racial hatred of servile blacks. For similar dynamics, see

Rael, *Black Identity, Black Protest*, 167. Whether St. Philip's connection to Trinity was overt and resented or covert and overlooked, the fact of black success spawned a backlash. Leonard Richards has noted that mob leaders tended to be well-educated members of established churches, including significant numbers of white Episcopalians. Many also worked in established trades that had traditionally earned their adherents a decent standard of living (Richards, *"Gentlemen of Property and Standing,"* 145–48, see also 167–70).

8. Richards, *"Gentlemen of Property and Standing,"* 114–15, 120–21; Rael, *Black Identity, Black Protest*, 169; Anbinder, *Five Points*, 12.

9. Wilder, *In the Company of Black Men*, 74; Perlman, "Organizations of the Free Negro," 191; Moses, *Alexander Crummell*, 14.

10. John Jay II, draft, "Funeral of the Rev. Peter Williams," New York, 1840, Jay Family Papers, Butler Library, Columbia University. Jay was the son of William, hence grandson of the statesman. Historians typically list his name with the Roman numeral II to distinguish him from his more famous relative. On the passport, see Hewitt, *Protest and Progress*, 37n54; and William C. Nell, *Colored Patriots of the American Revolution*, 320. The passport issuance is significant in that it implied citizenship, which the most ardent proslavery whites denied all blacks.

11. Moses, *Alexander Crummell*, 27; Townsend, *Faith in Their Own Color*, 73; Perlman, "Organizations of the Free Negro," 193n66. Barred from American medical schools, Smith trained in Scotland.

12. Hewitt, *Protest and Progress*, 87–88. Putting it in slightly different terms, Patrick Rael notes that, despite (or because of) black elites' attempts to promote respectability and uplift, "Sites of black elevation, such as racially mixed schoolhouses, often fell quickly to the mob" (Rael, *Black Identity, Black Protest*, 207).

13. Bishop Onderdonk to Rev. Peter Williams, July 12, 1834, reprinted in Woodson, ed., *Mind of the Negro*, 629; see also Townsend, *Faith in Their Own Color*, 53. Although the High Church vision of an expansive universal mission led Bishop Hobart to ordain Williams in the first place, the same theology now forced a different conclusion. I suggest that it is not so much individual differences—Hobart's openness versus Onderdonk's racism—that account for the change, but rather a changed social environment in which race relations were increasingly polarized. Organic inclusiveness could embrace other races in a smaller setting; but in the larger cityscape, racial reconciliation grew nearly impossible, without dramatically reconceptualizing the theology.

14. Peter Williams Jr., "To the Citizens of New York," July 14, 1834, reprinted in Woodson, ed., *Mind of the Negro*, 630–34. For criticisms of Williams's act, see Moses, *Alexander Crummell*, 23–24; and Carter G. Woodson, *The History of the Negro Church*, 96. For defenses from two Episcopal church historians, see Hewitt, *Protest and Progress*, 29–32; and Townsend, *Faith in Their Own Color*, 54–57.

15. Williams, "To the Citizens of New York"; Townsend, *Faith in Their Own Color*, 57. Williams complained to Gerrit Smith, a well-known, uncompromising abolitionist.

16. Townsend, *Faith in Their Own Color*, 56. Like his father, Williams remained an important go-between and aid for different black groups and causes until his death; such is well-covered throughout Hewitt, *Protest and Progress*. In the examples of Peter Williams, father and son, the organic ideal of community remained strong, but such remained individual, not institutional, expressions.

17. Onderdonk was essentially accused of sexual harassment/assault, as the bishop tended to caress female parishioners while speaking to them. The evidence against him was general knowledge to many churchmen, although some contemporary observers suggested that the charges were payback from Low Church adversaries tired of the bishop's harsh treatment (see Townsend, *Faith in Their Own Color*, 116–17).

18. This statement does not completely apply to all church laity, however; in an 1845 letter to the *National Anti-Slavery Standard*, several non-vestry laity, including Downing, affirmed their support for Jay (see Townsend, *Faith in Their Own Color*, 122–23).

19. Townsend, *Faith in Their Own Color*, 102–7. Townsend defends the parish by noting that St. Philip's denied white assistant ministers the title "rector," thus allowing the black vestry to retain power. But an examination of various controversies such as Alexander Crummell's failed application for employment reveals that assistant ministers wielded considerable influence behind the scenes, even if lacking formal title or full powers.

20. *Sixth Annual Report of the American Anti-Slavery Society,* 28–30.

21. Aileen S. Kraditor, *Means and Ends in American Abolitionism*, 57–58, 107–8; Ripley, ed., *The Black Abolitionist Papers*, vol. 3, *The United States, 1830–1846,* 22–23. The AFASS was doomed by poor timing at its inception—economic recession dried up contributions just after the group organized, and it remained a marginal institution with little influence.

22. "The First Colored Convention," in Bell, ed., *Minutes of the Proceedings of the National Negro Conventions.*

23. "Minutes and Proceedings of the First Annual Convention of the People of Colour," in Bell, ed. *Minutes of the Proceedings of the National Negro Conventions,* 7–8, 16; Ripley, ed., *Black Abolitionist Papers,* 3:452n2. My argument concerning Mother Zion's public retreat contrasts with a number of other scholars, including Graham Russell Hodges, *David Ruggles*; Wilder, *In the Company of Black Men*; and Washington, *Sojourner Truth's America.* I find that these works tend to assume black racial unity across class and gender lines, something difficult to assert given the scarce documentary record for Mother Zion in these later years. I suggest that the record indicates division as much as unity, and hence retreat as an institutional church body.

24. The denomination spread rapidly into the southern states after the Civil War. Today the church's headquarters are in North Carolina.

25. Townsend, *Faith in Their Own Color*, 8; Henry H. Mitchell, *Black Church Beginnings*, 189.

26. H. Mitchell, *Black Church Beginnings*, 189.

27. Ibid., 112–14.

28. Frederick Douglass, *Narrative of the Life of Frederick Douglass, an American Slave, Written by Himself* (1845), Douglass, *My Bondage and My Freedom* (1855), and Douglass, *Life and Times of Frederick Douglass, Written By Himself* (Boston 1893), all reprinted in Frederick Douglass, *Autobiographies*, ed. Henry Louis Gates Jr., 52, 54, 100, 231–24, 249–300, 719, 913–14.

29. Litwack, *North of Slavery*, 212–13. Late in life, Douglass also criticized the "superstition, bigotry, and priest-craft" of black religion (see Douglass, *Life and Times*, in *Autobiographies*, ed. Gates, 913–14).

30. Daniel Alexander Payne, *Recollections of Seventy Years*, 93–94, 80–81, 233–41.

31. "John Street 1840 Class Lists," vols. 238–239, Methodist Episcopal Church Records, NYPL.

32. The two best and most recent biographies of Sojourner Truth are Painter, *Sojourner Truth*; and Washington, *Sojourner Truth's America*. Painter's account of her early years occurs on pages 3–25; Washington's, on pages 9–47.

33. Painter, *Sojourner Truth*, 15–17; Washington, *Sojourner Truth's America*, 9–12.

34. [Olive Gilbert], *Narrative of Sojourner Truth, a Bondswoman of Olden Time*, 87; Washington, *Sojourner Truth's America*, 93. Washington's *Sojourner Truth's America* places Isabella firmly within an African, activist, abolitionist, and womanist community. In many important places, Washington's research admirably fills in the gaps that Carleton Mabee and Painter leave open, but her interpretation tends to gloss over the parts of Isabella's life that were not in direct harmony with other African, activist, abolitionist, or womanist actors.

35. *Narrative of Sojourner Truth*, 79–81; *New York Tribune*, September 7, 1853, in Fitch and Mandziuk, eds., *Sojourner Truth as Orator*, 145–47; Washington, *Sojourner Truth's America*, 84, 89, 92. Washington states that some blacks rejected Truth because they desired to hear whites, and claims white patriarchy as the corrupting force; this seems to neglect the clear patriarchal structures at Mother Zion. For another example, Newman, in *Freedom's Prophet*, 229–34, details the ambiguity and tension in Richard Allen's stance toward women leadership in the person of exhorter Jarena Lee.

36. Washington, *Sojourner Truth's America*, 93; Paul E. Johnson and Sean Wilentz, *The Kingdom of Matthias*; *Narrative of Sojourner Truth*, 100.

37. Painter, *Sojourner Truth*, 96–99; Carleton Mabee, *Sojourner Truth: Slave, Prophet, Legend*, 64, 66, 239–40, 245–46.

38. Painter, *Sojourner Truth*, 96–99.

39. "First Annual Meeting of the American Equal Rights Association, Church of the Puritans, New York City," reported in *New York Tribune*, May 10, 1867, reprinted in Fitch and Mandziuk, eds., *Sojourner Truth as Orator*, 123–24.

40. Mabee, *Slave, Prophet, Legend*, 64, 66, 239–40, 245–46; Painter, *Sojourner Truth*, 96–99. Mabee notes Truth staged some of her presentation to highlight her status as an exotic former slave. In private, Truth could slip into Dutch brogue as well as correct English delivery, but newspaper reports suggest that she used southern black argot in her public speaking.

41. *Longworth's 1839 Directory*; *Longworth's 1840 Directory*; "John Street 1840 Class Lists."

42. On nativist movements, see John Higham, *Strangers in the Land*; Tyler Anbinder, *Nativism and Slavery*; and Richard J. Carwardine, *Evangelicals and Politics in Antebellum America*.

43. Burrows and Wallace, *Gotham*, 632.

44. Nissenbaum, *Battle for Christmas*, 308–9.

45. For another example of this dynamic, see Gary J. Kornblith, "The Craftsman as Industrialist."

46. Lathrop Colgate Harper Papers, Box 1: Genealogy, New-York Historical Society.

47. Eugene Exman, *The Brothers Harper*, 4.

48. Thurlow Weed Barnes, *Life of Thurlow Weed*, vol. 2, *Memoir of Thurlow Weed*, 5.

49. Their first job was an English translation of Seneca's *Morals*, a Stoic philosophical treatise whose ethics closely paralleled the demands of Protestant living (Weed,

Life of Thurlow Weed, vol. 1, *Autobiography of Thurlow Weed,* 57). On the Harpers' business strategy, see Philip Hone, *Diary of Philip Hone,* 873.

50. Exman, *The Brothers Harper,* 1–2, 168.

51. George Templeton Strong, *Diary of George Templeton Strong,* 258.

52. Exman, *The Brothers Harper,* 345. In *Chants Democratic,* Sean Wilentz offers an unflattering portrait of James, depicting him as an intellectual lightweight who substituted nostalgic slogans for real solutions to the problems of an industrializing society. My emphasis here is that the changing society, which required affable businessmen, shaped James Harper, and reflected a changing focus among Methodist congregants.

53. On the decline of class fervor, see Hardt, *The Soul of Methodism,* 77–78; and "John Street 1840 Class Lists."

54. Seaman, *Annals of New York Methodism,* 321.

55. Information on Hall is taken from the admittedly inconsistent *Appleton's Cyclopedia of American Biography,* edited by James Grant Wilson and John Fiske. Hall is identified as a close friend of Nathan Bangs in the latter's biography, suggesting agreement with the new managerial vision.

56. Stevens, *Life of Nathan Bangs,* 313–23; see also Mathews, *Slavery and Methodism.*

57. Seaman, *Annals of New York Methodism,* 279.

58. Herman Melville, "The Two Temples," in *The Writings of Herman Melville,* vol. 9, *The Piazza Tales and Other Prose Pieces 1839–1860,* 303–15. The story was not published in Melville's lifetime.

59. Ibid., 303.

60. Pessen, *Riches, Class, and Power,* 175, 178.

61. Burrows and Wallace, *Gotham,* 714.

62. "Register of Members of the Corporation of Trinity Church New York Who Are Not Pew Holders," 1845–1868, Trinity Church Archives, New York City.

63. Strong, *Diary of George Templeton Strong,* 76–77, 307.

64. Hone, *Diary of Philip Hone,* 691–92.

65. Strong, *Diary of George Templeton Strong,* 228, 258.

66. One effort to reveal Strong's religious proclivities occurred in Courtney Cowart's General Theological Seminary thesis analyzing his diary. I was unable to examine her thesis during a long-lasting seminary library reconstruction, but the work is cited in Robert Bruce Mullin, "Trends in the Study of the History of the Episcopal Church."

67. Hone, *Diary of Philip Hone,* 134–35; Strong, *Diary of George Templeton Strong,* 200.

68. J. Robert Wright, Saint *Thomas Church Fifth Avenue,* 5.

Notes to the Conclusion

1. For a clear expression of evangelical unity, see Robert Baird, *Religion in America* (1844), quoted in McLoughlin, ed., *The American Evangelicals, 1800–1900,* 37–38. One colorful example of Methodist sectarianism, applied to a frontier setting, is found in Peter Cartwright, *Autobiography.*

2. Edward K. Spann, *The New Metropolis,* 395.

3. William C. Conant, *Narratives of Remarkable Conversions and Revival Incidents,* 357–58; Timothy L. Smith, *Revivalism and Social Reform in Mid-Nineteenth Century America,* 63–64; Stevens, *Life and Times of Nathan Bangs,* 406–7. See also Kathryn Teresa Long, *The Great Revival of 1857–58.*

4. Stevens, *Life and Times of Nathan Bangs,* 406.

5. Iver Bernstein, *The New York City Draft Riots*, 155.

6. On the Oxford Movement, see C. Brad Faught, *The Oxford Movement*. Butler, *Standing before the Whirlwind*, explains the differences between High Churchmen and the Tractarians; but as Butler notes, 137–38, many High Churchmen found themselves attracted to Oxford, and were often hesitant to condemn it.

7. Butler, *Standing before the Whirlwind*, explains the theological differences between the High Church and Broad Church. I suggest that the Broad Church, which emphasized rationality in worship and emotional experience, synthesized the competing parties and was possible because of the Episcopalian preference for unity.

8. Washington, *Sojourner Truth's America*, 89; Walls, *Reality of the Black Church*, 48–50, 70–76; Ripley, ed., *Black Abolitionist Papers*, 3:450, 455–56.

9. Graham Russell Hodges, *David Ruggles*, 7–8, 112–13. I stress class and gender differences that shaded disagreements in the black community, whereas Hodges tends to see black unity, typified by Ruggles's uncompromising stance.

10. Townsend, *Faith in Their Own Color*, 105–7. A similar interpretation of the effects of rejecting colonization is found in Moore, *Religious Outsiders*, 176–80. Moore's position, which coincides generally with black power protest traditions and positions arguing for cultural autonomy, has recently been countered by works such as Rael, *Black Identity, Black Protest*, 8–10.

11. St. Philip's drive for independence is well told in Townsend, *Faith in Their Own Color*.

12. On this, see chapter 8 of this work.

13. Lindsley, *This Planted Vine*, 209.

14. David W. Dunlap, *From Abyssinian to Zion*, 148–49, 242–43; Carla L. Peterson, *Black Gotham*, 248–49.

15. This gentrification was not without problems; Marcus Garvey derided St. Philip's for its social elitism and privileging light-skinned mulattoes (see Hill, ed., *The Marcus Garvey and Universal Negro Improvement Association Papers*, vol. 5, *September 1922–August 1924*, 437–39, 117n1). See also Thadious M. Davis, *Nella Larsen*, 127–28.

16. Seaman, *Annals of New York Methodism*, 279.

17. Ibid.

BIBLIOGRAPHY

Primary Sources

Published Works

Allen, Richard, and Absalom Jones. *A Narrative of the Proceedings of the Black People, during the Late Awful Calamity in Philadelphia, in the Year 1793, and a Refutation of Some Censures, Thrown upon Them in Some Late Publications*. Philadelphia: William W. Woodward, 1794.

Asbury, Francis. *The Journal of the Reverend Francis Asbury, Bishop of the Methodist Episcopal Church, from August 7, 1771 to December 7, 1815*. 3 vols. New York: N. Bangs and T. Mason, 1821.

Bangs, Nathan. *The Substance of a Sermon Preached on Opening the Methodist Church in John-Street, in the City of New-York, on the Morning of the 4th of January, 1818*. New York: John C. Totten, 1818.

Bell, Howard Holman, ed. *Minutes of the Proceedings of the National Negro Conventions 1830–1864*. New York: Arno, 1969.

Bowden, John. *The Essentials of Ordination Stated, in a Letter to a Friend; on the Subject of the Right Reverend Bishop Hobart's Consecration*. New York: James Oram, 1812.

Cartwright, Peter. *Autobiography of Peter Cartwright: The Backwoods Preacher*. New York: Hunt and Eaton, 1856.

Census of the Electors, and Total Population, of the City and County of New-York. New York: Henry C. Southwick, 1807.

The Charter of the Rector and Inhabitants of the City of New-York; Communion of the Protestant Episcopal Church in the State of New-York: Commonly Called the Charter of Trinity Church, with Notes by an Episcopalian of the City of New-York. New York: T. and J. Swords, 1813.

Conant, William C. *Narratives of Remarkable Conversions and Revival Incidents.* New York: Derby and Jackson, 1858.

Davis, Matthew L. *Report of the Case between the Reverend Cave Jones and the Rector and Inhabitants of the City of New-York in Communion of the Protestant Episcopal Church in the State of New York, as the Same was Argued before the Five Judges of the Supreme Court of the State of New-York—Arbitrators to Whom the Difference between the Parties Were Referred by a Rule of the Same Court.* New York: William A. Davis, 1813.

The Discipline of the Methodist Society, as Adopted in the City of New-York, 16th July, 1821. New York: Bolmore, 1821.

Douglass, Frederick. *Life and Times of Frederick Douglass, Written By Himself.* Boston, 1893. Reprinted in Frederick Douglass, *Autobiographies*, ed. Henry Louis Gates Jr. New York: Library of America, 1994.

———. *My Bondage and My Freedom.* 1855. Reprinted in Frederick Douglass, *Autobiographies*, ed. Henry Louis Gates Jr. New York: Library of America, 1994.

———. *Narrative of the Life of Frederick Douglass, an American Slave, Written by Himself.* 1845. Reprinted in Frederick Douglass, *Autobiographies*, ed. Henry Louis Gates Jr. New York: Library of America, 1994.

Downing, George T. "A Sketch of the Life and Times of Thomas Downing," *A.M.E. Church Review* 3, no. 4 (April 1887): 402–10.

An Episcopalian [pseud.]. *A Plain Address to Episcopalians on the Proposed Meeting at Mechanic-Hall.* New York, 1812.

First Annual Report of the American Anti-Slavery Society. New York: Dorr and Butterfield, 1834.

Garnet, Henry Highland. *A Memorial Discourse, by Rev. Henry Highland Garnet, Delivered in the Hall of the House of Representatives, Washington City, D.C., on Sabbath, February 12, 1865.* Philadelphia: J. M. Wilson, 1865.

[Gilbert, Olive]. *Narrative of Sojourner Truth, a Bondswoman of Olden Time.* 1878. Reprint, New York: Arno, 1968.

Hamilton, Alexander. *Papers of Alexander Hamilton.* Vol. 1. Edited by Harold C. Syrett and Jacob E. Cooke. New York: Columbia University Press, 1961.

Hammon, Jupiter. *An Address to the Negroes in the State of New-York.* New York: Carroll and Patterson, 1787.

Hastings, Hugh, ed. *Ecclesiastical Records, State of New York.* Vol. 6. Albany: J. B. Lyon, 1905.

Hieronymous [pseud.]. *Serious Thoughts on a Late Administration of Episcopal Orders, Submitted to the Calm Reflection of the Bishops of the Protestant Episcopal Church in the United States of America.* New York, 1812.

Hill, Robert A., ed. *The Marcus Garvey and Universal Negro Improvement Association Papers.* Vol. 5, *September 1922–August 1924.* Berkeley: University of California Press, 1986.

Hobart, John Henry. *An Address to Episcopalians on the Subject of the American Bible Society.* New York: T. and J. Swords, 1816.

———. [A Friend to Truth, pseud.]. *The Charter of the Corporation of Trinity Church Defended against the Attacks of a Late Pamphlet.* New York: T. and J. Swords, 1813.

———. *A Defence of the Essentials of Ordination in Answer to a Pamphlet Entitled Serious Thoughts on a Late Administration of Episcopal Orders.* New York: T. and J. Swords, 1812.

———. *Remarks on the Honorable John Jay's Letter, to the Reverend Cave Jones; In a Letter to a Friend.* New York: T. and J. Swords, 1812.

Hone, Philip. *The Diary of Philip Hone.* Edited by Allan Nevins. New York: Dodd and Mead, 1936.

Jay, John. "Anti-Slavery Papers of John Jay." Edited by Frank Monaghan. *Journal of Negro History* 17, no. 4 (October 1932): 491–93.

———. *The Correspondence and Public Papers of John Jay.* Vol. 4. Edited by Henry P. Johnston. New York: G. P. Putnam's Sons, 1893.

Jay, Sarah Livingston. *Selected Letters of John Jay and Sarah Livingston Jay.* Edited by Landa M. Freeman. Jefferson, N.C.: McFarland, 2004.

Jay, William. [An Episcopalian, pseud.]. *An Answer to Bishop Hobart's Pastoral Letter, on the Subject of Bible and Common Prayer-Book Societies, by an Episcopalian.* New York: Whiting and Watson, 1815.

———. *A Reply to a Second Letter to the Author; from the Right Rev. Bishop Hobart, with Remarks on His Hostility to Bible Societies with His Mode of Defending It; and Also on His Vindication of the Reverend Mr. Norris's Late Pamphlet.* New York: J. P. Haven, 1823.

Jones, Cave. *Dr. Hobart's System of Intolerance Exemplified in the Late Proceedings against His Colleague, the Author.* New York: D. & G. Bruce, 1811.

———. *A Solemn Appeal to the Church Being a Plain Statement of Facts in the Matters Pending between Dr. Hobart with others, and the Author.* New York, 1811.

King, Rufus. *Life and Correspondence of Rufus King.* Vol. 1, *1755–1794*, edited by Charles King. New York: G. P. Putnam's Sons, 1894.

Maclay, William. *The Journal of William Maclay, United States Senator from Pennsylvania, 1789–1791.* New York: A. and C. Boni, 1927.

Manross, William Wilson, ed. *The Fulham Papers in the Lambeth Palace Library, American Colonial Section Calendar and Indexes.* Oxford: Clarendon, 1965.

McLoughlin, William H., ed. *The American Evangelicals, 1800–1900: An Anthology.* Gloucester, Mass.: Peter Smith, 1976.

Melville, Herman. "The Two Temples." In *The Writings of Herman Melville*, vol. 9, *The Piazza Tales and Other Prose Pieces 1839–1860.* Evanston and Chicago: Northwestern University Press and Newberry Library, 1987.

Minutes of the Common Council of the City of New-York 1784–1831. 31 vols. New York: City of New York, 1917.

Payne, Daniel Alexander. *Recollections of Seventy Years*. 1888. Reprint, New York: Arno, 1968.

Pintard, John. *Census of the Electors, and Total Population, of the City and County of New-York*. New York: Henry C. Southwick, 1807.

———. *Enumeration of the Inhabitants of the City of New-York*. New York, 1806.

Porter, Dorothy, ed. *Early Negro Writing 1760–1837*. Boston: Beacon, 1971.

Proceedings of a Meeting of the Citizens of New-York and Others, Convened in the City-Hall on the 13th of May, 1816 at the Request of the Board of Managers of the American Bible Society, with the Speeches of George Griffin and Peter A. Jay, Esquires Delivered on the Occasion. New York: American Bible Society, 1816.

The Resolutions Adopted at a Meeting of the Episcopalians at Mechanic Hall also Two Letters from the Honorable John Jay to the Reverend Cave Jones. New York, 1812.

Ripley, C. Peter, ed. *The Black Abolitionist Papers*. Vol. 3, *The United States, 1830–1846*. Chapel Hill: University of North Carolina, 1991.

Rush, Christopher. *A Short Account of the Rise and Progress of the African Methodist Episcopal Church in America*. New York: published by the author, 1843.

Seabury, Samuel. *Letters of a Westchester Farmer, 1774–1775*. Edited by C. H. Vance. 1930. Reprint, New York: Da Capo, 1970.

Seabury, Samuel, III. *Moneygripe's Apprentice: The Personal Narrative of Samuel Seabury III*. Edited by Robert Bruce Mullin. New Haven: Yale University Press, 1989.

Seton, Elizabeth. *Elizabeth Seton: Selected Writings*. Edited by Ellin Kelly and Annabelle Melville. New York: Paulist Press, 1987.

———. *Memoir, Letters and Journal of Elizabeth Seton: Convert to the Catholic Faith and Sisters of Charity*. 2 vols. Edited by Robert Seton. New York: P. O'Shea, 1869.

[———]. *Memoirs of Mrs. S******. Elizabeth, N.J.: Isaac A. Kollock, 1817.

Sixth Annual Report of the American Anti-Slavery Society with the Speeches Delivered at the Anniversary Meeting, Held in the City of New-York on the 7th of May, 1838. New York: William S. Dorr, 1839.

Stilwell, Samuel. *Historical Sketches of the Rise and Progress of the Methodist Society, in the City of New-York*. New York: Bolmore, 1821.

Strong, George Templeton. *The Diary of George Templeton Strong: Young Man in New York, 1835–1849*. Edited by Allan Nevins and Milton Hasley Thomas. New York: Macmillan, 1952.

Weed, Thurlow. *Life of Thurlow Weed*. Vol. 1, *Autobiography of Thurlow Weed*, edited by Harriet A. Weed. 1883. Reprint, New York: Da Capo, 1970.

———. *Life of Thurlow Weed*. Vol. 2, *Memoir of Thurlow Weed*, edited by Thurlow Weed Barnes. 1884. Reprint, New York: Da Capo, 1970.

Wesley, John. *The Letters of the Reverend John Wesley, A.M.* Vol. 5, edited by John Telford. London: Epworth, 1931.

———. *Works of the Reverend John Wesley.* Vol. 7. New York: B. Waugh and T. Mason, 1835.

White, George. *A Brief Account of the Life, Experience, Travels, and Gospel Labours of George White, an African.* 1810. Reprinted in Graham Russell Hodges, ed. *Black Itinerants of the Gospel: The Narratives of John Jea and George White.* Madison, Wisc.: Madison House, 1993.

Woodson, Carter G., ed. *The Mind of the Negro as Reflected in Letters Written during the Crisis.* 1926. Reprint, New York: Russell and Russell, 1969.

Newspapers, Periodicals, and Directories

Anglo-African Magazine. Vol. 1, 1859.

Argus, and Greenleaf's New Daily Advertiser. New York. 1796.

Centinel of Freedom. Newark, N.J. 1796.

Colored American. New York. 1837–1841.

Franks, David. *The New-York Directory.* New York: Shepard Kollock, 1786.

———. *The New-York Directory.* New York: Samuel and John Loudon, 1787.

Freedom's Journal. Vol. 1. 1827.

Friendly Visitor. Vol. 1. 1825. Edited by William Stilwell.

Longworth, David. *The American Almanack, New-York Register, and City Directory, for the Twenty-First Year of American Independence.* New York: David Longworth, 1796.

———. *Longworth's American Almanac, New-York Register, and City-Directory, for the Twenty-Seventh Year of American Independence.* New York: David Longworth, 1802.

———. *Longworth's American Almanac, New-York Register, and City-Directory, for the Twenty-Sixth Year of American Independence.* New York: David Longworth, 1801.

Longworth, Thomas. *Longworth's American Almanac, New-York Register, and City Directory, for the Fiftieth Year of American Independence.* New York: Thomas Longworth, 1825.

———. *Longworth's American Almanac, New-York Register, and City Directory, for the Fifty-Fifth Year of American Independence.* New York: Thomas Longworth, 1830.

———. *Longworth's American Almanac, New-York Register, and City Directory, for the Fifty-Ninth Year of American Independence.* New York: Thomas Longworth, 1839.

———. *Longworth's American Almanac, New-York Register, and City Directory, for the Forty-Fourth Year of American Independence.* New York: Thomas Longworth, 1819.

———. *Longworth's New York Directory, for the Forty-Seventh Year of American Independence.* New York: Thomas Longworth, 1822.

———. *Longworth's American Almanac, New-York Register, and City Directory, for the Sixtieth Year of American Independence*. New York: Thomas Long-worth, 1840.

Massachusetts Mercury. Boston. 1797.

New Hampshire Gazette. Portsmouth. 1797.

Newport Mercury. 1797.

The New-York Directory, and Register, for the Year 1790. New York: Hodge, Allen, and Campbell, 1790.

The New-York Directory, and Register, for the Year 1795. New York: T. and J. Swords, 1795.

New-York Evening Post. 1821.

New York Herald. 1796.

New-York Mercury. 1766.

New York Minerva, & Mercantile Evening Advertiser. Vol. 3, 1796.

New York Times. 1866.

Political Gazette. Newburyport, Mass. 1797.

Archival Sources

1801 Communicant List. Trinity Church Archives, New York City.

Arcularius, Philip J. "October 30, 1805, To the Honorable Common Council the Representation of the Superintendent of the Alms House." Common Council Papers, Box 26, Folder 722, Almshouse 1805, New York Municipal Archives.

Assessed Valuation of Real Estate Collection. New York City Municipal Archives.

Catalog of the Records of the Christian Faith Society, 1691–1792. Lambeth Palace Library, London.

Lathrop Colgate Harper Family Papers. New-York Historical Society.

Jay Family Papers. Butler Library, Columbia University.

John Jay Papers. Butler Library, Columbia University.

Methodist Episcopal Church Records, New York City. New York Public Library.

Miller, Kristin, comp. "A List of Methodist and Episcopalian Bible Society Officers." American Bible Society Archives, New York City.

Office of the County Clerk, New York County, Religious Incorporations 1784–1836. Vol. 1. New York City Municipal Archives.

Papers of the Society for the Propagation of the Gospel in Foreign Parts. Lambeth Palace Library, London.

Papers of the Society for the Relief of Poor Widows with Small Children. Vol. 1. New-York Historical Society.

"Petition of the African Society on the Subject of two Lots purchased for burial ground." Petitions May–August 1795, Box 15, Folder 465, Common Council Papers, New York Municipal Archives.

Pew Rents for Trinity Parish, and St. Paul's and St. John's chapels. Second Trinity Church Building, before 1828. Record 17905. Trinity Church Archives, New York City.

Records of the Society for the Propagation of the Gospel, Letters Series B, 1701–1786. Accessed from the University of Minnesota Library.

"Register of Members of the Corporation of Trinity Church New York Who Are Not Pew Holders." 1845–1868. Trinity Church Archives, New York City.

Saint Philip's Church Petition to the Corporation of Trinity Church, 8 November 1826. Trinity Church Archives, New York City.

St. Philip's Record Books, Baptisms 1819–1829, Schomburg Center for African American History, New York Public Library, New York City.

Trinity Church General Register of Baptisms. Trinity Church Archives, New York City.

Trinity Vestry Minutes. Trinity Church Archives, New York City.

Secondary Sources

Books, Dissertations, and Edited Collections

Albion, Robert Greenhalgh. *The Rise of New York Port, 1815–1860.* With Jennie Barnes Pope. New York: Scribner's Sons, 1939.

Allgor, Catherine. *Parlor Politics: In Which the Ladies of Washington Help Build a City and a Government.* Charlottesville: University Press of Virginia, 2000.

Anbinder, Tyler. *Five Points: The Nineteenth-Century New York City Neighborhood That Invented Tap Dance, Stole Elections, and Became the World's Most Notorious Slum.* New York: Free Press, 2001.

———. *Nativism and Slavery: The Northern Know-Nothings and the Politics of the 1850s.* New York: Oxford University Press, 1992.

Andrews, Dee. *The Methodists in Revolutionary America, 1776–1800.* Princeton, N.J.: Princeton University Press, 2000.

Appleby, Joyce. *Inheriting the Revolution: The First Generation of Americans.* Cambridge: Harvard University Press, 2000.

Balmer, Randall. *A Perfect Babel of Confusion: Dutch Religion and English Culture in the Middle Colonies.* New York: Oxford University Press, 2002.

Barnes, Brooks Miles, and Barry R. Truitt, eds. *Seashore Chronicles: Three Centuries of the Virginia Barrier Islands.* Charlottesville: University Press of Virginia, 1997.

Ben-Atar, Doron, and Barbara B. Oberg, eds. *Federalists Reconsidered.* Charlottesville: University Press of Virginia, 1998.

Berlin, Ira. *Many Thousands Gone: The First Two Centuries of Slavery in North America.* Cambridge: Harvard University Press, 1998.

Bernstein, Iver. *The New York City Draft Riots: Their Significance for American Society and Politics in the Age of the Civil War.* New York: Oxford University Press, 1990.

Berrian, William. *A Historical Sketch of Trinity Church, New York.* New York: Stanford and Swords, 1847.

Bethune, Divie. *The Power of Faith: Exemplified in the Life and Writings of the*

Late Mrs. Isabella Graham of New-York. 2nd ed. New York: Kirk and Mercein, 1817.

Bilhartz, Terry. *Urban Religion and the Second Great Awakening: Church and Society in Early National Baltimore.* Rutherford, N.J.: Farleigh Dickinson University Press, 1986.

Blackmar, Elizabeth. *Manhattan for Rent, 1785–1850.* Ithaca, N.Y.: Cornell University Press, 1989.

Blassingame, John W. *The Slave Community: Plantation Life in the Antebellum South.* Rev. ed. New York: Oxford University Press, 1979.

Blumin, Stuart M. *The Emergence of the Middle Class: Social Experience in the American City, 1790–1900.* Cambridge: Cambridge University Press, 1989.

Bolster, Jeffrey. *Black Jacks: African American Seamen in the Age of Sail.* Cambridge: Harvard University Press, 1998.

Bonomi, Patricia U. *Under the Cope of Heaven: Religion, Society, and Politics in Colonial America.* New York: Oxford University Press, 1986.

Bradley, David Henry, Sr. *A History of the A.M.E. Zion Church, Part I, 1796–1872.* Nashville: Parthenon, 1956.

Brandt, Clare. *An American Aristocracy: The Livingstons.* Garden City, N.Y.: Doubleday, 1986.

Brooke, John L. *Columbia Rising: Civil Life on the Upper Hudson from the Revolution to the Age of Jackson.* Chapel Hill: University of North Carolina Press, 2010.

Brooks, Geraldine. *Dames and Daughters of the Young Republic.* New York: Crowell, 1901.

Bruce, Dickson D., Jr. *The Origins of African American Literature, 1680–1865.* Charlottesville: University of Virginia Press, 2001.

Burrows, Edwin G., and Michael Wallace. *Gotham: A History of New York City to 1898.* New York: Oxford University Press, 1999.

Butler, Diana Hochstedt. *Standing against the Whirlwind: Evangelical Episcopalians in Nineteenth-Century America.* New York: Oxford University Press, 1995.

Butler, Jon. *Awash in a Sea of Faith: Christianizing the American People.* Cambridge: Harvard University Press, 1990.

Carwardine, Richard J. *Evangelicals and Politics in Antebellum America.* New Haven: Yale University Press, 1993.

Chopra, Ruma. *Unnatural Rebellion: Loyalists in New York City during the Revolution.* Charlottesville: University of Virginia Press, 2011.

Chorley, E. Clowes. *Men and Movements in the American Episcopal Church.* 1946. Reprint, Hamden, Ct.: Archon, 1961.

Cray, Robert E., Jr. *Paupers and Poor Relief in New York City and Its Rural Environs, 1700–1830.* Philadelphia: Temple University Press, 1988.

Davis, David Brion. *The Problem of Slavery in the Age of Revolution.* Ithaca, N.Y.: Cornell University Press, 1975.

Davis, Thadious M. *Nella Larsen, Novelist of the Harlem Renaissance: A Woman's Life Unveiled.* Baton Rouge: Louisiana State University Press, 1996.

Davis, Thomas J. *Rumor of Revolt: The Great Negro Plot in Colonial New York.* New York: Free Press, 1985.

De Costa, B. F. *Three Score and Ten: The Story of St. Philip's Church, New York.* New York, 1889.

Dirvin, Joseph I. *Mrs. Seton: Foundress of the American Sisters of Charity.* New York: Farrar, Strauss, and Cudahy, 1962.

Disosway, Gabriel P. *The Earliest Churches of New York.* New York: J. G. Gregory, 1865.

Dix, Morgan. *A History of the Parish of Trinity Church in the City of New York.* 5 vols. New York: G. P. Putnam and Sons, 1898–1906.

Doll, Peter M. *Revolution, Religion, and National Identity: Imperial Anglicanism in British North America, 1745–1795.* Cranbury, N.J.: Fairleigh Dickinson University Press, 2000.

Dorsey, Bruce. *Reforming Men and Women: Gender in the Antebellum City.* Ithaca, N.Y.: Cornell University Press, 1992.

Dunlap, Angela H. *Voices of the Freedom Church.* Durham, N.C.: A. H. Dunlap, 1996.

Dunlap, David W. *From Abyssinian to Zion: A Guide to Manhattan's Houses of Worship.* New York: Columbia University Press, 1994.

Egerton, Douglas R. *Death or Liberty: African Americans and Revolutionary America.* New York: Oxford University Press, 2009.

Exman, Eugene. *The Brothers Harper: A Unique Publishing Partnership and Its Impact upon the Cultural Life of America from 1817 to 1853.* New York: Harper and Row, 1965.

Faught, C. Brad. *The Oxford Movement: A Thematic History of the Tractarians and Their Times.* University Park: Pennsylvania State University Press, 2003.

Fischer, David Hackett. *The Revolution of American Conservatism: The Federalist Party in the Era of Jeffersonian Democracy.* New York: Harper and Row, 1965.

Fitch, Suzanne Pullon, and Roseann M. Mandzuik, eds. *Sojourner Truth as Orator: Wit, Story, and Song.* Westport, Ct.: Greenwood, 1997.

Flanagan, Kathleen. "The Influence of John Henry Hobart on the Life of Elizabeth Ann Seton." Ph. D. diss., Union Theological Seminary, 1978.

Fleming, Thomas. *Duel: Alexander Hamilton, Aaron Burr, and the Future of America.* New York: Basic, 1999.

Foote, Thelma Wills. *Black and White Manhattan: The History of Racial Formation in Colonial New York City.* New York: Oxford University Press, 2004.

Foster, Charles J. *An Errand of Mercy: The Evangelical United Front 1790–1837.* Chapel Hill: University of North Carolina Press, 1960.

Fox, Dixon Ryan. *The Decline of Aristocracy in the Politics of New York, 1801–1840*. Edited by Robert V. Remini. 1919. Reprint, New York: Kraus, 1965.

Frederickson, George M. *The Black Image in the White Mind: The Debate on Afro-American Character and Destiny, 1817–1914*. 1971. Reprint, Hanover, N.H.: Wesleyan University, 1987.

Frey, Sylvia. *Water from the Rock: Black Resistance in a Revolutionary Age*. Princeton, N.J.: Princeton University Press, 1991.

Fulop, Timothy E., ed. *African American Religion: Interpretive Essays in History and Culture*. New York: Routledge, 1997.

Geertz, Clifford. *The Interpretation of Cultures*. New York: Basic, 1973.

Gellman, David N. *Emancipating New York: The Politics of Slavery and Freedom, 1777–1827*. Baton Rouge: Louisiana State University Press, 2006.

Genealogies of Virginia Families, from the William and Mary College Quarterly Historical Meeting. Vol. 2. Baltimore: Genealogical Publishing, 1982.

Genovese, Eugene D. *Roll Jordan Roll: The World the Slaves Made*. New York: Pantheon, 1974.

George, Carol V. R. *Segregated Sabbaths: Richard Allen and the Emergence of Independent Black Churches 1760–1840*. New York: Oxford University Press, 1973.

Gibson, Campbell, and Kay Jung. *Historical Census Statistics on Population Totals by Race, 1790 to 1990, and by Hispanic Origin, 1970 to 1990, for the United States, Regions, Divisions, and States*. Washington, D.C.: U.S. Census Bureau, 2002.

Gilfoyle, Timothy J. *City of Eros: New York City, Prostitution, and the Commercialization of Sex, 1790–1820*. New York: Norton, 1992.

Gilje, Paul. *The Road to Mobocracy: Popular Disorder in New York City, 1763–1834*. Chapel Hill: University of North Carolina Press, 1987.

Gilje, Paul A., and William Pencak, eds. *New York in the Age of the Constitution 1775–1800*. Rutherford, N.J.: Fairleigh Dickinson University Press, 1992.

Gilje, Paul A., and Howard B. Rock, eds. *Keepers of the Revolution, New Yorkers at Work in the Early Republic*. Ithaca, N.Y.: Cornell University, 1992.

Goodfriend, Joyce D. *Before the Melting Pot: Society and Culture in Colonial New York City, 1664–1730*. Princeton, N.J.: Princeton University Press, 1994.

Goodman, Paul. *Of One Blood: Abolitionism and the Origins of Racial Equality*. Berkeley: University of California Press, 1998.

Griffin, Clifford S. *Their Brothers' Keepers: Moral Stewardship in the United States, 1800–1865*. New Brunswick, N.J.: Rutgers University Press, 1960.

Hall, David D., ed. *Lived Religion in America: Toward a History of Practice*. Princeton, N.J.: Princeton University Press, 1997.

———. *Worlds of Wonder, Days of Judgment: Popular Religious Belief in Early New England*. New York: Knopf, 1989.

Hall, Stephen G. *A Faithful Account of the Race: African American Historical*

Writing in Nineteenth-Century America. Chapel Hill: University of North Carolina Press, 2009.

Halttunen, Karen. *Murder Most Foul: The Killer and the American Gothic Imagination*. Cambridge: Harvard University Press, 1998.

Hamilton, Allan McLane. *The Intimate Life of Alexander Hamilton*. New York: Scribner's Sons, 1910.

Hardt, Philip F. *The Soul of Methodism: The Class Meeting in Early New York City Methodism*. Lanham, Md.: University Press of America, 2000.

Harris, Leslie M. *In the Shadow of Slavery: African Americans in New York City, 1626–1863*. Chicago: University of Chicago Press, 2003.

Harris, Matthew, and Thomas Kidd, eds. *The Founding Fathers and the Debate over Religion in Revolutionary America: A History in Documents*. New York: Oxford University Press, 2011.

Hatch, Nathan O. *The Democratization of American Christianity*. New Haven: Yale University Press, 1989.

Heimert, Alan. *Religion and the American Mind from the Great Awakening to the Revolution*. Cambridge: Harvard University Press, 1966.

Hempton, David. *Methodism: Empire of the Spirit*. New Haven: Yale University Press, 2005.

Hewitt, John H., Jr. *Protest and Progress: New York's First Black Episcopal Church Fights Racism*. New York: Garland, 2000.

Heyrman, Christine Leigh. *Southern Cross: The Beginnings of the Bible Belt*. New York: Knopf, 1997.

Higham, John. *Strangers in the Land: Patterns of American Nativism 1860–1925*. New Brunswick, N.J.: Rutgers University Press, 1955.

Hirrel, Leo P. *Children of Wrath: New School Calvinism and Antebellum Reform*. Lexington: University of Kentucky Press, 1998.

Hodges, Graham Russell. *David Ruggles: A Radical Black Abolitionist and the Underground Railroad in New York City*. Chapel Hill: University of North Carolina Press, 2012.

———. *New York City Cartmen, 1667–1850*. New York: New York University Press, 1986.

———. *Root and Branch: African Americans in New York and East Jersey, 1613–1863*. Chapel Hill: University of North Carolina Press, 1999.

Hoffer, Peter. *The Great New York Conspiracy of 1741*. Lawrence: University of Kansas Press, 2003.

Hood, James Walker. *One Hundred Years of the African Methodist Episcopal Zion Church; or, The Centennial of African Methodism*. New York: A.M.E. Zion Book Concern, 1895.

———. *Sketch of the Early History of the African Methodist Episcopal Zion Church, with Jubilee Souvenir and Appendix*. Charlotte, N.C.: A.M.E. Zion Publication House, 1914.

Howe, Daniel Walker. *What Hath God Wrought: the Transformation of America, 1815–1848*. New York: Oxford University Press, 2007.

Isaac, Rhys. *The Transformation of Virginia, 1740–1790*. Chapel Hill: University of North Carolina Press, 1982.

Jasanoff, Maya. *Liberty's Exiles: American Loyalists in the Revolutionary World*. New York: Knopf, 2011.

Johnson, Curtis D. *Islands of Holiness: Rural Religion in Upstate New York, 1790–1860*. Ithaca, N.Y.: Cornell University Press, 1989.

Johnson, Paul E. *A Shopkeeper's Millennium: Society and Revivals in Rochester, 1815–1837*. New York: Hill and Wang, 1978.

Johnson, Paul E., and Sean Wilentz. *The Kingdom of Matthias*. New York: Oxford University Press, 1994.

Jordan, Ryan P. *Slavery and the Meetinghouse: The Quakers and the Abolitionist Dilemma, 1820–1865*. Bloomington: Indiana University Press, 2007.

Jordan, Winthrop D. *White over Black: American Attitudes toward the Negro, 1550–1812*. New York: Oxford University Press, 1974.

Kerber, Linda K. *Federalists in Dissent: Imagery and Ideology in Jeffersonian America*. Ithaca, N.Y.: Cornell University Press, 1970.

———. *No Constitutional Right to Be Ladies: Women and the Obligations of Citizenship*. New York: Hill and Wang, 1998.

Keyssar, Alexander. *The Right to Vote: The Contested History of Democracy in the United States*. New York: Basic, 2000.

Klingberg, Frank. *Anglican Humanitarianism in Colonial New York*. Philadelphia: Church Historical Society, 1940.

Kraditor, Aileen S. *Means and Ends in American Abolitionism: Garrison and His Critics on Strategy and Tactics, 1834–1840*. New York: Pantheon, 1967.

Lamb, Martha J. *History of the City of New York: Its Origins, Rise, and Progress*. 3 vols. New York and Chicago: A. S. Barnes, 1877, 1880, 1921.

Lawrence, Anna M. *One Family under God: Love, Belonging, and Authority in Early Transatlantic Methodism*. Philadelphia: University of Pennsylvania Press, 2011.

Lee, Shin Ja. "The Practice of Spiritual Direction in the Life and Writings of St. Elizabeth Ann Seton." Ph.D. diss., Catholic University of America, 2010.

Lepore, Jill. *New York Burning: Liberty, Slavery, and Conspiracy in Eighteenth-Century Manhattan*. New York: Vintage, 2005.

Lindsley, James Elliott. *This Planted Vine: A Narrative History of the Episcopal Diocese of New York*. New York: Harper and Row, 1984.

Little, Lawrence S. *Disciples of Liberty: The African Methodist Episcopal Church in the Age of Imperialism, 1884–1916*. Knoxville: University of Tennessee Press, 2000.

Litwack, Leon F. *North of Slavery: The Negro in the Free States, 1790–1860*. Chicago: University of Chicago Press, 1961.

Lobody, Diane. "Lost in the Ocean of Love: The Mystical Writings of Catherine Livingston Garrettson." Ph.D. diss., Drew University, 1990.

Long, Kathryn Teresa. *The Great Revival of 1857–58: Interpreting an American Religious Awakening.* New York: Oxford University Press, 1998.

Loveland, Anne C., and Otis B. Wheeler. *From Meetinghouse to Megachurch: A Material and Cultural History.* Columbia: University of Missouri Press, 2003.

Mabee, Carleton. *Sojourner Truth: Slave, Prophet, Legend.* New York: New York University Press, 1993.

Mathews, Donald G. *Slavery and Methodism: A Chapter in American Morality, 1780–1845.* Princeton, N.J.: Princeton University Press, 1965.

May, Henry F. *The Enlightenment in America.* New York: Oxford University Press, 1976.

McCarthy, Timothy Patrick, and John Stauffer, eds. *Prophets of Protest: Reconsidering the History of American Abolitionism.* New York: New Press, 2006.

McDonald, Forrest. *Alexander Hamilton.* New York: Norton, 1979.

McManus, Edgar J. *A History of Negro Slavery in New York.* Syracuse: Syracuse University Press, 1966.

McMurray, George, and Ndugu G. B. T'Ofori-Atta. *Mother Zion: African Methodist Episcopal Zion Church: Two Hundred Years of Evangelism and Liberation: the Birth Story of a Denomination.* Charlotte, N.C.: A.M.E. Zion Publishing House, 1996.

Mills, Frederick V., Sr. *Bishops by Ballot: An Eighteenth-Century Ecclesiastical Revolution.* New York: Oxford University Press, 1978.

Milner, Clyde A., II, Carol A. O'Connor, and Martha A. Sandweiss, eds. *The Oxford History of the American West.* New York: Oxford University Press, 1994.

Mitchell, Broadus. *Alexander Hamilton: A Concise Biography.* New York: Oxford University Press, 1976.

Mitchell, Henry H. *Black Church Beginnings: The Long-Hidden Realities of the First Years.* Grand Rapids, Mich.: Eerdman's, 2004.

Mohl, Raymond. *Poverty in New York, 1783–1825.* New York: Oxford University Press, 1971.

Moore, R. Laurence. *Religious Outsiders and the Making of Americans.* New York: Oxford University Press, 1986.

Morgan, Edmund. *American Slavery, American Freedom: The Ordeal of Colonial Virginia.* New York: Norton, 1975.

Moses, Wilson Jeremiah. *Alexander Crummell: A Study of Civilization and Discontent.* New York: Oxford University Press, 1989.

Mullin, Robert Bruce. *Episcopal Vision/American Reality: High Church Theology and Social Thought in Evangelical America.* New Haven: Yale University Press, 1986.

Nash, Gary. *Forging Freedom: The Formation of Philadelphia's Black Community, 1720–1840*. Cambridge: Harvard University Press, 1991.

———. *Red, White, and Black: The Peoples of Early North America*. 3rd ed. Englewood Cliffs, N.J.: Prentice Hall, 1992.

Nell, William C. *Colored Patriots of the American Revolution*. 1855. Reprint, New York: Arno, 1968.

Nelson, William H. *The American Tory*. 1961. Reprint, Westport, Ct.: Greenwood, 1980.

Newman, Richard S. *Freedom's Prophet: Bishop Richard Allen, the AME Church, and the Black Founding Fathers*. New York: New York University Press, 2008.

Nissenbaum, Stephen. *The Battle for Christmas*. New York: Knopf, 1996.

North, Elizabeth Mason. *Consecrated Talents: or, the Life of Mary W. Mason*. 1870. Reprint, New York: Garland, 1987.

Norton, Mary Beth. *Liberty's Daughters: The Revolutionary Experience of American Women, 1750–1800*. Boston: Little, Brown, 1980.

———. *Separated by Their Sex: Women in Public and Private in the Colonial Atlantic World*. Ithaca, N.Y.: Cornell University Press, 2011.

O'Day, Rosemary. *Women's Agency in Early Modern Britain and the American Colonies: Patriarchy, Partnership, and Patronage*. New York: Pearson Longman, 2007.

Painter, Nell Irvin. *Sojourner Truth: A Life, A Symbol*. New York: Norton, 1996.

Pessen, Edward. *Riches, Class, and Power before the Civil War*. Lexington, Mass.: Heath, 1973.

Peterson, Carla L. *Black Gotham: A Family History of African Americans in Nineteenth-Century New York*. New Haven: Yale University Press, 2011.

Pointer, Richard W. *Protestant Pluralism and the New York Experience: A Study of Eighteenth-Century Religious Diversity*. Bloomington: Indiana University Press, 1988.

Pomerantz, Sidney I. *New York, an American City 1783–1803: A Study of Urban Life*. 2nd ed. New York: I. J. Friedman, 1965.

Rael, Patrick. *Black Identity & Black Protest in the Antebellum North*. Chapel Hill: University of North Carolina Press, 2002.

Rankin, Richard. *Ambivalent Churchmen and Evangelical Churchwomen: The Religion of the Episcopal Elite in North Carolina, 1800–1860*. Columbia: University of South Carolina Press, 1993.

Ranlet, Philip. *The New York Loyalists*. Knoxville: University of Tennessee Press, 1986.

Rediker, Marcus, and Peter Linebaugh. *Many-Headed Hydra: Sailors, Slaves, Commoners, and the Hidden History of the Revolutionary Atlantic*. Boston: Beacon, 2000.

Richards, Leonard L. *"Gentlemen of Property and Standing": Anti-Abolition Mobs in Jacksonian America*. New York: Oxford University Press, 1970.

Richter, Daniel K. *Before the Revolution: America's Ancient Pasts*. Cambridge: Harvard University Press, 2011.

Roberts, Rita. *Evangelicalism and the Politics of Reform in Northern Black Thought, 1776–1863*. Baton Rouge: Louisiana State University Press, 2010.

Rock, Howard B. *Artisans of the New Republic: The Tradesmen of New York City in the Age of Jefferson*. New York: New York University Press, 1979.

Rothschild, Nan A. *New York City Neighborhoods: The Eighteenth Century*. San Diego: Academic Press, 1990.

Ryan, Mary P. *Cradle of the Middle Class: The Family in Oneida County, New York, 1790–1865*. Cambridge: Cambridge University Press, 1981.

Schneider, Gregory A. *The Way of the Cross Leads Home: The Domestication of American Methodism*. Bloomington: Indiana University Press, 1993.

Seaman, Samuel A. *Annals of New York Methodism, Being a History of the Methodist Episcopal Church in the City of New York from A.D. 1766 to A.D. 1890*. New York: Hunt and Eaton, 1892.

Sellers, Charles. *The Market Revolution: Jacksonian America, 1815–1846*. New York: Oxford University Press, 1991.

Sensbach, Jon F. *Rebecca's Revival: Creating Black Christianity in the Atlantic World*. Cambridge: Harvard University Press, 2005.

———. *A Separate Canaan: The Making of an Afro-Moravian World in North Carolina, 1763–1840*. Chapel Hill: University of North Carolina Press, 1998.

Shaw, Gwendolyn DuBois. *Portraits of a People: Picturing African Americans in the Nineteenth Century*. Andover, Mass., and Seattle: Addison Gallery of American Art in association with University of Washington Press, 2006.

Shorto, Russell. *The Island at the Center of the World: The Epic Story of Dutch Manhattan and the Forgotten Colony That Shaped America*. New York: Vintage, 2005.

Sidbury, James. *Becoming African in America: Race and Nation in the Early Black Atlantic*. New York: Oxford University Press, 2007.

Simpson, Craig M. *A Good Southerner: The Life of Henry Wise of Virginia*. Chapel Hill: University of North Carolina Press, 1985.

Simpson, Robert Drew, ed. *American Methodist Pioneer: The Life and Journals of the Rev. Freeborn Garrettson, 1752–1827*. Madison, N.J., and Rutland, Vt.: Drew University Library, 1984.

Smith, Timothy L. *Revivalism and Social Reform in Mid-Nineteenth Century America*. New York: Abigdon Press, 1957.

Soderlund, Jean R. *Quakers & Slavery: A Divided Spirit*. Princeton, N.J.: Princeton University Press, 1985.

Spann, Edward K. *The New Metropolis: New York City, 1840–1857*. New York: Columbia University Press, 1981.

St. George, Robert Blair, ed. *Possible Pasts: Becoming Colonial in Early America*. Ithaca, N.Y.: Cornell University Press, 2000.

Stansell, Christine. *City of Women: Sex and Class in New York, 1789–1860*. New York: Knopf, 1986.

Stevens, Abel. *Life and Times of Nathan Bangs, D.D.* New York: Carlton and Porter, 1863.

———. *The Women of Methodism: Its Three Foundresses, Susanna Wesley, the Countess of Huntingdon, and Barbara Heck, with Sketches of their Female Associates and Successors in the Early History of the Denomination.* New York: Carlton and Porter, 1866.

Still, Bayrd. *Mirror for Gotham: New York as Seen by Contemporaries from Dutch Days to the Present.* New York: New York University Press, 1956.

Stokes, I. N. Phelps. *The Iconography of Manhattan Island.* 5 vols. 1915. Reprint, New York: Arno, 1967.

———. *New York Past and Present: Its History and Landmarks, 1524–1939.* New York: Plantin Press, 1939.

The Story of Old John Street Church. New York: Raynor R. Rogers, 1984.

Sutton, William R. *Journeymen for Jesus: Evangelical Artisans Confront Capitalism in Jacksonian Baltimore.* University Park: Pennsylvania State University Press, 1998.

Swift, David E. *Black Prophets of Justice: Activist Clergy before the Civil War.* Baton Rouge: Louisiana State University, 1989.

Taylor, Alan. *American Colonies.* New York: Viking, 2001.

Taylor, Clarence. *Black Religious Intellectuals: The Fight for Equality from Jim Crow to the Twenty-First Century.* New York: Routledge, 2002.

Taylor, George Rogers. *The Transportation Revolution, 1815–1860.* New York: Rinehart, 1951.

Thompson, E. P. *The Making of the English Working Class.* New York: Pantheon, 1963.

Tiedemann, Joseph S. *Reluctant Revolutionaries: New York City and the Road to Independence, 1763–1776.* Ithaca, N.Y.: Cornell University Press, 1997.

Townsend, Craig D. *Faith in Their Own Color: African Episcopalians in New York City.* New York: Columbia University Press, 2005.

———. "An Inexpedient Time: Race and Religion among New York City's Episcopalians." Ph.D. diss., Harvard University, 1998.

Wakeley, J. B. *Lost Chapters Recovered from the Early History of American Methodism.* New York: Carlton and Porter, 1858.

Waldstreicher, David. *In the Midst of Perpetual Fetes: The Making of American Nationalism, 1776–1820.* Chapel Hill: University of North Carolina Press, 1997.

Walker, Clarence E. *Rock in a Weary Land: The African Methodist Episcopal Church during the Civil War and Reconstruction.* Baton Rouge: Louisiana State University Press, 1982.

Walls, William J. *The African Methodist Episcopal Zion Church: Reality of the Black Church.* Charlotte, N.C.: A.M.E. Zion Publishing House, 1974.

Walters, Ronald G. *American Reformers, 1815–1860.* New York: Hill and Wang, 1978.

Washington, Margaret. *Sojourner Truth's America.* Urbana: University of Illinois Press, 2009.

Wheeler, B. F. *The Varick Family: With Many Family Portraits.* Mobile, Ala., 1906.

White, Shane. *Somewhat More Independent: The End of Slavery in New York City, 1770–1810.* Athens: University of Georgia Press, 1991.

———. *Stories of Freedom in Black New York.* Cambridge: Harvard University Press, 2002.

White, Shane, and Graham White. *Stylin': African American Expressive Culture from Its Beginnings to the Zoot Suit.* Ithaca, N.Y.: Cornell University Press, 1998.

Wigger, John. *Taking Heaven by Storm: Methodism and the Rise of Popular Christianity in America.* New York: Oxford University Press, 1998.

Wilder, Craig Steven. *In the Company of Black Men: The African Influence on African American Culture in New York City.* New York: New York University Press, 2001.

Wilentz, Sean. *Chants Democratic: New York City and the Rise of the American Working Class, 1788–1850.* New York: Oxford University Press, 1984.

Williams, Johnny E. *African American Religion and the Civil Rights Movement in Arkansas.* Jackson: University Press of Mississippi, 2008.

Wilson, James Grant, and John Fiske, eds. *Appleton's Cyclopedia of American Biography.* 6 vols. New York: D. Appleton, 1888–1900.

Wilson, Sherrill D. *New York City's African Slaveholders: A Social and Material Culture History.* New York: Garland, 1994.

Wind, James P., and James W. Lewis, eds. *American Congregations.* Vol. 2, *New Perspectives in the Study of Congregations.* Chicago: University of Chicago Press, 1994.

Wood, Betty. *Slavery in Colonial America, 1619–1776.* Lanham, Md.: Rowman and Littlefield, 2005.

Wood, Gordon. *The Radicalism of the American Revolution.* New York: Knopf, 1992.

Woodson, Carter. *History of the Negro Church.* 2nd ed. Washington, D.C.: Associated Publishers, 1921.

Wosh, Peter J. *Spreading the Word: The Bible Business in Nineteenth-Century America.* Ithaca, N.Y.: Cornell University Press, 1994.

Wright, J. Robert. *Saint Thomas Church Fifth Avenue.* Grand Rapids, Mich.: Eerdman's, 2001.

Journal Articles

Aptheker, Herbert. "The Quakers and Negro Slavery." *Journal of Negro History* 25, no. 3 (July 1940): 331–62.

Barratt, Carrie Rebora. "Faces of a New Nation: American Portraits of the 18th and Early 19th Centuries." *Metropolitan Museum of Art Bulletin* 61, no. 1 (Summer 2003): 3–56.

Boylan, Anne M. "Timid Girls, Venerable Widows and Dignified Matrons: Life Cycle Patterns among Organized Women in New York and Boston, 1797–1840." *American Quarterly* 38, no. 5 (Winter 1986): 779–97.

———. "Women in Groups: An Analysis of Women's Benevolent Organizations in New York and Boston, 1797–1840." *Journal of American History* 71, no. 3 (December 1984): 497–523.

Bratt, James D. "The Reorientation of American Protestantism, 1835–1845." *Church History* 67, no. 1 (March 1998): 52–82.

Butler, Jon. "Communities and Congregations: The Black Church in St. Paul, 1860–1900." *Journal of Negro History* 56, no. 2 (April 1971): 118–34.

———. "Religion in New York City: Faith That Could Not Be." *U.S. Catholic Historian* 22, no. 2 (Spring 2004): 51–61.

Cott, Nancy F. "Young Women in the Second Great Awakening in New England." *Feminist Studies* 3, no. 1/2 (Autumn 1975): 15–29.

De Jong, Gerald Francis. "The Dutch Reformed Church and Negro Slavery in Colonial America." *Church History* 40, no. 4 (December 1971): 423–36.

Deyle, Steven. "The Irony of Liberty: Origins of the Domestic Slave Trade." *Journal of the Early Republic* 12, no. 1 (Spring 1992): 37–62.

Gerardi, Donald F. M. "The King's College Controversy 1753–1756 and the Ideological Roots of Toryism in New York." *Perspectives in American History* 11 (1977): 147–96.

Gravely, Will B. "The Dialectic of Double-Consciousness in Black American Freedom Celebrations, 1808–1863." *Journal of Negro History* 67, no. 4 (Winter 1982): 302–17.

Gregory, Jeremy. "Refashioning Puritan New England: The Church of England in British North America, c. 1680–1770." *Transactions of the Royal Historical Society*, 6th ser., vol. 20 (2010): 85–112.

Griffin, Clifford S. "Religious Benevolence as Social Control, 1815–1860." *Mississippi Valley Historical Review* 44, no. 3 (December 1957): 423–44.

Harmon, J. H., Jr. "The Negro as a Local Business Man." *Journal of Negro History* 14, no. 2 (April 1929): 116–55.

Hessinger, Rodney. "'A Base and Unmanly Conspiracy': Catholicism and the Hogan Schism in the Gendered Religious Marketplace of Philadelphia." *Journal of the Early Republic* 31, no. 3 (Fall 2011): 357–96.

Isaac, Rhys. "Evangelical Revolt: The Nature of the Baptists' Challenge to the Traditional Order in Virginia, 1765 to 1775." *William and Mary Quarterly* 31, no. 3 (July 1974): 345–68.

Kerber, Linda K. "The Republican Mother: Women and the Enlightenment—An American Perspective." *American Quarterly* 28, no. 2 (Summer 1976): 187–205.

Kornblith, Gary J. "The Craftsman as Industrialist: Jonas Chickering and the Transformation of American Piano Making." *Business History Review* 59, no. 3 (Autumn 1985): 349–68.

Mullin, Robert Bruce. "Trends in the Study of the History of the Episcopal Church." *Anglican and Episcopal History* 72, no. 2 (June 2003): 153–65.

Perlman, Daniel. "Organizations of the Free Negro in New York City, 1800–1860." *Journal of Negro History* 56, no. 3 (July 1971): 181–97.

Polgar, Paul J. "'To Raise Them to an Equal Participation': Early National Abolitionism, Gradual Emancipation, and the Promise of African American Citizenship." *Journal of the Early Republic* 31, no. 2 (Summer 2011): 229–58.

Price, Jacob M. "Economic Function and the Growth of American Port Towns in the Eighteenth Century." *Perspectives in American History* 8 (1974): 123–86.

Schmidt, Leigh Eric. "'A Church-Going People are a Dress-Loving People': Clothes, Communication, and Religious Culture in Early America." *Church History* 58, no. 1 (March 1989): 36–51.

Swan, Robert J. "John Teasman: African-American Educator and the Emergence of Community in Early Black New York City, 1787–1815." *Journal of the Early Republic* 12, no. 3 (Autumn 1992): 331–56.

———. "Prelude and Aftermath of the Doctors' Riot of 1788: A Religious Interpretation of White and Black Reaction to Grave Robbing." *New York History* 81, no. 4 (October 2000): 417–56.

Weston, Rob N. "Alexander Hamilton and the Abolition of Slavery in New York." *Afro-Americans in New York Life and History* 18, no. 1 (January 31. 1994): 31–45.

White, Shane. "A Question of Style: Blacks in and around New York City in the Late 18th Century." *Journal of American Folklore* 102, no. 403 (January–March 1989): 23–44.

Index

About the Author

Kyle T. Bulthuis is an assistant professor of early American history at Utah State University. He lives with his wife and two daughters in Logan, Utah.

EARLY AMERICAN PLACES

Colonization and Its Discontents: Emancipation,
Emigration, and Antislavery in Antebellum Pennsylvania
Beverly C. Tomek

Empire at the Periphery: British Colonists, Anglo-Dutch Trade, and the
Development of the British Atlantic, 1621—1713
Christian J. Koot

Slavery before Race: Europeans, Africans, and Indians
at Long Island's Sylvester Manor Plantation, 1651–1884
Katherine Howlett Hayes

Faithful Bodies: Performing Religion and Race in the Puritan Atlantic
Heather Miyano Kopelson

Against Wind and Tide: The African American Struggle
against the Colonization Movement
Ousmane K. Power-Greene

Four Steeples over the City Streets: Religion and Society in New York's
Early Republic Congregations
Kyle T. Bulthuis